SAFETY NOTICE

Hiking, scrambling, and all forms of outdoor recreation involve inherent risks and an element of unpredictability. Many of the hikes in this guidebook are not for novices and may not be safe for your party. There are dangers on every trail, route, and road, and conditions can change at any time. While every effort has been made to ensure accuracy at time of writing, this book may contain errors and omissions. You assume full responsibility for your safety and health in and around the backcountry. The author, publisher, and distributors accept no liability for any loss, damage, injury, or death arising from the use of this book. Check current conditions, carry the 10 essentials, exercise caution, and stay within your limits.

• REVISED AND UPDATED SECOND EDITION •

105 HIKES

IN AND AROUND SOUTHWESTERN BRITISH COLUMBIA

STEPHEN HUI

Foreword by

SI:YÉMIYA ALBERT (SONNY) MCHALSIE

GREYSTONE BOOKS
Vancouver/Berkeley/London

For Stefan, Esther, Verena, and Julius, who introduced me to knödel,
and for the builders and stewards of the Sunshine Coast Trail, where we first met

---

25 26 27 28 29 5 4 3 2 1

Greystone Books Ltd.
greystonebooks.com

Cataloguing data available from Library and Archives Canada
ISBN 978-1-77840-226-5 (pbk.)
ISBN 978-1-77840-227-2 (epub)

Editing by Lucy Kenward
Copy editing by Meg Yamamoto
Proofreading by Alison Strobel
Indexing by Stephen Ullstrom
Cover and text design by Fiona Siu
Front cover photograph by EB Adventure Photography/Shutterstock.com
Back cover and interior photographs by Stephen Hui, except where credited otherwise
Cartography by Steve Chapman, Canadian Map Makers

Printed and bound in Malaysia on FSC® certified paper at Papercraft Sdn. Bhd.
The FSC® label means that materials used for the product have been responsibly sourced.

Greystone Books thanks the Canada Council for the Arts, the British Columbia Arts Council, the Province of British Columbia through the Book Publishing Tax Credit, and the Government of Canada for supporting our publishing activities.

MIX
Paper | Supporting responsible forestry
FSC® C016973

Greystone Books gratefully acknowledges the xʷməθkʷəy̓əm (Musqueam), Sḵwx̱wú7mesh (Squamish), and səlilwətaɬ (Tsleil-Waututh) peoples on whose land our Vancouver head office is located.

FACING: Rohr Lake, Marriott Lake, and Mount Marriott from Mount Rohr (Hike 49).

CONTENTS

LIONS BAY

SQUAMISH

CHEAKAMUS RIVER

WHISTLER

PEMBERTON

Hikes South of Vancouver

FACING: Looking down at Suxwi:ts from Porcupine Rock (Hike 67).

FOREWORD

by Si:yémiya Albert (Sonny) McHalsie

TRAILS HAVE long fascinated me. My Nlaka'pamux (Nl'akapmx) and Stó:lō ancestors used trails for many purposes. Today, trails are key to my work as a Stó:lō cultural adviser and historian.

Accordingly, I'm delighted to open the second edition of Stephen Hui's *105 Hikes In and Around Southwestern British Columbia*. Over thousands of years, Indigenous Peoples have blazed countless trails across the region. Many of today's hiking paths take advantage of these routes.

My understanding of the importance of trails began with the many paths my family used to access our various fishing grounds. Today, we fish at Eyxel (meaning "at the foot" in the Halq'eméylem language) on the Stó:lō (Fraser River), as well as at a spot near the Fraser-Hope Bridge, where we have constructed safer and easier trails.

My Nlaka'pamux father told me stories about the trails that he used as a boy along with my grandfather. He spoke of a trail that led to a spring known as S'expen (meaning "cracked head" in the Nłeʔkepmxcín language). Boys from the village ran there for a spiritual bath as part of their puberty training. My grandfather, Antoine, had a trapline trail that extended from the Anderson River up to his cabin at the headwaters of the East Anderson River; it was also used to access huckleberry patches.

A trail near Scuzzy Creek was the site of the last raid of the S'atchenko (Stó:lō) against the Nlaka'pamux before European contact. When the Stó:lō warriors reached the top of the trail, the Nlaka'pamux warriors ambushed them. My grandfather had a trail to his fishing rock and wind-drying rack below the China Bar Tunnel, where we also had a trail to harvest pine mushrooms. As a young man, he also had a trail to his cabin at Inkawthia Lake near Spuzzum.

In the course of my work for the Stó:lō Research and Resource Management Centre, I learned of a trail to Xoletsa (Frozen Lakes), an important blueberry and huckleberry picking area above Yale. Access to Indigenous right holders is now obstructed by a "No Trespassing" sign and a locked gate. A trail behind Chowéthel (Chawathil) was used to access the huckleberries on Q'aw (Howling Mountain); it zigzagged all the way to the top. Every year, my late uncle Bill Pat Charlie and his cousins, Gilbert Ewen and James Peters, had to clear the trail as well as set up a camp for the Elders.

The late Agnes Kelly, a Stó:lō knowledge keeper, spoke of a trail, which ran from Skw'átets up the ridge behind Jones Lake, that was used by many people from Skw'átets, Shxw'ōwhámél, Chowéthel, and Ruby Creek. Every year, people used this trail to harvest blueberries at lower elevations for two weeks and then black huckleberries in the subalpine for four weeks. Two other important trails led to the women's and men's fasting grounds on the mountain between Hunter Creek and Lorenzetta Creek. There is some interest within Shxw'ōwhámel First Nation in re-establishing these three trails.

I've spent many years recording the Halq'eméylem names of places across Stó:lō territory. It's good to see place names in Halq'eméylem and other Indigenous languages prominently featured in *105 Hikes*. Halq'eméylem place names such as Kw'ekw'e'i:qw (Sumas Mountain), Lhílheqey (Cheam Peak), and St'ám'ya (Hope Mountain) connect the Stó:lō to our ancestors, our culture, our land, our stories, and our values.

As you hike the trails, I'd like to remind you that First Nations and Tribes hold jurisdiction over these lands. Many trails come uncomfortably close to our sacred and cultural sites. Please take care and show respect everywhere you hike.

SI:YÉMIYA ALBERT (SONNY) MCHALSIE *is the cultural adviser and sxweyxwiyam (historian) at the Stó:lō Research and Resource Management Centre. He co-authored* A Stó:lō–Coast Salish Historical Atlas. *McHalsie has received honorary degrees from the University of Victoria and University of the Fraser Valley. A member of the Shxw'ōwhámél First Nation, McHalsie is of Nlaka'pamux and Stó:lō heritage and lives in the Fraser Valley. In this foreword, McHalsie represents only his personal and family interest and knowledge.*

PREFACE

WRITING A hiking guidebook was a long-time dream that became reality with the first edition of *105 Hikes In and Around Southwestern British Columbia*. The idea first came to me in high school, when hiking became my favourite pastime. Early on, I started taking photos and keeping notes on my trips to places such as T'ak̲'t'ak̲'múy̓íṅ tl'a Iṅiny̓áx̲a7n (The Black Tusk) and Qoqó:lem (Vedder Mountain).

When making plans, my friends and I often relied on the fourth edition of *103 Hikes in Southwestern British Columbia*, authored by Mary and David Macaree and published in 1994. My brother, Patrick, brought home a copy, which I read cover to cover. At the time, you could say it was my favourite book of any genre. Anyway, I permanently borrowed Patrick's copy and still have it, held together by packing tape, today.

I'm not alone in my love for the inviting prose and quaint sketch maps of the Macarees, who immigrated from Scotland to Canada in 1955. Indeed, many a local hiker has referred to *103 Hikes* (first published in 1973) as a "bible" of sorts—one indelibly linked to fond memories of mountains and meadows. After the fourth edition, the Macarees passed the torch to fellow British Columbia Mountaineering Club (BCMC) member Jack Bryceland (1940–2024), who completed the fifth and sixth editions. (As a journalist at the *Georgia Straight* newspaper, I was thrilled to interview Bryceland about the publication of the sixth—and final—edition in 2008.)

When Greystone Books founding publisher Rob Sanders came calling in 2016 and invited me to write a new guidebook to succeed *103 Hikes*, I jumped at the opportunity. Taking on *105 Hikes* has been both challenging and rewarding. Undoubtedly, the Macarees set a high bar, and readers understandably have high expectations.

I learned plenty from putting together the first edition, published in 2018, as well as from readers' feedback. It's been especially gratifying to receive encouragement from folks who hiked with the Macarees. After writing *Destination Hikes In and Around Southwestern British Columbia* and then *Best Hikes and Nature Walks With Kids In and Around Southwestern British Columbia*, it was time for me to revisit *105 Hikes* and produce this revised and updated second edition.

Through *103 Hikes*, Mary (1922–2008) and David (1919–1998) inspired many to venture into the forests and mountains, tread lightly on the trails, and gain a healthy appreciation and concern for wild places. It's an honour to follow in their footsteps. In the spirit of the Macarees, a portion of the proceeds from sales of this book will go to the BCMC, of which I'm also a member, for conservation purposes.

INTRODUCTION

WELCOME TO THE second edition of *105 Hikes In and Around Southwestern British Columbia*. This guidebook covers rewarding hiking trails and routes in the Coast Mountains and Cascade Range and around the Salish Sea, extending across the Canada-U.S. border into northwestern Washington. This completely revised and updated edition introduces 36 new hikes and includes major changes to several trails.

The hikes I've selected are located north, east, west, and south of Vancouver, B.C., which lies in the Indigenous territories of the Musqueam (xʷməθkʷəy̓əm), Squamish (Sḵwx̱wú7mesh), and Tsleil-Waututh (səlilwətaɬ) First Nations. However, the trails span the territories of many First Nations and Tribes among the Coast Salish, St'át'imc, Nlaka'pamux, Syilx, Tŝilhqot'in, and Secwépemc peoples, the stewards of these lands and waters since time immemorial. Indeed, many hiking trails trace ancient Indigenous pathways. The cultures, economies, histories, and languages of the First Nations and Tribes are intertwined with the coast and mountains, which remain subject to Indigenous governance—and, where signed, treaties—today.

105 Hikes features hikes new and old, long and short, popular and sleepy. Whether it's the classic trails of Garibaldi, Golden Ears, and E.C. Manning Provincial Parks; scrambles to North Shore peaks; wildflower hikes in the Chilliwack Valley; hill walks of Vancouver Island; or sections of the Owl-Tenquille Traverse and Sunshine Coast Trail, there's no shortage of options for your next adventure.

The trips vary widely in quality and difficulty, but they generally fit within the following parameters (with a few exceptions):

- Are accessible as a day or weekend trip from Vancouver.
- Are doable in a day on foot, though some are better suited to overnighters.

A subalpine meadow on Snow Camp Mountain (see Hike 82).

- Take a minimum of 3 hours (with at least 150 m/490 ft of elevation gain) and a maximum of 12 hours.
- Deserve at least a "worthwhile" rating; there are no "poor" hikes in the book.
- Require no more than Class 3 scrambling. (In the Yosemite Decimal System, Class 1 denotes foot travel; Class 2 involves some use of hands; Class 3 entails easier climbing that's typically tackled unroped; Class 4 indicates steeper, more exposed climbing, where a belay is recommended; and Class 5 applies to technical climbing on vertical or nearly vertical rock.)

Additional hikes meeting these parameters are described in the companion volume, *Destination Hikes In and Around Southwestern British Columbia*. My other book, *Best Hikes and Nature Walks With Kids In and Around Southwestern British Columbia*, highlights shorter and easier trails suitable for all ages and experience levels.

Lofty summits, turquoise lakes, ancient forests, and blooming meadows—many a fair-weather hiker tries to pack in as many of these natural spectacles as possible between the long weekends of May and October, the so-called hiking season in these parts. Indeed, Vancouver averages 160 days with rainfall a year, and many high-elevation trails are snow-free only from July to October. Therefore, being a dedicated hiker means donning gaiters, waterproof gear, and traction aids or snowshoes, and persevering through all kinds of weather.

I've hiked every trail in the book, and I've striven for accuracy in my descriptions. However, little is static in the backcountry. Conditions vary depending on the weather and time of day, season, and year. Trails are rerouted, roads get rougher, bridges are washed away, logging and landslides obliterate paths, signs fade, and markers disappear. Therefore, take care.

This guide is intended for use with AdventureSmart's three Ts (trip planning, training, and taking the essentials) and more than a modicum of caution. No one plans to get lost or injured in the backcountry. Take the time to learn about avalanche and wildlife safety. Make sure to leave a trip plan with a reliable person, to help search and rescue teams find you in the event of an emergency. Before heading out, consult trail reports, avalanche bulletins (from Avalanche Canada or the Northwest Avalanche Center), and weather forecasts, and take note of sunset time.

Once on the trail, please endeavour not to spoil the experience for others. Unfortunately, more hikers often equals more problems: litter, poop, noise, human-wildlife conflict, disturbance of Indigenous cultural sites, environmental damage, and so on. Indeed, a little knowledge of backcountry ethics and etiquette goes a long way. For starters, respect the posted regulations, silence your cellphone, keep your music to yourself, put that drone away, and refrain from building inuksuit. Heed guidance from First Nations stewards. Yield to horse riders and, when going downhill, to uphill hikers.

The minimum-impact practices championed by the Leave No Trace Center for Outdoor Ethics include hiking in small groups (10 people or fewer), sticking to established campsites and trails (don't shortcut switchbacks), packing out all food and waste, leaving natural and historical objects in place, never feeding wildlife, and keeping dogs under control at all times (and carrying out their poop) or leaving them at home. In light of the climate emergency, highway bottlenecks, and overcrowded parking lots, please consider using transit, carpooling, car-sharing, ride-hailing, cycling, and other alternative transportation options where possible. Let's be inclusive on the trails. Everyone should feel welcome in the outdoors, regardless of ability, age, class, ethnicity, gender, sexual orientation, or size.

Many favoured hiking spots are places of cultural, economic, historical, and spiritual importance to First Nations. Indeed, many mountains, rivers, lakes, islands, and rocks have storyful names, old and new, in Indigenous languages—including Halq'eméylem, hən̓q̓əmin̓əm̓, and Hul'q'umi'num'; Sḵwx̱wú7mesh Sníchim; St̓át̓imcets and Ucwalmícwts; Nłeʔkepmxcín; nsyilxcən; she shashishalhem; ʔayʔaǰuθəm; ləkʷəŋən, SENĆOŦEN, Xwlemi Chosen, and Xws7ámeshqen; nəxʷsƛ̓ay̓əmúcən; Lhéchelesem; dxʷləšucid and txʷəlšucid; Nenqayni Ch'ih; and Secwepemctsín. Thanks to the work of Stó:lō historian (and foreword writer) Si:yémiya Albert (Sonny) McHalsie, *A Stó:lō–Coast Salish Historical Atlas* records more than 700 Halq'eméylem place names in the Lower Mainland; a number of these toponyms are reproduced in this guidebook.

Respect these sacred places—and the rights and responsibilities of Indigenous people of the territory to care for, use, and occupy them (regardless of park status). Though hiking is often viewed as a low-impact activity, the popularity of hiking and outdoor recreation has a big impact on First Nations whose ancestral lands and waters are rendered unavailable or unsuitable for hunting, fishing, medicine gathering, forest gardening, ritual bathing, vision questing, and other cultural practices.

In this context, it is heartening to see some fruitful collaborations between outdoor recreation organizations and First Nations, acknowledging shared interests in responsible recreation and environmental stewardship, and recognizing First Nations' jurisdiction. For example, the B.C. Marine Trails Network Association created the Marine Trail Code of Conduct—informed by its work with N̲anwak̲olas Council—which encourages respect for First Nations cultural heritage on paddling routes. In 2022, the Squamish Nation and Squamish Off-Road Cycling Association signed a memorandum of understanding, committing to co-operate on the stewardship of mountain-biking trails. We need to see more hiking groups doing relationship-building in the same vein.

We have the vision and leadership of First Nations to thank for protecting some of our most cherished wildlands. Back in 1989, the Líl̓wat and Lytton (Tl'kemtsin) First Nations declared the establishment of Stein Valley Tribal Heritage Park. Along with public pressure, this action led to the B.C. government creating Stein Valley Nlaka'pamux Heritage Park, co-managed by the Lytton First Nation and B.C. Parks, in 1995. In 2014, the Xeni Gwet'in and Yuneŝit'in First Nations announced Nexwagwezʔan (Dasiqox Tribal Park), north of South Chilcotin Mountains Provincial Park, in Tŝilhqot'in territory.

More recently, the Líl̓wat and N'Quatqua First Nations partnered with B.C. Parks on much-needed visitor use management strategies for Pipi7íyekw (Joffre Lakes Provincial Park) and Háwint (Tenquille Lake)—both beloved hiking areas under threat from overuse. In 2022, the Lower Similkameen Indian Band designated the entire nʔaysnúlaʔxʷ snxaʔcnitkʷ (Ashnola River watershed), including kʷaniɬkʷaʔitkʷ (Cathedral Provincial Park), as a sməlqmíx Protected and Conserved Area. Meanwhile, in the Fraser Canyon, the Kanaka Bar Band (T'eqt'aqtn'mux) is developing the T'eqt'aqtn Indigenous Protected and Conserved Area, next door to the Sti'yen (Stein River) watershed.

Many other First Nations are setting up new Indigenous protected and conserved areas in B.C. and employing Indigenous guardians to monitor and restore their lands and waters and uphold Indigenous laws and protocols. These are welcome developments for all of us who love nature and want to foster a healthier relationship between communities, lands, and waters.

It takes a lot of people working together to protect wild places, build and maintain trails, and make sure parks get the staffing and funding they need. I hope *105 Hikes* leads you down new paths, encourages you to recreate safely and responsibly, feeds your interest in the nature and culture of these lands and waters, and inspires you to speak out or lend a hand in support of our parks, trails, and wildlands.

GET INFORMED

AdventureSmart
adventuresmart.ca

Avalanche Canada
avalanche.ca

B.C. Parks
bcparks.ca

B.C. Search and Rescue Association
bcsara.com

Canadian Parks and Wilderness Society–B.C.
cpawsbc.org

Federation of Mountain Clubs of B.C.
mountainclubs.org

First Peoples' Map of B.C.
maps.fpcc.ca

Leave No Trace Center for Outdoor Ethics
lnt.org

Northwest Avalanche Center
nwac.us

Outdoor Recreation Council of B.C.
orcbc.ca

Squamish Atlas
squamishatlas.com

Washington Trails Association
wta.org

FACING: Sun God Mountain looms behind One Duck Lake (Hike 44).

PRIORITIZING YOUR SAFETY ON THE TRAILS

by Kayla Brolly and Douglas Pope

WHETHER YOU ARE an experienced hiker or a newcomer stepping onto the trail for the first time, the prospect of hiking in the mountains of the Pacific Northwest is filled with the potential of breathtaking views, fresh air, and a profound connection with nature. Yet, as you prepare to immerse yourself in the great outdoors, we cannot overstate the importance of prioritizing your safety and well-being.

As search and rescue technicians, we bear witness to what happens when things don't go as planned. We hope you can avoid misadventure by being prepared, telling someone where you are going, and staying where you are if you become lost.

The North Shore mountains, for example, while captivating, can be deceptively challenging. Close proximity to populated areas and seemingly straightforward access to trailheads might mislead some into assuming these trails are easy and equipped with cell service—which is often not the case. In truth, these trails are rugged and surrounded by heavily forested, steep, and demanding terrain. And the weather—we can't forget about the weather. They don't call it Raincouver for nothing. Which means it can become dark very quickly, the ground can be very, very wet and slippery, and there's the additional challenge of snow and ice at higher elevations.

Broadly, preparedness involves three main components: adequate training, proper equipment, and trip planning. It is of critical importance to align your training and fitness level with your hiking objectives. Realistic assessments of your capabilities and those of your group are essential. The peaks have stood for millennia and will await your return as you progressively build the stamina and confidence to meet your objectives and enjoy this beautiful corner of the globe.

The proper footwear and equipment are not optional accessories but the linchpin between a successful outing and potential injury or worse. This includes essential survival gear for situations when becoming lost, injured, or benighted could turn a pleasant hike into an emergency situation. By ensuring you have the necessary gear and supplies, you create a safety net that can make all the difference in challenging circumstances.

In our experience, many people could avoid the need for rescue by ensuring they have the following equipment on their hike: sturdy hiking footwear, extra layers of clothing, a headlamp, microspikes or crampons, an extra battery for the cellphone, and a satellite communication device. Another tip: Even if you lose cell reception, if you need help, still try to call 911, as 911 calls go to any provider's cell tower.

Finally, the importance of trip planning cannot be emphasized enough. Meticulously planning your route, understanding the terrain, and being aware of environmental conditions are foundational to a safe and enjoyable journey. Leaving a trip plan with a responsible person—including where you are going, who you are with, what equipment you have, and what time you are expected to return—is essential.

Consider two scenarios: In the first, you find yourself lost or injured without anyone aware of your whereabouts. You are alone, it's getting dark and cold, and you realize no one knows you are missing, and you have no idea when someone will notice you are missing and call for help. Now, imagine a second scenario, where someone knows your plan and will call for help when they realize you have not returned. You can await rescue with the assurance that help will be activated.

Accidents do not discriminate based on experience level. We've rescued people who are out for the first time as well as those who have summited peaks all over the world. We are here to tell you it can happen to you. Whether you're a novice or a seasoned hiker, unforeseen challenges like bad weather, early darkness, or unexpected injuries can turn an easy hike into a prolonged crisis. Preparedness is the key to ensuring a positive backcountry experience.

In the unfortunate event that you find yourself lost or injured, resist the instinct to press on. Remaining where you are increases the likelihood of rescue. On the North Shore, descending often leads to perilous natural drainages marked by dense vegetation, steep cliffs, and waterfalls. Descending also increases the chance of losing cell service. Many rescues involve individuals stranded in these treacherous areas, emphasizing the importance of staying put. If you become lost, don't panic, remain in place, and maintain a positive mental attitude.

As you explore the beauty of the North Shore and the Coast Mountains, we sincerely hope you won't need our services. However, should you find yourself in need, we will come.

KAYLA BROLLY *is a registered nurse who has been volunteering with North Shore Rescue since 2013. In her previous life, she was a professional ski patroller and rappel forest firefighter. On North Shore Rescue, Brolly has held the roles of ground search team leader, executive officer, medical advisory committee member, swift-water rescue technician, helicopter rescue team member, social media coordinator, and educator and is the co-creator and co-manager of the advanced medical provider program. When she's not working, training, or rescuing, she loves hiking, skiing, puzzling, reading, and making dinosaur noises with her baby daughter. She lives in North Vancouver.*

DOUGLAS POPE *is a retired professional engineer who has been volunteering with North Shore Rescue since 2004. He is a search manager for the team. In his spare time, Pope likes to hike, mountain bike, and play with his granddaughter, Alaia. He has lived on the North Shore since he was eight years old and has been exploring the creeks and mountains ever since.*

10 ESSENTIALS FOR BACKCOUNTRY TRAVEL

1. **Navigation** (map, compass, GPS)
2. **Headlamp** (extra batteries)
3. **Sun protection** (sunglasses, sun hat, sunscreen)
4. **First-aid kit** (bandages, blister pads, pain-relief medication)
5. **Knife** (repair kit, multi-tool, duct tape)
6. **Fire starter** (waterproof matches, lighter)
7. **Shelter** (tent, emergency blanket)
8. **Extra food** (energy bars)
9. **Extra water** (purifier)
10. **Extra clothes** (insulating layers, rain gear)

FACING: Fall colour on Skywalk North (Hike 40) below Rainbow Mountain.

TAKING CARE OF NATURE

by Tori Ball

THE BEAUTIFUL AND extraordinary places we visit to hike, swim, and camp host a remarkable diversity of plants and animals. B.C. boasts the highest biodiversity of any province or territory in Canada. This diversity of plant and animal life is mirrored in the diversity of Indigenous Peoples across B.C.—including over 200 distinct First Nations, more than 30 First Nations languages, and many dialects. Diverse stories, cultural practices, and ceremonies demonstrate a deep knowledge, responsibility, and connection to land unique to each place and community.

Parks and protected areas across B.C. and Canada have a dark history—including forced removal and attempted separation of First Nations from their lands and cultures. The modern view of conservation recognizes that humans and nature have evolved together over thousands of years. This view has led to a long-awaited shift to supporting and recognizing Indigenous practices, rights, and leadership in the protection and stewardship of lands and waters.

As visitors to these places, it is important for us to learn both of these histories. Both B.C. Parks and Parks Canada have been on journeys to better reflect and include First Nations in decision-making and create space to honour their histories and ongoing connections.

This book provides a jumping-off point for learning about First Nations whose traditional territories host amazing outdoor experiences. I encourage you to deepen your knowledge by learning about the history and ongoing culture of the First Nations that are inseparable from the lands that host you for your wander among large trees, open grasslands, or coastal vistas.

No matter how lightly you tread, all outdoor recreation activities leave an impact. We all share a responsibility to leave places better than we found them. The Seven Principles of Leave No Trace are a great starting place to learn about stewardship as an outdoor adventurer.

Taking care of the places that are important for recreation, as well as clean air and water, goes beyond our personal responsibility. Nature is in crisis. While B.C. boasts the highest biodiversity in Canada, it also has the most species at risk. Expanding our protected areas, in partnership with First Nations, is a proven way to slow rapid climate change and reverse biodiversity loss.

We have a collective responsibility and power to ensure that wildlife, nature, and landscapes that offer us so much are protected and well managed for the long term. This means sustained government resources and making sure that nature conservation doesn't drop off the list of priorities. Politics goes through cycles, yet our enthusiasm for conservation must be steadfast.

If you appreciate your time hiking in the outdoors, I encourage you to share that with your local political representatives—and let them know that nature needs more attention and protection.

TORI BALL *grew up flatwater canoe tripping in Ontario, spending weeks on the move on waterways. This experience led her to a career in climate and nature conservation advocacy. When she isn't wandering outside, she is working with all levels of government to address the biodiversity crisis and helping fellow nature lovers speak up to protect the lands and waters we all depend on. Ball is the conservation director for the Land and Fresh Water Program at the Canadian Parks and Wilderness Society-British Columbia (CPAWS-BC). She spends much of her free time in the forests, rivers, and ocean throughout coastal B.C. with her toddler and partner. She lives in Squamish, in the unceded, traditional territory of the Sḵwx̱wú7mesh (Squamish) Nation.*

SEVEN PRINCIPLES OF LEAVE NO TRACE

1. Plan ahead and prepare.
2. Travel and camp on durable surfaces.
3. Dispose of waste properly.
4. Leave what you find.
5. Minimize campfire impacts.
6. Respect wildlife.
7. Be considerate of other visitors.

HOW TO USE THIS GUIDE

THE 105 HIKES in this book are categorized by regions north, east, west, and south of Vancouver and arranged by distance from the city. To select a hike, start with the Overview Map and Hikes at a Glance table—or consult the Hikes by Distance table on page 256. (You can also find Hikes by Time, Hikes by Elevation Gain, and Hikes by High Point tables; a bibliography; and other resources on my website at *105Hikes.com*.)

Each numbered trip comes with feature icons, statistics and ratings, a topographic map, hiking and driving directions, and a photograph. I've included transit options where available.

What follows are explanations of the feature icons, statistics, and ratings used in this guide, as well as information to help clarify the hiking and driving directions.

FEATURES

Icons draw your attention to the features of each numbered trip.

Dogs:

Yes: Dogs are permitted. Hikers with dogs should keep them on the trail, close, and under control at all times. Pick up and pack out dog poop; don't leave it in bags, even temporarily, along the trail. Keep dogs out of streams and wetlands to protect wildlife.

Leash required: Dogs must be leashed for all or a significant portion of the hike. Respect the posted regulations. Hikers with dogs yield to other hikers.

No: Dogs are prohibited on all or part of the route. Leave your furry friends at home.

Transit: The hike is accessible via public bus or private shuttle, running on a regular schedule.

Good for a rainy day: The hike is still rewarding in moderate rain, and the terrain is somewhat suitable for wet weather.

Backpacking: The hike can be done as part of an overnight (or multi-day) trip, due to at least one backcountry campsite on the described route or a connected trail.

STATISTICS

Distance: The length of the hike as described is provided in metric and imperial units.

Time: Everyone hikes at their own pace. Once you've completed several of the hikes in the book, you'll get an idea of how your times compare with the estimates listed. I've indicated whether a given time (and distance) refers to an out-and-back trip or a loop, lollipop, circuit, or other type of trip. The estimates include enough time for an average hiker to take short breaks for snacks, lunch, and viewpoints. (Budget extra time for swimming!)

Elevation gain: The net elevation gain is simply the difference between the highest and lowest points encountered on the hike. Some hikes have many ups and downs that are not reflected in this statistic. Although both metric and imperial elevations are noted in the text, the maps show contour lines in metric only.

High point: This statistic represents the highest elevation above mean sea level attained on the hike—often, but not always, a summit.

Season: The time of year when conditions are typically—but not always—favourable for the hike is indicated. That is, the trail should be mostly snow-free, so no need for snowshoes or traction aids.

Maps: The small maps in this guide are no substitute for large, printed maps. For each hike, the relevant map sheets from Natural Resources Canada's National Topographic System (NTS) or the U.S. Geological Survey (USGS) are noted. Where appropriate, I also recommend maps from publishers such as Canadian Map Makers, Clark Geomatics, Green Trails Maps, John Baldwin, Square One Maps, and Trail Ventures BC.

Trailhead: The geographic position of the start of the hike is given in degrees, minutes, and seconds using the World Geodetic System 1984 (WGS84) datum. The trailhead is often, but not necessarily, near the parking area.

RATINGS

This book and the companion volume, *Destination Hikes In and Around Southwestern British Columbia*, share the same rating system for difficulty. Each hike is assigned a quality rating and a difficulty rating, with which you may vehemently disagree. Both are inherently subjective, but might help you select the right trip for a given day.

Quality

★ **Worthwhile:** A decent leg-stretcher or thigh-burner.

★★ **Good:** A tad low on the reward-to-effort ratio, but definitely has its moments.

★★★ **Very good:** Great views for the effort required.

★★★★ **Excellent:** An incredibly scenic and satisfying trip.

★★★★★ **Amazing:** Among the very best experiences in the book.

Difficulty

● **Easy:** Minimal elevation gain on well-marked trails.

■ **Moderate:** A workout with decent elevation gain on reasonably obvious paths.

◆ **Difficult:** Strenuous due to large elevation gain, some route-finding challenges, and/or easy scrambling with little exposure.

◆◆ **Advanced:** Extremely demanding with tricky route-finding, substantial off-trail travel, and/or exposed scrambling—for experienced parties only.

THE HIKE

Trails are not described in winter conditions. River directions (for example, "river left" and "right bank") are given from the perspective of looking downstream. A "lollipop" hike features a loop at its far end; the same route (the "stem") is followed to the loop and back to the trailhead.

GETTING THERE

Transit: Before you travel, make sure to verify routes, schedules, stops, and fares on transit-agency or bus-company websites. TransLink (*translink.ca*) operates public transit in Metro Vancouver; B.C. Transit (*bctransit.com*) handles service elsewhere in the province. Parkbus (*parkbus.ca*) offers scheduled service on select dates to a few major trailheads in provincial parks.

Vehicle: Driving directions are provided from major highways. When vehicle access involves gravel roads, I've noted whether two-wheel drive (2WD), four-wheel drive (4WD), and/or high clearance is required (at time of writing). Road conditions are subject to dramatic change. I've also indicated if a park pass is required, pay parking is in effect, or a trailhead toilet is available.

The following locations are shorthand for particular intersections:

- **Downtown Squamish (S<u>k</u>wx̱wú7mesh):** Highway 99 (Sea to Sky Highway) and Cleveland Avenue/Loggers Lane.
- **Mount Currie:** Main Street and Lillooet Lake Road, where northbound Highway 99 traffic turns right (for Duffey Lake Road).
- **Sechelt Village (ch'atlich):** Sunshine Coast Highway/Dolphin Street and Wharf Avenue, where northbound Highway 101 traffic turns left (for Earls Cove).
- **Whistler Village:** Highway 99 (Sea to Sky Highway) and Village Gate Boulevard.

FUN FACT: On Trans-Canada Highway 1 in the Lower Mainland and Yellowhead Highway 5 (Coquihalla Highway), exit numbers correspond to the distance in kilometres east of Horseshoe Bay.

KEY TO MAP SYMBOLS

- Parking
- Bus Stop
- Ferry Dock
- 4-Wheel-Drive
- Toilet
- Waterfall
- Viewpoint
- Camping
- Backcountry Hut
- Chalet/Lodge
- Warning
- No Public Access
- Primary Highway
- Mountain Peak
- Direction of Travel / Off-Map Destination

- Road
- Track
- Trail
- Described Route
- Described Route (Off -Trail)
- Chairlift/Gondola/Tram
- Railroad
- Major Contour Line (100 m)
- Minor Contour Line (20 m)
- Creek/Stream
- Forest
- River/Lake/Ocean
- Alpine/Rock/Open Terrain
- Wetland
- Glacier

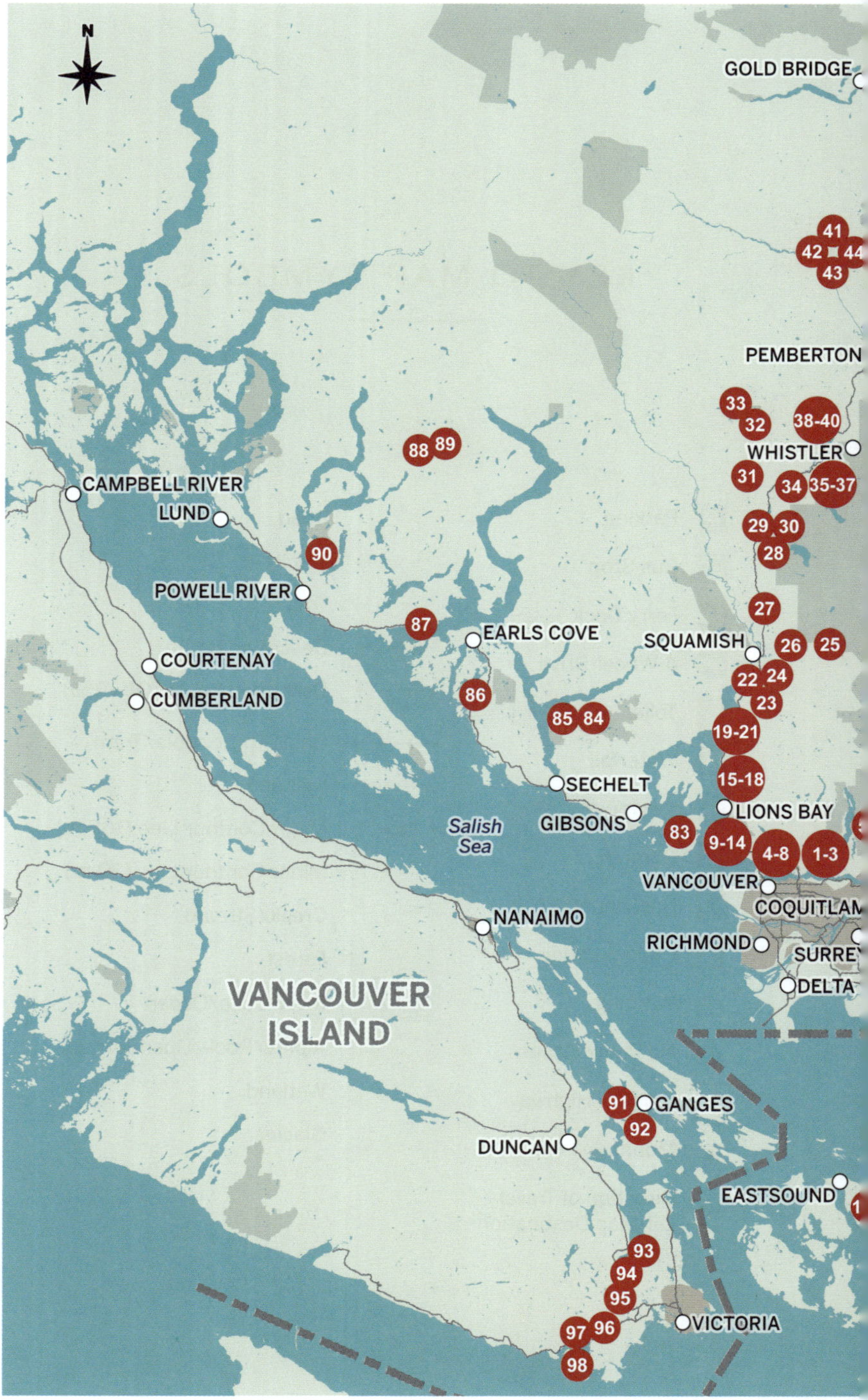
N
GOLD BRIDGE
PEMBERTON
WHISTLER
CAMPBELL RIVER
LUND
POWELL RIVER
EARLS COVE
SQUAMISH
COURTENAY
CUMBERLAND
SECHELT
GIBSONS
LIONS BAY
Salish Sea
VANCOUVER
COQUITLAM
NANAIMO
RICHMOND
SURREY
DELTA
VANCOUVER ISLAND
GANGES
DUNCAN
EASTSOUND
VICTORIA
41
42
43
33
32
38-40
88
89
31
34
35-37
29
30
28
90
27
87
26
25
22
24
86
85
84
23
19-21
15-18
83
9-14
4-8
1-3
91
92
93
94
95
96
97
98

CACHE CREEK
KAMLOOPS
LILLOOET
SPENCES BRIDGE
MERRITT
British Columbia
BOSTON BAR
YALE
PRINCETON
HOPE
AGASSIZ
CHILLIWACK
APLE RIDGE
ISSION
ABBOTSFORD
CANADA
USA
SUMAS
GLACIER
BELLINGHAM
Washington
NACORTES
MOUNT VERNON
49
8
47
71
72
73
74
75
56
55
54
57
58
60
69
70
76
59
65
63
61
64
66
67
68
62
77
81
79
78
82
80
104
103
105
99
100
0
20
40 km
0
10
20 mi

Hike	Quality	Difficulty	Distance	Time
HIKES NORTH OF VANCOUVER				
North Vancouver				
1 Devil's Peak	★★	◆	8 km (5 mi)	5 hours
2 Mount Seymour	★★★	■	8 km (5 mi)	4.5 hours
3 Mount Elsay	★★★★	◆	13 km (8.1 mi)	10 hours
4 Norvan Falls	★★	●	14.5 km (9 mi)	5 hours
5 Mount Burwell	★★	◆	25 km (15.5 mi)	11 hours
6 Mount Fromme	★	■	10 km (6.2 mi)	5 hours
7 Goat Mountain	★★	■	14 km (8.7 mi)	7.5 hours
8 Crown Mountain	★★★★	◆◆	16 km (9.9 mi)	8.5 hours
West Vancouver				
9 Hollyburn Mountain	★★	■	12 km (7.5 mi)	4 hours
10 Mount Strachan	★★★	◆	9 km (5.6 mi)	5 hours
11 Unnecessary Mountain	★★★	◆	18 km (11.2 mi)	8 hours
12 Black Mountain and Eagle Bluff	★★★	●	9.5 km (5.9 mi)	4.5 hours
13 West Knob	★★	■	10 km (6.2 mi)	5 hours
14 Donut Rock	★	◆	12 km (7.5 mi)	6.5 hours
Lions Bay				
15 Ken's Bluffs	★★★	■	9 km (5.6 mi)	5 hours
16 Mount Harvey	★★	◆	12.5 km (7.8 mi)	7.5 hours
17 Tunnel Bluff	★★★★	●	11 km (6.8 mi)	4 hours
18 Brunswick Mountain	★★★	◆◆	14.5 km (9 mi)	8.5 hours
19 Deeks Bluff	★★	■	7.5 km (4.7 mi)	4 hours
20 Stl'álk̲em Stak̲w (Deeks Lake)	★★	■	13.5 km (8.4 mi)	7.5 hours
21 Beth Lake	★★	■	18 km (11.2 mi)	7 hours
Squamish				
22 Sea to Summit Trail	★★	■	6.5 km (4 mi)	4 hours
23 Neverland Falls	★★★	■	9 km (5.6 mi)	5.5 hours
24 Siy̓ám̓ Smánit (Stawamus Chief Mountain)	★★★★	■	14 km (8.7 mi)	5 hours
25 Watersprite Lake	★★★★★	■	17 km (10.6 mi)	7 hours
26 Elfin Lakes	★★★★	■	20 km (12.4 mi)	6.5 hours
27 Tantalus View Lookout	★★★	●	12 km (7.5 mi)	5 hours
Cheakamus River				
28 Garibaldi Lake and Black Tusk Meadows	★★★★★	■	21 km (13 mi)	6.5 hours

Elevation Gain (or Loss)	High Point	Season	Dogs	Transit	Good for a Rainy Day	Back-packing
100 m (330 ft)	630 m (2,070 ft)	April to November	Leash		✓	
390 m (1,280 ft)	1,455 m (4,770 ft)	July to October	Leash			
500 m (1,640 ft)	1,422 m (4,665 ft)	July to October	Leash			
230 m (755 ft)	430 m (1,410 ft)	March to November	Yes	✓	✓	
1,340 m (4,400 ft)	1,544 m (5,070 ft)	July to October	Leash	✓		
810 m (2,660 ft)	1,171 m (3,840 ft)	June to November	Yes	✓	✓	
1,110 m (3,640 ft)	1,401 m (4,600 ft)	July to October	No	✓		
1,210 m (3,970 ft)	1,501 m (4,925 ft)	July to October	No	✓		
430 m (1,410 ft)	1,326 m (4,350 ft)	July to November	Leash			
540 m (1,770 ft)	1,459 m (4,790 ft)	July to October	Leash			
630 m (2,070 ft)	1,548 m (5,080 ft)	July to October	Leash			✓
310 m (1,020 ft)	1,224 m (4,020 ft)	June to November	Leash		✓	
655 m (2,150 ft)	760 m (2,490 ft)	April to November	Leash	✓	✓	
975 m (3,200 ft)	1,080 m (3,540 ft)	May to November	Leash	✓		
400 m (1,310 ft)	610 m (2,000 ft)	March to November	Yes	✓		
1,420 m (4,660 ft)	1,652 m (5,420 ft)	July to October	Yes	✓		
470 m (1,540 ft)	700 m (2,300 ft)	March to November	Yes	✓		
1,560 m (5,120 ft)	1,788 m (5,870 ft)	July to October	Leash	✓		
410 m (1,345 ft)	470 m (1,540 ft)	Most of the year	Leash		✓	✓
980 m (3,215 ft)	1,040 m (3,410 ft)	May to November	Leash		✓	✓
1,010 m (3,310 ft)	1,060 m (3,480 ft)	May to November	Yes		✓	
850 m (2,790 ft)	885 m (2,900 ft)	April to November	Yes	✓		
420 m (1,380 ft)	1,290 m (4,230 ft)	June to October	Yes	✓		
625 m (2,050 ft)	702 m (2,300 ft)	March to November	Yes	✓		
650 m (2,130 ft)	1,450 m (4,760 ft)	July to October	No			✓
620 m (2,030 ft)	1,590 m (5,220 ft)	July to October	No			✓
170 m (560 ft)	400 m (1,310 ft)	Most of the year	Leash		✓	
1,080 m (3,540 ft)	1,650 m (5,410 ft)	July to October	No	✓		✓

Hike	Quality	Difficulty	Distance	Time
29 T'ak̲'t'ak̲'múy̓ín̓ tl'a Il̓hiny̓áx̲a7n (The Black Tusk)	★★★★★	◆◆	27 km (16.8 mi)	10.5 hours
30 Panorama Ridge	★★★★★	◆	30 km (18.6 mi)	10.5 hours
31 Brandywine Mountain	★★★★★	◆◆	10 km (6.2 mi)	5.5 hours
32 Conflict Lake	★★★★	■	12 km (7.5 mi)	4 hours
33 Cirque Lake	★★★★★	◆	4 km (2.5 mi)	3 hours
Whistler				
34 Crater Rim Trail	★★★	■	11.5 km (7.1 mi)	5.5 hours
35 Flute Summit	★★★★	■	9 km (5.6 mi)	4 hours
36 Blackcomb Burn	★★★	◆	6.2 km (3.9 mi)	3 hours
37 Decker Tarn	★★★★	■	9 km (5.6 mi)	4 hours
38 Rainbow Pass	★★★★	■	18 km (11.2 mi)	7 hours
39 Skywalk South	★★★★	◆	18 km (11.2 mi)	6.5 hours
40 Skywalk North	★★★★★	■	18 km (11.2 mi)	8 hours
Pemberton				
41 Háwint (Tenquille Lake)	★★★★	■	13 km (8.1 mi)	4.5 hours
42 Copper Mound	★★★★	◆◆	14 km (8.7 mi)	6 hours
43 Mount McLeod	★★★★	◆	15.5 km (9.6 mi)	7 hours
44 One Duck Lake	★★★★★	◆◆	25 km (15.5 mi)	11.5 hours
45 Upper Fowl Lake	★★★★★	◆	15 km (9.3 mi)	7 hours
46 Valentine Lake	★★★★	◆	12 km (7.5 mi)	5.5 hours
Líl̓wat Lake to Duffey Lake				
47 Wetscín'atkwa (Lizzie Creek)	★★	◆	27 km (16.8 mi)	10 hours
48 Pipi7íyekw (Joffre Lakes)	★★★★★	●	9.5 km (5.9 mi)	4 hours
49 Mount Rohr	★★★★★	◆◆	12 km (7.5 mi)	8 hours
Bridge River				
50 Cinnabar Ridge	★★★	■	14.5 km (9 mi)	6.5 hours
HIKES EAST OF VANCOUVER				
Port Moody and Coquitlam				
51 Little Horn Mountain	★★	■	18 km (11.2 mi)	6.5 hours
52 Coquitlam Lake View Trail	★★	■	12.5 km (7.8 mi)	5.5 hours
Maple Ridge				
53 Alouette Mountain	★★★	■	22 km (13.7 mi)	9 hours
54 Evans Peak	★★★★	◆	8 km (5 mi)	5 hours
55 Gold Creek	★★	■	11.5 km (7.1 mi)	3.5 hours

Elevation Gain (or Loss)	High Point	Season	Dogs	Transit	Good for a Rainy Day	Backpacking
1,745 m (5,725 ft)	2,315 m (7,595 ft)	July to October	No	✓		✓
1,560 m (5,120 ft)	2,133 m (7,000 ft)	July to October	No	✓		✓
860 m (2,820 ft)	2,213 m (7,260 ft)	July to October	No			
180 m (590 ft)	1,370 m (4,495 ft)	July to October	No			
330 m (1,080 ft)	1,530 m (5,020 ft)	July to October	Leash			
320 m (1,050 ft)	920 m (3,020 ft)	April to November	Yes	✓	✓	
455 m (1,490 ft)	2,182 m (7,160 ft)	July to September	No	✓		✓
1,165 m (3,820 ft)	1,850 m (6,070 ft)	July to September	No	✓		
240 m (790 ft)	2,050 m (6,730 ft)	July to September	No	✓		
840 m (2,760 ft)	1,510 m (4,950 ft)	July to October	No			✓
1,050 m (3,445 ft)	1,790 m (5,870 ft)	July to October	No	✓		
1,050 m (3,445 ft)	1,790 m (5,870 ft)	July to October	No	✓		
445 m (1,460 ft)	1,710 m (5,610 ft)	July to October	No			✓
890 m (2,920 ft)	2,157 m (7,080 ft)	July to September	No			✓
890 m (2,920 ft)	2,158 m (7,080 ft)	July to September	No			✓
775 m (2,540 ft)	2,040 m (6,690 ft)	July to September	No			✓
510 m (1,670 ft)	1,730 m (5,680 ft)	July to October	Yes			✓
670 m (2,200 ft)	1,770 m (5,810 ft)	July to October	Yes			✓
1,220 m (4,000 ft)	1,610 m (5,280 ft)	July to October	Yes			✓
360 m (1,180 ft)	1,570 m (5,150 ft)	July to October	No	✓		✓
1,030 m (3,380 ft)	2,423 m (7,950 ft)	July to October	Leash			✓
1,000 m (3,280 ft)	2,213 m (7,260 ft)	July to September	Yes			
350 m (1,150 ft)	451 m (1,480 ft)	March to November	Leash	✓		
600 m (1,970 ft)	930 m (3,050 ft)	May to November	Leash		✓	
1,110 m (3,640 ft)	1,361 m (4,465 ft)	July to October	Yes		✓	
950 m (3,120 ft)	1,132 m (3,710 ft)	June to November	No	✓		
210 m (690 ft)	360 m (1,180 ft)	Most of the year	Leash	✓	✓	✓

Hike	Quality	Difficulty	Distance	Time
56 x̣ε'εc'εnxʷ (Golden Ears)	★★★★	◆◆	24 km (14.9 mi)	11 hours
Mission to Harrison Hot Springs				
57 79 Grind	★★	■	6.5 km (4 mi)	4 hours
58 Hoover Bluff	★★	■	11 km (6.8 mi)	4.5 hours
59 Leq'á:mel (Nicomen Mountain)	★★	◆	16 km (9.9 mi)	8 hours
60 Campbell Lake	★	■	10 km (6.2 mi)	6 hours
Abbotsford and Chilliwack				
61 Kw'ekw'e'i:qw (Sumas Mountain)	★★★	■	14.5 km (9 mi)	6.5 hours
62 Qoqó:lem (Vedder Mountain)	★★	■	11.5 km (7.1 mi)	5 hours
63 Gloria Lookout	★★★	◆	11 km (6.8 mi)	6.5 hours
Chilliwack River				
64 Mount Thurston	★★★	◆	16 km (9.9 mi)	7 hours
65 Lhílheqey (Cheam Peak)	★★★★★	■	9 km (5.6 mi)	4 hours
66 Ford Mountain	★	■	12 km (7.5 mi)	5.5 hours
67 Porcupine Rock	★★★	◆	6 km (3.7 mi)	4.5 hours
68 Flora Peak	★★★★	◆	12 km (7.5 mi)	7 hours
Hope and Fraser Canyon				
69 St'ám'ya (Hope Mountain)	★★★★	■	8.5 km (5.3 mi)	6 hours
70 Wells Peak	★★★★	■	6 km (3.7 mi)	4.5 hours
71 Tikwalus Heritage Trail	★★★	■	12.5 km (7.8 mi)	7 hours
Coquihalla Pass to Tulameen River				
72 Zupjok Peak	★★★★	■	10 km (6.2 mi)	4.5 hours
73 The Flatiron	★★★★	■	10 km (6.2 mi)	5.5 hours
74 Illal Mountain	★★★★★	◆	18 km (11.2 mi)	8.5 hours
75 Podunk Creek	★★	■	23 km (14.3 mi)	7 hours
E.C. Manning Provincial Park				
76 Skagit Bluffs	★	●	12 km (7.5 mi)	4.5 hours
77 Three Brothers Mountain	★★★★★	■	21 km (13 mi)	6.5 hours
78 Windy Joe Mountain	★★	■	15 km (9.3 mi)	5 hours
79 Frosty Mountain	★★★★★	■	21 km (13 mi)	7.5 hours
80 Skwa-kwa-eets (Lightning Lakes)	★★★	■	19.5 km (12.1 mi)	6.5 hours
81 Skyline Summit	★★★	■	14 km (8.7 mi)	5.5 hours
82 Lone Goat Mountain	★★★★	■	22 km (13.7 mi)	8 hours

Elevation Gain (or Loss)	High Point	Season	Dogs	Transit	Good for a Rainy Day	Back-packing
1,540 m (5,050 ft)	1,716 m (5,630 ft)	July to October	Yes	✓		✓
530 m (1,740 ft)	700 m (2,300 ft)	March to November	Leash			
300 m (980 ft)	490 m (1,610 ft)	Most of the year	Leash		✓	
1,210 m (3,970 ft)	1,221 m (4,010 ft)	June to October	Yes			
675 m (2,215 ft)	690 m (2,260 ft)	April to November	Leash	✓	✓	
750 m (2,460 ft)	910 m (2,990 ft)	May to November	Leash		✓	
365 m (1,200 ft)	925 m (3,035 ft)	May to October	Yes		✓	
1,125 m (3,690 ft)	1,455 m (4,770 ft)	June to October	Yes			
1,000 m (3,280 ft)	1,630 m (5,350 ft)	June to October	Leash			
690 m (2,260 ft)	2,104 m (6,900 ft)	July to October	Leash			
1,010 m (3,310 ft)	1,421 m (4,660 ft)	June to October	Yes		✓	
640 m (2,100 ft)	1,240 m (4,070 ft)	June to October	No			
1,310 m (4,300 ft)	1,952 m (6,405 ft)	July to October	Leash			✓
690 m (2,260 ft)	1,844 m (6,050 ft)	July to October	Yes			
700 m (2,300 ft)	1,863 m (6,110 ft)	July to October	Yes			
790 m (2,590 ft)	910 m (2,990 ft)	May to October	Yes			✓
655 m (2,150 ft)	1,835 m (6,020 ft)	July to October	Leash			
690 m (2,260 ft)	1,898 m (6,230 ft)	July to October	Leash			
870 m (2,850 ft)	2,020 m (6,630 ft)	July to October	Yes			✓
215 m (705 ft)	1,470 m (4,820 ft)	June to October	Yes		✓	✓
350 m (1,150 ft)	930 m (3,050 ft)	April to November	Leash		✓	
480 m (1,575 ft)	2,272 m (7,450 ft)	July to October	Leash			✓
665 m (2,180 ft)	1,825 m (5,990 ft)	July to October	Leash		✓	✓
1,170 m (3,840 ft)	2,409 m (7,900 ft)	July to October	Leash			✓
100 m (330 ft)	1,260 m (4,130 ft)	May to October	Leash		✓	✓
750 m (2,460 ft)	1,996 m (6,550 ft)	July to October	Leash			✓
640 m (2,100 ft)	2,004 m (6,575 ft)	July to October	Leash			✓

3

MOUNT ELSAY

Distance: 13 km (8.1 mi)
Time: 10 hours (lollipop)
Elevation gain: 500 m (1,640 ft)
High point: 1,422 m (4,665 ft)
Season: July to October

Quality: ★★★★
Difficulty: ◆
Maps: NTS 92-G/7 Port Coquitlam; Trail Ventures BC North Shore
Trailhead: 49°22′03″ N, 122°56′57″ W

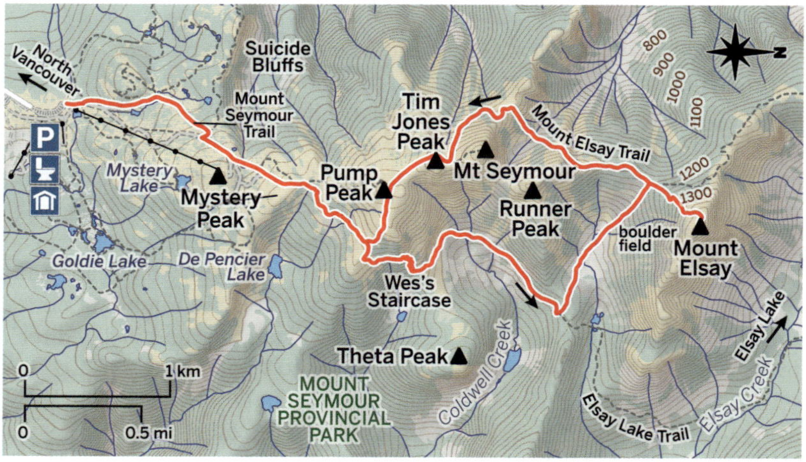

BECKONING WITH panoramic views, Mount Elsay is the next major peak north of Mount Seymour (Hike 2) in the Fannin Range. Rising in the territories of the Musqueam (xʷməθkʷəy̓əm), Squamish (Sḵwx̱wú7mesh), and Tsleil-Waututh (səlilwətaɬ) First Nations, the mountain chain constitutes a drainage divide—with the Seymour River (Jol-gul-hook in the hən̓q̓əmin̓əm̓ language of the Tsleil-Waututh Nation) to the west and xʔəl̓ilwətaʔɬ (Indian River) and səl̓ilw̓ət (Indian Arm) to the east.

From the B.C. Parks kiosk at the top of Parking Lot 4 (1,067 m/3,500 ft), follow the Mount Seymour Trail north for 1 hour (2.5 km/1.6 mi) to a junction east of Pump Peak. Embarking on a strenuous counterclockwise loop, head right on the Elsay Lake Trail. Enter the wild backcountry of Mount Seymour Provincial Park. In winter, this trail (adopted by the Vancouver Korean Hiking Club) is closed due to extreme avalanche hazard.

Plunge down Wes's Staircase. Start a descending traverse of the wide bowl at the headwaters of Coldwell Creek. With the cliffs of Pump Peak, Tim Jones Peak (c̓ew̓əyəɬəm), Mount Seymour, and Runner Peak looming above, cross three boulder fields separated by trees. After 1 hour on the Elsay Lake Trail, make an ascending traverse of a fourth boulder field with smaller rocks.

Hiking on Mount Elsay, with The Needles in the background.

Back in the trees, the first large orange diamond on the left indicates the turnoff (49°23′53″ N, 122°55′48″ W) for the fun ascent, 4.8 km (3 mi) from the parking lot. With some flagging, the Mount Elsay route climbs steeply in the woods to emerge in a bowl with a peaceful tarn. Cross a clear creek that feeds it, and clamber up a big boulder field all the way to the Elsay-Runner col.

Turn right and head up the rooty forest path, easy slabs, and lingering snow to the summit cairn (5 hours up; 49°24′25″ N, 122°56′16″ W). Your 360-degree payoff includes Mount Bishop due north and Elsay Lake far below, Eagle Ridge across səl̓ilw̓ət, the Fraser River (stal̓əw̓), Mount Seymour behind Runner Peak, downtown Vancouver, and The Needles.

Backtrack to the col. Continue the counterclockwise loop on the rugged, slippery, and wickedly steep Mount Elsay Trail. Sticking to the west side of the ridge, cross boulder gullies, and drop to bypass Runner Peak.

Finally, after 9 km (5.6 mi) of intense hiking, climb to the Seymour–Tim Jones col (49°23′29″ N, 122°56′38″ W). Turn right on the Mount Seymour Trail and head south on easier terrain to the trailhead.

No drones, feeding wildlife, fires, flower or mushroom picking, horses, littering, smoking, or vaping. Dogs must be leashed; however, B.C. Parks discourages bringing dogs to the backcountry.

GETTING THERE

Vehicle: Westbound on Trans-Canada Highway 1 in North Vancouver, north of Ironworkers Memorial Second Narrows Crossing, take Exit 22B. Turn right on Mount Seymour Parkway. (Eastbound on Highway 1, take Exit 21 for Mountain Highway. Go left on East Keith Road.) In 4.4 km (2.7 mi), turn left on Mount Seymour Road and drive up to the ski area (toilet available). Park as close as you can to the top. Winter tires are required from October to March. In summer, overnight parking is limited to Lot 2.

4

NORVAN FALLS

Distance: 14.5 km (9 mi)
Time: 5 hours (out and back)
Elevation gain: 230 m (755 ft)
High point: 430 m (1,410 ft)
Season: March to November

Quality: ★★
Difficulty: ●
Maps: NTS 92-G/6 North Vancouver; Trail Ventures BC North Shore
Trailhead: 49°21′37″ N, 123°01′41″ W

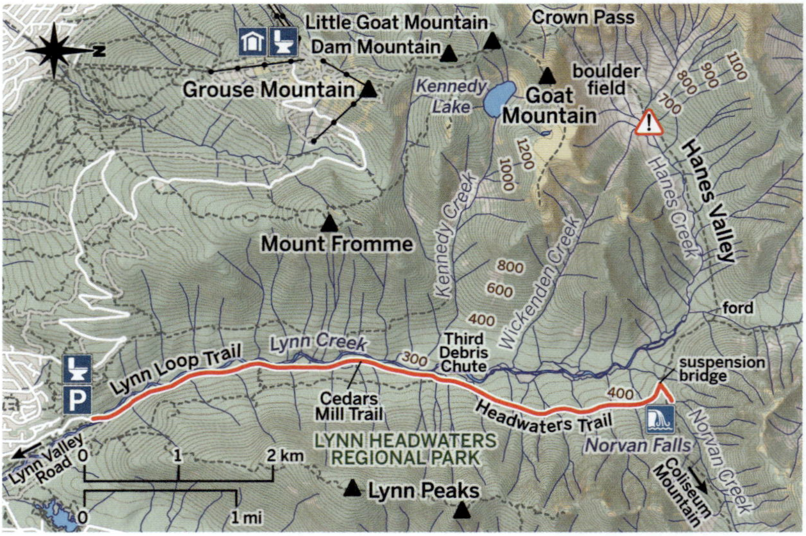

VISIT LYNN HEADWATERS Regional Park in spring or fall and you're likely to encounter apricot jelly, woody bracket, and other interesting fungi. One of the seven principles espoused by the Leave No Trace Center for Outdoor Ethics is "Leave what you find." This guideline also applies to the rusty logging relics you'll see on this shoulder-season, transit-friendly outing in the territories of the Musqueam (xʷməθkʷəy̓əm), Squamish (Sḵwx̱wú7mesh), and Tsleil-Waututh (səlilwətaɬ) First Nations.

From the park entrance (200 m/660 ft), site of the historic B.C. Mills House, cross Lynn Creek on a bridge by the remains of a water intake dam. Lynn Creek is known as X̱a7élcha Swá7elt in Sḵwx̱wú7mesh Sníchim to the Squamish Nation and Kan-ul-cha in hən̓q̓əmin̓əm̓ to the Tsleil-Waututh Nation. Fill out a form at the hiker registration kiosk on the east side. Go north (left) on the wide Lynn Loop Trail for 1.8 km (1.1 mi) and, ignoring a trail to your right, continue onto the pretty Cedars Mill Trail. Here is the site of a logging mill closed in 1927.

Reach the Third Debris Chute in 2.1 km (1.3 mi). Join the northern leg of the Headwaters Trail (left), an old logging road that leads you deeper into the pleasing forest. Heavy rain can make it unsafe to cross a creek with a damaged bridge. In 3 km (1.9 mi), the challenging route to Coliseum Mountain (see Hike 5) strikes off to the right; ignore this turnoff. Before going right at the next junction (49°24′51″ N, 123°02′00″ W), look left to check out the nifty suspension bridge over Norvan Creek.

The suspension bridge over Norvan Creek.

Head upstream to Norvan Falls (2.5 hours up), where signs warn hikers to keep back from the steep cliff. After lunch, retrace your steps to the park entrance.

On the far side of the suspension bridge, the trail continues to a junction. Rough routes (for summer and experienced hikers only) carry on to the Hanes Valley (left) and seldom-visited Lynn Lake (right). The difficult Hanes route closes in winter and makes headlines for all the wrong reasons: lost, unprepared, injured, and dead hikers. To cross over to Grouse Mountain (Múm̓tem in Sḵwx̱wú7mesh), ford Lynn Creek, head up the Hanes Valley, and ascend the big boulder field to Crown Pass. Turn left for the steep trail up Little Goat Mountain (see Hike 7), and follow the Alpine Trail or Ridge Trail to the ski area (no dogs), 16 km (9.9 mi) from the Lynn Headwaters entrance. Ride the Skyride aerial tramway (ticket required) or hike down the BCMC Trail to the transit-serviced Grouse Mountain base.

GETTING THERE

Transit: Take TransLink Bus 209, 210 (Upper Lynn Valley), or 228 (Lynn Valley) to Underwood Avenue at Evelyn Street. Walk east on the Evelyn Park path and Evelyn Street and cross Lynn Valley Road. Don't enter the park gate; go down Rice Lake Road and turn left on Marion Road. Hike the Varley Trail (1.5 km/0.9 mi) to the park entrance.

Vehicle: On Trans-Canada Highway 1 in North Vancouver, take Exit 19 and turn right on Lynn Valley Road. Alternatively, from Exit 21 (eastbound) or 22A (westbound), head north on Mountain Highway and turn right on Lynn Valley Road. Drive through the park gate and continue to the park entrance (toilet available), using an overflow lot if necessary. Pay parking is in effect March to October. No overnight parking; check park hours.

5

MOUNT BURWELL

Distance: 25 km (15.5 mi)
Time: 11 hours (out and back)
Elevation gain: 1,340 m (4,400 ft)
High point: 1,544 m (5,070 ft)
Season: July to October

Quality: ★★
Difficulty: ◆
Maps: NTS 92-G/6 North Vancouver; Trail Ventures BC North Shore
Trailhead: 49°21′37″ N, 123°01′41″ W

IN 1908, a B.C. Mountaineering Club party made the first recorded ascent of a pleasant peak at the north end of the Seymour River–Lynn Creek divide and called it White Mountain. Mount Burwell, as it is now known, stands in the territories of the Musqueam (xʷməθkʷəy̓əm), Squamish (Sḵwx̱wú7mesh), and Tsleil-Waututh (səlilwətaɬ) First Nations, who have climbed the North Shore mountains for thousands of years.

From the Lynn Headwaters Regional Park entrance (200 m/660 ft), cross the Lynn Creek bridge and fill out a form at the hiker registration kiosk. Lynn Creek is known as X̱a7élcha Swá7elt in Sḵwx̱wú7mesh Sníchim to the Squamish Nation and Kan-ul-cha in hən̓q̓əmin̓əm̓ to the Tsleil-Waututh Nation. Go north (left) on the easy Lynn Loop Trail (1.8 km/1.1 mi), Cedars Mill Trail (2.1 km/1.3 mi), and Headwaters Trail (3 km/1.9 mi).

Just before the Norvan Falls (Hike 4) junction, take the gruelling Coliseum Mountain route (4.6 km/2.9 mi) on the right (49°24′51″ N, 123°01′58″ W). For 2 hours or so, tackle the relentlessly steep path up the Norvan Creek basin. Encounter a little waterfall and pool, as well as Norvan Meadows at the base of a rockslide. At Norvan Pass, a viewpoint overlooking the Seymour Valley lies off to the right. The Seymour River is known as Ch'ích'elxwi7ḵw Staḵw

Cathedral Mountain (left) and Mount Burwell from Thunderbird Ridge.

in Sk̲wx̲wú7mesh and Jol-gul-hook in hən̓q̓əmin̓əm̓. (Ch'ích'elxwi7k̲w is a village site at the river's mouth.)

Continue north along the divide, merging with a rough route from the Lower Seymour Conservation Reserve (via Paton Lookout). Eventually, arrive on a subalpine ridge with a few small ponds. While the mountaintop appears to keep moving backwards, the blocky summit of Coliseum Mountain (1,446 m/4,740 ft; 49°26′02″ N, 123°00′24″ W) finally comes 4 hours from the Headwaters Trail.

Mount Burwell (6.5 hours up; 49°26′33″ N, 123°00′55″ W) is higher and tantalizingly close (1 km/0.6 mi). Descend to nearby ponds. Follow flagging along the ridge extending north, with the Cornett Lakes below to your right. The straightforward (Class 2) scramble parallels a drop-off. From the summit, marvel at the gully-incised south face of Cathedral Mountain and peer down at Palisade Lake. Retrace your steps.

For many hikers, the punishing ascent to Coliseum Mountain—and the impressive views—is more than enough. Turn around at this lesser summit for a 10-hour (23 km/14.3 mi) round trip.

Dogs must be leashed on the Coliseum Mountain route.

GETTING THERE

Transit: Take TransLink Bus 209, 210 (Upper Lynn Valley), or 228 (Lynn Valley) to Underwood Avenue at Evelyn Street. Walk east on the Evelyn Park path and Evelyn Street and cross Lynn Valley Road. Don't enter the park gate; go down Rice Lake Road and turn left on Marion Road. Hike the Varley Trail (1.5 km/0.9 mi) to the park entrance.
Vehicle: On Trans-Canada Highway 1 in North Vancouver, take Exit 19 and turn right on Lynn Valley Road. Alternatively, from Exit 21 (eastbound) or 22A (westbound), head north on Mountain Highway and turn right on Lynn Valley Road. Drive through the park gate and continue to the park entrance (toilet available), using an overflow lot if necessary. Pay parking is in effect March to October. No overnight parking; check park hours.

6
MOUNT FROMME

Distance: 10 km (6.2 mi)
Time: 5 hours (out and back)
Elevation gain: 810 m (2,660 ft)
High point: 1,171 m (3,840 ft)
Season: June to November
Quality: ★
Difficulty: ■
Maps: NTS 92-G/6 North Vancouver; Trail Ventures BC North Shore
Trailhead: 49°20′57″ N, 123°03′58″ W

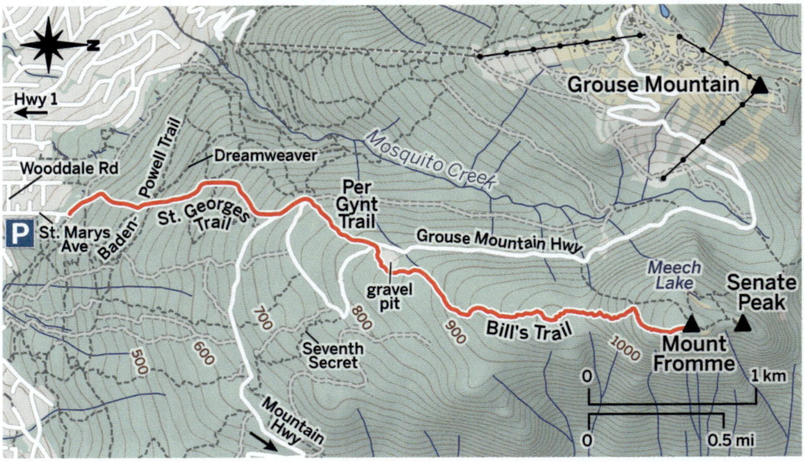

MOST HIKERS can't pick Mount Fromme out of a lineup, but it's the epicentre of freeride mountain biking on the North Shore and far beyond. Formerly known as Timber Mountain and Dome Mountain, Fromme is heavily scarred by logging. Still, it's an enjoyable hike that's doable without snowshoes earlier in the season than higher North Shore summits. Rising in the territories of the Musqueam (xʷməθkʷəy̓əm), Squamish (Sḵwx̱wú7mesh), and Tsleil-Waututh (səlilwətaɬ) First Nations, Fromme stands east of Grouse Mountain (Múm̓tem in Sḵwx̱wú7mesh Sníchim, the Squamish language).

One trailhead lies at the top of St. Marys Avenue (360 m/1,180 ft). Head west (left) on the power-line access road and past two gates. Quickly fork right, passing Skid Road (right) and a fenced-off radio antenna (left), to find the signed start of the St. Georges Trail (hiking only). Briefly go left on Dreamweaver (watch out for bikers), then continue right and uphill on St. Georges.

Cross the Baden-Powell Trail (with a bench to the left) and Ramble On. Reach the old Grouse Mountain Highway, which opened as a toll road in 1926. Head left on the gravel road, passing Executioner (left). At the next bend, exit left on a logging road (Lower Grouse Mountain Highway); immediately, go right on the Per Gynt Trail.

Snow on Mount Fromme in summer.

Re-emerge on the Grouse Mountain Highway, 2.5 km (1.6 mi) from St. Marys Avenue, at the hike's halfway point. Across the road, spot pink flagging tapes, slightly to the left. Cross the ditch and use a fixed cable to start up Bill's Trail (820 m/2,690 ft; 49°21′57″ N, 123°03′48″ W). Pass a gravel pit and gradually rise in the lovely woods. Steeply zigzag uphill amid old-growth cedars and firs.

Hit a four-way junction. Left is Wally's Trail (the upper section of Per Gynt), coming from farther up the Grouse Mountain Highway. Straight is a path down to Meech Lake. Go right for the summit of Mount Fromme (2.5 hours up; 49°23′00″ N, 123°03′23″ W). Trees foil the panorama, but the view includes Crown Mountain (Hike 8), Mount Burwell (Hike 5), Lynn Creek (X̱a7élcha Swá7elt in Sḵwx̱wú7mesh; Kan-ul-cha in hən̓q̓əmin̓əm̓ to the Tsleil-Waututh Nation), and Mount Seymour (Hike 2).

Senate Peak, Fromme's lower north summit, beckons across a steep gap. Several options are possible for the descent. However, you're less likely to get lost and need North Shore Rescue's help if you retrace your steps on familiar paths of the Mosquito Creek (Eslha7án̓ Swá7elt in Sḵwx̱wú7mesh; Tla-mau-ulk in hən̓q̓əmin̓əm̓) basin.

Incorporated in 1998, the North Shore Mountain Bike Association maintains Dreamweaver and other bike trails on Fromme.

GETTING THERE

Transit: From Lonsdale Quay, take TransLink Bus 230 (Upper Lonsdale) to the 200 block of East Braemar Road. Walk up the stairs at the crosswalk to St. Marys Avenue and continue north (600 m/0.4 mi).

Vehicle: On Trans-Canada Highway 1 in North Vancouver, take Exit 18. Go north on Lonsdale Avenue. Turn right on East Braemar Road, left on St. Georges Avenue, and right on Balmoral Road, which curves left and becomes St. Marys Avenue. Park near the intersection of St. Marys and Wooddale Road.

7

GOAT MOUNTAIN

Distance: 14 km (8.7 mi)
Time: 7 hours (circuit)
Elevation gain: 1,110 m (3,640 ft)
High point: 1,401 m (4,600 ft)
Season: July to October

Quality: ★★
Difficulty: ■
Maps: NTS 92-G/6 North Vancouver; Trail Ventures BC North Shore
Trailhead: 49°22′16″ N, 123°05′54″ W

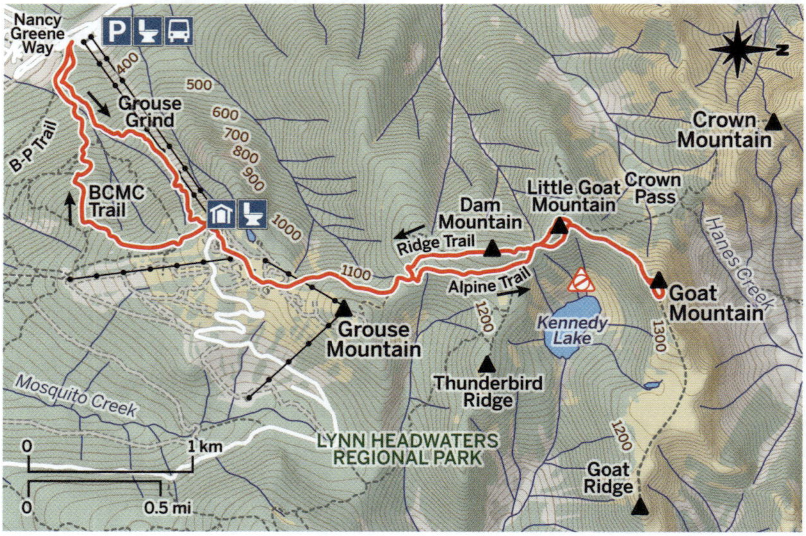

GROUSE MOUNTAIN Regional Park is home to two wildly popular workout hikes: the Grouse Grind and the BCMC (B.C. Mountaineering Club) Trail. These super-steep paths facilitate (free) access to higher terrain behind Grouse Mountain (Múmtem in Sḵwx̱wú7mesh Sníchim, the language of the Squamish Nation [Sḵwx̱wú7mesh Úxwumixw]) in Lynn Headwaters Regional Park.

Find the trailhead gate (290 m/950 ft; closed at night and all winter) above Parking Lot D. Follow the crowd left onto the Grouse Grind (no dogs or downhill hiking). In 1.5 hours or so (the record is 23 minutes, 48 seconds), ascend 800 m (2,625 ft) over 2.5 km (1.6 mi), with the help of 2,830 stairs, paralleling the Skyride aerial tramway and new gondola lift. Reach the Peak Chalet (1,100 m/3,610 ft), then walk north for 1.2 km (0.7 mi) through the resort, passing right of the grizzly bear enclosure.

Take the rocky road (part of the Snowshoe Grind in winter) to looker's left of the Lower Peak ski run. Go under the Peak Chair and continue to Whistler Pass, the col between Dam Mountain and Grouse Mountain. After gaining some height on Dam, follow the Alpine Trail right. Ignore the Thunderbird

Crown Mountain (left), The Camel, and Spindle Peak from the summit.

Trail leaving to the right. Keep right at junctions with paths to Little Goat Mountain and Crown Pass.

Now on the trail to Goat Mountain, pass ponds and a helipad. Clamber up a rooty incline to earn a view of Kennedy Lake far below. Above two fixed chains, there's a fork. Go left, starting a clockwise loop, and tackle the final scrambly section with yellow handlines for aid.

At a mountaintop signpost, go left and through the rocks to the summit of Goat Mountain (49°24′13″ N, 123°04′44″ W), 2 hours (3.6 km/2.2 mi) from the chalet. Soak up the majestic view of Crown Mountain (Hike 8).

On the descent, take the trail dropping east from the summit, then turn right at the Goat Ridge junction to return to Grouse. (The Goat Ridge route extends 1.6 km/1 mi east to tarns, a minor summit, and a viewpoint.) Close the Goat Mountain loop at the fixed chains.

Head back to the junction with the trail to Crown Pass; keep left, then immediately go right. Follow the Ridge Trail over insignificant Little Goat Mountain (1,323 m/4,340 ft). Keep right to surmount Dam Mountain (1,349 m/4,430 ft; 49°23′39″ N, 123°04′52″ W), which overlooks the Capilano River (Xwmélts'stn Stáḵw in Sḵwx̱wú7mesh; xʷməθkʷəy̓əmaʔɬ in hən̓q̓əmin̓əm̓ to the Musqueam [xʷməθkʷəy̓əm] Nation). Follow a water pipe to reunite with the Alpine Trail and return to the ski area.

Below the chalet, find the BCMC Trail (2.9 km/1.8 mi) entrance to the left of the Grouse Grind. Descend the steep and loose path (hiking poles advised) to the Baden-Powell Trail and go right to complete the circuit. Paying customers can ride the Skyride (return trip or download) to skip the Grouse Grind and/or BCMC Trail. Goat Mountain is a 4.5-hour round trip from the chalet.

GETTING THERE

Transit: Take TransLink Bus 232, 236, or 247 (Grouse Mountain) to the Skyride base. (In summer, the Grouse Mountain resort runs a free shuttle daily between Canada Place and the Skyride base.)

Vehicle: On Trans-Canada Highway 1 in North Vancouver, take Exit 14 and head north on Capilano Road, which turns into Nancy Greene Way. Find pay parking at the base of the Grouse Mountain ski area (6400 Nancy Greene Way; car-share parking, electric-vehicle charging, and toilet available).

8

CROWN MOUNTAIN

Distance: 16 km (9.9 mi)
Time: 8.5 hours (circuit)
Elevation gain: 1,210 m (3,970 ft)
High point: 1,501 m (4,925 ft)
Season: July to October

Quality: ★★★★
Difficulty: ◆◆
Maps: NTS 92-G/6 North Vancouver; Trail Ventures BC North Shore
Trailhead: 49°22′16″ N, 123°05′54″ W

CROWN MOUNTAIN is one of the most distinctive summits on the North Shore. Rising in the territories of the Musqueam (xʷməθkʷəy̓əm), Squamish (Sḵwx̱wú7mesh), and Tsleil-Waututh (səlilwətaɬ) First Nations, the main peak is aptly named The Pyramid. A curiously shaped rock formation, The Camel, sits on its shoulder.

Novices and young kids have no business here. Summiting Crown requires exposed scrambling. It's best left for a day without rain, snow, or significant wind. One slip on this peak, north of Grouse Mountain (Múm̓tem in Sḵwx̱wú7mesh Sníchim, the language of the Squamish Nation), could do you in.

From the trailhead gate (290 m/950 ft; closed at night and all winter) above Parking Lot D, set off on the Baden-Powell Trail. Ignore the mob instantly going left on the Grouse Grind. Take the next left and climb the ragged BCMC (B.C. Mountaineering Club) Trail (no dogs). In 1.5 hours or more (the record is 32 minutes, 30 seconds), ascend 800 m (2,625 ft) over 2.9 km (1.8 mi) in the Mackay Creek (Tl'alhemá7elkw Swá7elt in Sḵwx̱wú7mesh; ƛ̓əɬəməɬqəʔ in hən̓q̓əmin̓əm̓ to the Musqueam Nation) drainage.

Reach the Peak Chalet (1,100 m/3,610 ft), then walk north on the plateaus. Take the rocky road to looker's left of the Lower Peak ski run. On Dam

The Camel and Hanes Valley from the summit.

Mountain, follow the Alpine Trail right. Ignore the Thunderbird Trail leaving to the right. Keep right at junctions for Little Goat Mountain.

In 2.9 km (1.8 mi), head left at a signpost for the Hanes Valley route (where right goes to Goat Mountain, Hike 7) and quickly earn a princely view of your objective. Plunge down the super-steep and slippery path, with assistance from fixed chains. At Crown Pass (1,030 m/3,380 ft), the Hanes Valley route descends a big boulder field to the right. However, go straight ahead.

The trail rises in the woods. Scramble across and up slabs following paint smears on rock. (Do not attempt this unless the slabs are dry.) Pick your way through a boulder field and up to a shoulder above the Crater Rim arête. The loose path leads up the ridge until it's time for the Class 3 scramble to the top of The Pyramid. Another option is to stay left of the crest and shinny up the back.

Gain Crown's knife-edge summit (49°24′36″ N, 123°05′31″ W), 3 hours (5 km/3.1 mi) from the chalet. The North Shore mountains surround you. Spot snow-capped Mount Baker (Xwsa7k̲ in Sk̲wx̲wú7mesh; χe:t̓ᶿenəxʷ in hən̓q̓əmin̓əm̓) on the horizon.

After clambering out of Crown Pass on the way back, keep right to get on the Ridge Trail. Go over Little Goat Mountain (1,323 m/4,340 ft) and Dam Mountain (1,349 m/4,430 ft) en route to the chalet. Descend the BCMC Trail (hiking poles advised) and turn right on the B-P Trail to finish the day's adventure. Paying customers can ride the Skyride (return trip or download) to skip the BCMC Trail. Crown Mountain is a 6-hour round trip from the chalet.

GETTING THERE

Transit: Take TransLink Bus 232, 236, or 247 (Grouse Mountain) to the Skyride base. (In summer, the Grouse Mountain resort runs a free shuttle daily between Canada Place and the Skyride base.)

Vehicle: On Trans-Canada Highway 1 in North Vancouver, take Exit 14 and head north on Capilano Road, which turns into Nancy Greene Way. Find pay parking at the base of the Grouse Mountain ski area (6400 Nancy Greene Way; car-share parking, electric-vehicle charging, and toilet available).

9

HOLLYBURN MOUNTAIN

Distance: 12 km (7.5 mi)
Time: 4 hours (lollipop)
Elevation gain: 430 m (1,410 ft)
High point: 1,326 m (4,350 ft)
Season: July to November

Quality: ★★
Difficulty: ■
Maps: NTS 92-G/6; Friends of Cypress Provincial Park Southern Section
Trailhead: 49°22′45″ N, 123°11′30″ W

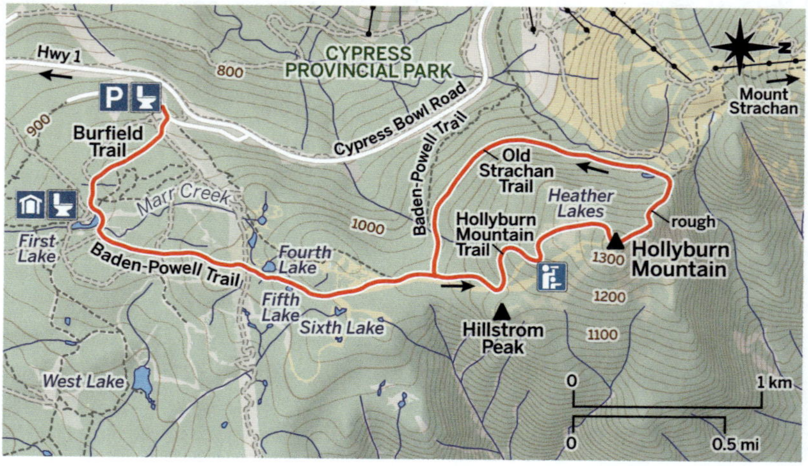

ON TOP OF Hollyburn Mountain, you're likely to be visited by whisky-jacks and ravens looking for a free lunch. Other birds you might see on this hike include the chestnut-backed chickadee, red-breasted sapsucker, sooty grouse, and winter wren.

From the B.C. Parks kiosk at the Nordic ski area (900 m/2,950 ft), head under the power line, briefly go left on a gravel road, and bear right on the Burfield Trail. Find the historic Hollyburn Lodge, opened in 1927 and rebuilt in 2017 by the Hollyburn Heritage Society, at First Lake. Take a path going left and around the lake's north shore.

Turn left on the Baden-Powell Trail to head up Hollyburn Ridge. Over the next 1.9 km (1.2 mi), cross the Sitzmark Trail and pass a warming hut, Fourth Lake, and Fifth Lake. Where the B-P Trail turns west, continue straight ahead (north) on the steeper Hollyburn Mountain Trail for 1.8 km (1.1 mi), coming close to minor Hillstrom Peak (1,159 m/3,800 ft), earning a viewpoint, and visiting Heather Lakes.

Enjoy the sight of the Twin Sisters (Ch'ich'iyúy in Sḵwx̱wú7mesh Sníchim, the language of the Squamish Nation [Sḵwx̱wú7mesh Úxwumixw]; a.k.a. The

Snowshoe tracks on Hollyburn Mountain in winter.

Lions) and Crown Mountain (Hike 8)—or fog—from Hollyburn's summit knob (2 hours up; 49°24′02″ N, 123°10′58″ W). Examine the outcrops for chlorite schist, quartz veins, and hornblende diorite dikes surrounded by metasedimentary rock. Don't feed the wildlife—it's more harmful than helpful.

Feel free to go back the way you came, but it's more interesting (and challenging) to plunge northwest down a decidedly rough, overgrown path to the dank col between Mount Strachan (Hike 10) and Hollyburn Mountain. Keep left and descend south on the Old Strachan Trail amid old-growth western hemlock and yellow cedar trees, including the Hollyburn Giant. Turn left on the B-P Trail and retrace your steps to First Lake and the Burfield Trail.

During ski season, snowshoers can plod the (free) hikers' access trail from the Nordic base to the summit for a round trip of 6 km (3.7 mi). It is marked with wands, stays outside the Cypress Mountain ski-area boundary, and is glorious after a snowfall. Heed the posted avalanche bulletins.

Hollyburn Mountain lies in the territories of the Musqueam (xʷməθkʷəy̓əm), Squamish (Sḵwx̱wú7mesh), and Tsleil-Waututh (səlilwətaɬ) First Nations. No camping, drones, fires, flower or mushroom picking, horses, littering, mountain biking, smoking, or vaping. Dogs must be leashed.

GETTING THERE

Vehicle: On Trans-Canada Highway 1 in West Vancouver, take Exit 8. Head north on Cypress Bowl Road into Cypress Provincial Park. In 13 km (8.1 mi), just past the 1,200-year-old Roadside Yellow Cedar, turn right and park at the cross-country ski area (toilet available). (In winter, Cypress Coach Lines offers shuttle service from the Vancouver Art Gallery, Lonsdale Quay, and Park Royal to the ski area.)

10

MOUNT STRACHAN

Distance: 9 km (5.6 mi)
Time: 5 hours (loop)
Elevation gain: 540 m (1,770 ft)
High point: 1,459 m (4,790 ft)
Season: July to October

Quality: ★★★
Difficulty: ◆
Maps: NTS 92-G/6; Friends of Cypress Provincial Park Southern Section
Trailhead: 49°23′48″ N, 123°12′16″ W

ON A CLEAR DAY, the satisfying panorama from Mount Strachan (pronounced "strahn") extends deep into the Coast Mountains and far across the Salish Sea. Getting there is super fun too, if you climb up the back side and do this hike as a clockwise loop. Mount Strachan is one of the three peaks that rim Cypress Bowl in the territories of the Musqueam (xʷməθkʷəy̓əm), Squamish (Sḵwx̱wú7mesh), and Tsleil-Waututh (səlilwətaɬ) First Nations.

Find the trailhead kiosk (916 m/3,005 ft) past the Cypress Creek Lodge and Olympic rings (a legacy of Vancouver's 2010 Winter Games). To the right, set off on the Howe Sound Crest Trail (HSCT), which quickly splits into west (no dogs) and east branches; fork right for the old (east) trail. Briefly join Pumphouse Road. West and east reunite by a kiosk paying tribute to Paul Binkert (1908–1995), a legendary trail builder.

Head north on the HSCT, traversing forested slopes to lovely Strachan Meadows at the 2.4 km (1.5 mi) mark. Between two bridges at Montizambert Creek (49°24′49″ N, 123°12′14″ W), an overgrown path to the right strikes off toward Christmas Gully, where snow lingers in the shadows. The rough route

Ch'ich'iyúy from the north peak.

rockets up the obvious couloir—ducking in and out of the trees to emerge in the saddle between Mount Strachan's north and south peaks.

Go left to the higher summit (2 hours up; 49°24′47″ N, 123°11′36″ W), after 3.4 km (2.1 mi) on foot. Strachan's gift to you is an excellent view of the Twin Sisters, a.k.a. The Lions—a sacred mountain known as Ch'ich'iyúy in Sḵwx̱wú7mesh Sníchim, the language of the Squamish Nation.

Backtrack to the saddle and gain the south peak (1,442 m/4,730 ft), which sits atop the Cypress Mountain downhill ski area. The base is 2.5 hours (5.1 km/3.2 mi) away on our Tour du Mont Strachan. Follow flagging and established paths south, keeping the SkyQuad Chairlift to your right. Pay attention to signs and markers; it's too easy to wander off-trail.

Encounter—but don't disturb—the remains of a Royal Canadian Navy T-33 jet that crashed in 1963, killing two pilots. Cross wet meadows. Keep left to avoid ending up on the Collins ski run. Descend to the dank col between Mount Strachan and Hollyburn Mountain (Hike 9). Stick with the Old Strachan Trail as it descends south, passing the old yellow cedar known as the Hollyburn Giant. Turn right on the Baden-Powell Trail to return to the downhill ski base in 2 km (1.2 mi).

No drones, fires, flower or mushroom picking, horses, littering, mountain biking, smoking, or vaping. Dogs must be leashed. Founded in 1990, the Friends of Cypress Provincial Park Society advocates for the preservation of the park's natural and historical features.

GETTING THERE

Vehicle: On Trans-Canada Highway 1 in West Vancouver, take Exit 8. Head north on Cypress Bowl Road into Cypress Provincial Park. Drive 15 km (9.3 mi) up to the downhill ski area (6000 Cypress Bowl Road; electric-vehicle charging and toilet available) and park as close to the road's end as possible. Overnight parking is limited to Lot 3B.

11

UNNECESSARY MOUNTAIN

Distance: 18 km (11.2 mi)
Time: 8 hours (out and back)
Elevation gain: 630 m (2,070 ft)
High point: 1,548 m (5,080 ft)
Season: July to October

Quality: ★★★
Difficulty: ◆
Maps: NTS 92-G/6 North Vancouver; Trail Ventures BC North Shore
Trailhead: 49°23′48″ N, 123°12′16″ W

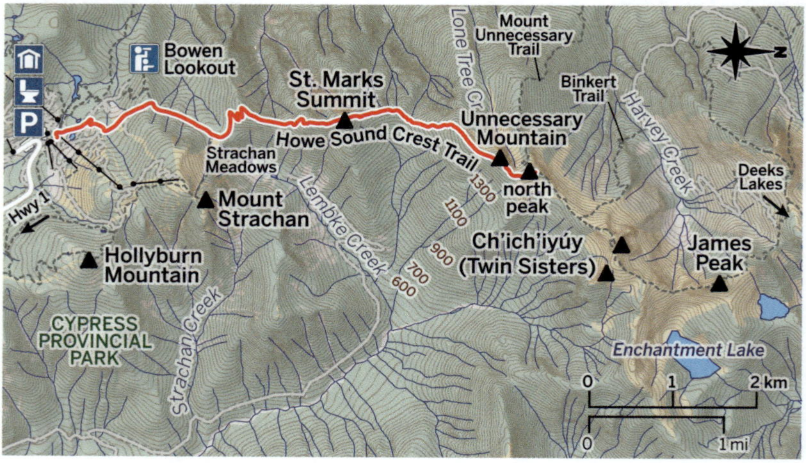

SCALING THE iconic Twin Sisters is taxing enough. Imagine having to surmount another peak on the way there and back. Historically, approaching the Sisters from Lions Bay required going up and over Unnecessary Mountain—hence its name. These days, nobody's forcing anyone to visit Unnecessary Mountain, but it's a worthy destination in its own right. Take a strenuous hike on the Howe Sound Crest Trail (HSCT), in Cypress Provincial Park and the territories of the Musqueam (xʷməθkʷəy̓əm), Squamish (Sḵwx̱wú7mesh), and Tsleil-Waututh (səlilwətaɬ) First Nations.

Find the trailhead kiosk (916 m/3,005 ft) past the Olympic rings. To the right, set off on the HSCT, which quickly splits into west (no dogs) and east branches; fork right for the old (east) trail. The branches reunite at the Paul Binkert memorial kiosk, east of the Bowen Lookout.

Head north on the HSCT, crossing Montizambert Creek at Strachan Meadows. Switchback up a wooded bump, perhaps spotting an American three-toed woodpecker. Continue north along the divide between Howe Sound (Átl'ḵa7tsem in Sḵwx̱wú7mesh Sníchim, the language of the Squamish Nation) and the Capilano River (Xwmélts'stn Stáḵw in Sḵwx̱wú7mesh; xʷməθkʷəy̓əmaʔɬ in hən̓q̓əmin̓əm̓ to the Musqueam Nation).

In 5.5 km (3.4 mi), arrive at St. Marks Summit (1,371 m/4,500 ft; 49°25′41″ N, 123°12′23″ W). Towering cliffs overlook Átl'k̲a7tsem (stay away from the edge), and the vantage of the Twin Sisters (Ch'ich'iyúy in Sk̲wx̲wú7mesh), a.k.a. The Lions, is dynamite. Turn back here for a moderate, 4.5-hour round trip.

Chá7elk̲wnech in Átl'k̲a7tsem from St. Marks Summit.

Continuing toward Unnecessary Mountain, the best and worst are yet to come. Drop 170 m (560 ft) to a dark col in the forest, only to regain it and more on the wickedly steep and rugged ascent. At last, a magnificent ridge walk to the south peak (49°26′41″ N, 123°12′01″ W)—the true summit—or farther to the north peak (1,543 m/5,060 ft) rewards your sweat.

From Unnecessary Mountain, formerly known as Mount St. Marks, gaze upon the vertically jointed hornblende diorite, rounded by glacial abrasion, of the Twin Sisters. Peer down at Bowen Island (Nex̲wlélex̲wem in Sk̲wx̲wú7mesh; č̓əw̓č̓əw̓ʔiqən̓ in hən̓q̓əmin̓əm̓) and Gambier Island (Chá7elk̲wnech in Sk̲wx̲wú7mesh) in Átl'k̲a7tsem. Retrace your steps to Cypress Bowl.

In full, the HSCT is a 29 km (18 mi) backpacking trip. The trail goes between the Twin Sisters and ends south of Porteau Cove (Xwáw̓chayay). There are designated campsites at Magnesia Meadows, Brunswick Lake, and Deeks Lake (Stl'álk̲em Stak̲w, Hike 20).

In winter and spring, beware of dangerous avalanche terrain on the trail to St. Marks Summit and Unnecessary Mountain. During ski season, snowshoers must pick up a free backcountry access corridor tag at the Black Mountain Lodge to pass through the ski area.

GETTING THERE

Vehicle: On Trans-Canada Highway 1 in West Vancouver, take Exit 8. Head north on Cypress Bowl Road into Cypress Provincial Park. Drive 15 km (9.3 mi) up to the downhill ski area (6000 Cypress Bowl Road; electric-vehicle charging and toilet available) and park as close to the road's end as possible. Overnight parking is limited to Lot 3B.

12

BLACK MOUNTAIN AND EAGLE BLUFF

Distance: 9.5 km (5.9 mi)
Time: 4.5 hours (circuit)
Elevation gain: 310 m (1,020 ft)
High point: 1,224 m (4,020 ft)
Season: June to November

Quality: ★★★
Difficulty: ●
Maps: NTS 92-G/6; Friends of Cypress Provincial Park Southern Section
Trailhead: 49°23′48″ N, 123°12′16″ W

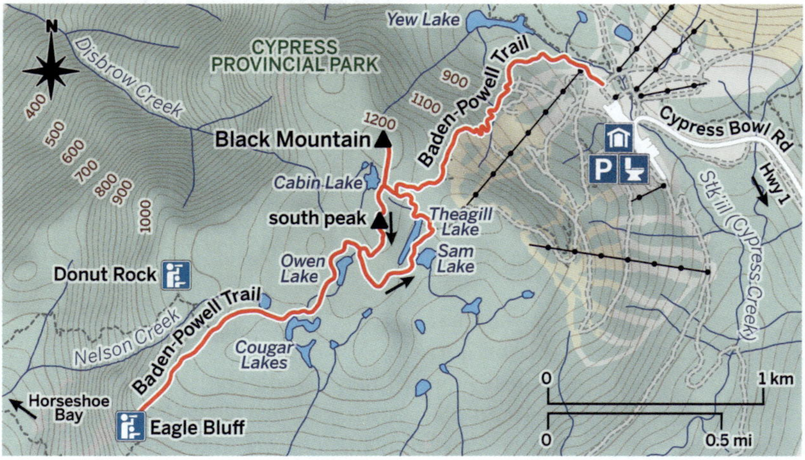

FOR SOME, the cloudy days of fall signal that it's time to put away the hiking boots. Not so fast. Lace 'em up and head to Cypress Provincial Park, in the territories of the Musqueam (xʷməθkʷəy̓əm), Squamish (Sḵwx̱wú7mesh), and Tsleil-Waututh (səlilwətaɬ) First Nations. Autumn is ideal for paying a visit to Black Mountain's pretty lakes and woods.

Find the trailhead kiosk (916 m/3,005 ft) past the Olympic rings. To the right, set off on the Baden-Powell Trail. Keep left at three turnoffs—for the Howe Sound Crest Trail and Yew Lake Trail (no dogs)—in the headwaters of Cypress Creek (Stk̲'iil in Sḵwx̱wú7mesh Sníchim, the language of the Squamish Nation). Switchback up the gravel path, signed as the Black Mountain Trail in winter.

Reach a major junction in 2.1 km (1.3 mi). Leaving the B-P Trail, turn right for Cabin Lake and right again to visit the Yew Lake Lookout on Black Mountain's north and highest summit (49°23′39″ N, 123°13′08″ W). Back at Cabin Lake, continue on the Black Mountain Loop (counterclockwise) to the south summit outcrop (1,218 m/4,000 ft). Rejoin the B-P Trail farther south.

The Baden-Powell Trail on Black Mountain.

Go west (right) for 1.6 km (1 mi), passing Owen Lake and Cougar Lakes, and spurning a rightward turnoff for Donut Rock (Hike 14). (Donut Rock is an optional side quest, 15 minutes off the B-P via a flagged but rough trail.)

Break out of the trees at wide-open Eagle Bluff (2 hours up; 1,050 m/3,445 ft). Feast your eyes on Point Grey (ʔəlqsən in hən̓q̓əmin̓əm̓ to the Musqueam Nation) and Point Atkinson (xʷməq̓məq̓əs), guarding the entrance to Burrard Inlet (səl̓ilw̓ət), and beyond to Mount Baker (χe:t̓ᶿenəxʷ). While you're enthralled with the big view, a raven might drop in to steal your lunch. (Don't feed the wildlife.)

For the return, stick with the B-P Trail eastbound all the way back to the trailhead. That way, you'll see Sam Lake and Theagill Lake and complete the scenic loop of the Black Mountain Plateau.

The B-P Trail, which this excursion samples, traverses the North Shore mountains for 48 km (30 mi), from Horseshoe Bay (Ch'ax̱áy in Sḵwx̱wú7mesh) to Deep Cove (Sp'eḵ'náy). Built in 1971 by Boy Scouts and Girl Guides, it's typically day hiked in four sections by completists—or dashed in a matter of hours during the Knee Knackering North Shore Trail Run. (The fastest time is 4 hours, 32 minutes.)

During ski season, snowshoers must pick up a free backcountry access corridor tag at the Black Mountain Lodge to pass through the ski area.

GETTING THERE

Vehicle: On Trans-Canada Highway 1 in West Vancouver, take Exit 8. Head north on Cypress Bowl Road into Cypress Provincial Park. Drive 15 km (9.3 mi) up to the downhill ski area (6000 Cypress Bowl Road; electric-vehicle charging and toilet available) and park as close to the road's end as possible. (In winter, Cypress Coach Lines offers shuttle service from the Vancouver Art Gallery, Lonsdale Quay, and Park Royal to the ski area.)

13
WEST KNOB

Distance: 10 km (6.2 mi)
Time: 5 hours (out and back)
Elevation gain: 655 m (2,150 ft)
High point: 760 m (2,490 ft)
Season: April to November

Quality: ★★
Difficulty: ■
Maps: NTS 92-G/6 North Vancouver; Trail Ventures BC North Shore
Trailhead: 49°21′40″ N, 123°15′34″ W

WHYTE LAKE PARK preserves old-growth trees and provides a vital link between Nelson Canyon Park and Cypress Provincial Park. This shoulder-season hike to Whyte Lake and the West Knob of Black Mountain visits all three parks, in the territories of the Musqueam (xʷməθkʷəy̓əm), Squamish (Sḵwx̱wú7mesh), and Tsleil-Waututh (səlilwətaɬ) First Nations.

From the Whyte Lake parking lot (115 m/380 ft), take the service road under the Nelson Canyon bridge to a water tank. Don't cross the old Highway 1 bridge; go right on the Trans Canada Trail—unpopularly rebranded as The Great Trail between 2016 and 2021. Continue straight onto a path (as the double track bends left to dead-end at the West Vancouver Streamkeeper Society's Nelson Creek salmon hatchery).

Soon the easy Whyte Lake Trail strikes off left, bridging Nelson Creek and Whyte Creek. Visit the lovely dock at Whyte Lake, a habitat for beavers and blue-listed westslope cutthroat trout (no fishing). Turn right at the outhouse junction (280 m/920 ft), 45 minutes (2.3 km/1.4 mi) from the start. Pass a lakeshore access spur. Bear right on the Baden-Powell Trail above the lake. Follow Whyte Creek and fleur-de-lys markers up the dark lower slopes

The view of ʔəlqsən and the Salish Sea from the West Knob.

of Black Mountain (passing the south end of the rough Mountain Abyss Traverse Trail, which connects to the Sunset Trail and Lions Bay).

Look for a fork (615 m/2,020 ft; 49°23′03″ N, 123°14′44″ W), 1 hour (2.2 km/1.4 mi) past Whyte Lake. "WK" is painted in orange on a boulder, and an old metal plate on a tree indicates "Eagle Ridge"; Eagle Bluff (Hike 12) lies 60 minutes farther up the B-P Trail. However, go left on the rough and sometimes ill-defined Donut Rock Trail (Hike 14).

In 15 minutes (400 m/0.2 mi), take a left turnoff (690 m/2,260 ft; 49°23′11″ N, 123°14′31″ W) and follow yellow signs through the salal to the West Knob viewpoint. Several steps before the viewpoint, a boot path goes right and climbs steeply to a cairn atop the treed summit (2.5 hours up; 49°23′18″ N, 123°14′32″ W).

Back at the viewpoint, peer over the shore pines at Point Grey (ʔəlqsən in the hən̓q̓əmin̓əm̓ language of the Musqueam and Tsleil-Waututh; Elḵsn in Sḵwx̱wú7mesh Sníchim); Passage Island (Smelhmelhél̓ch—"waves go over it all the time"—in Sḵwx̱wú7mesh); and Mount Elphinstone on the Sunshine Coast. Return the way you came.

GETTING THERE

Transit: From downtown Vancouver or Park Royal, take TransLink Bus 250 (Horseshoe Bay) to the 6300 block of Marine Drive. Walk north to the roundabout and cross the highway overpass. Turn right on Horseshoe Bay Drive and find the Black Mountain trailhead and parking area on the left (49°22′01″ N, 123°16′29″ W). Hike up the Baden-Powell Trail, merging with the Whyte Lake approach in 2 km (1.2 mi).

Vehicle: On Trans-Canada Highway 1 in West Vancouver, take Exit 4. On the north side of the highway, turn left on Westport Road. In 1.8 km (1.1 mi), go under the highway and turn right into the busy Whyte Lake parking lot.

14

DONUT ROCK

Distance: 12 km (7.5 mi)
Time: 6.5 hours (out and back)
Elevation gain: 975 m (3,200 ft)
High point: 1,080 m (3,540 ft)
Season: May to November

Quality: ★
Difficulty: ◆
Maps: NTS 92-G/6 North Vancouver; Trail Ventures BC North Shore
Trailhead: 49°21′40″ N, 123°15′34″ W

DONUT ROCK rises from the forest on Black Mountain. The trail to this outcrop with a vista—in the territories of the Musqueam (xʷməθkʷəy̓əm), Squamish (Sḵwx̱wú7mesh), and Tsleil-Waututh (səlilwətaɬ) First Nations—is really rough and very steep. Through a gap in the trees, watch ferries ply Howe Sound (Átl'ḵa7tsem in Sḵwx̱wú7mesh Sníchim, the language of the Squamish Nation).

From the Whyte Lake parking lot (115 m/380 ft), take the service road under the Nelson Canyon bridge to a water tank. Don't cross the old Highway 1 bridge; go right on the Trans Canada Trail (TCT). Continue straight onto a path where the double track bends left to a dead end. Soon the easy Whyte Lake Trail leaves the TCT to the left. Visit the lovely dock at Whyte Lake (no fishing).

Turn right at the outhouse junction (280 m/920 ft), 45 minutes (2.3 km/1.4 mi) from the start. Pass a lakeshore access spur. Bear right on the Baden-Powell Trail. Follow fleur-de-lys markers into Cypress Provincial Park (passing the south end of the rough Mountain Abyss Traverse Trail).

Look for a fork (615 m/2,020 ft; 49°23′03″ N, 123°14′44″ W), 1 hour (2.2 km/1.4 mi) past Whyte Lake. "WK" is painted in orange on a boulder, and an old metal plate on a tree indicates "Eagle Ridge"; Eagle Bluff (Hike 12)

Hikers atop Donut Rock.

lies 60 minutes farther up the B-P Trail. However, go left on the rough and sometimes ill-defined Donut Rock Trail.

In 15 minutes (400 m/0.2 mi), pass the left-hand turnoff (690 m/2,260 ft; 49°23′11″ N, 123°14′31″ W) for the West Knob (Hike 13). From here, the Donut Rock Trail gets tougher. Cross two branches of Nelson Creek. Zigzag through mossy outcrops with licorice ferns. Fixed lines—a shoelace and rope—assist with slippery, scrambly bits.

Top out at Donut Rock (3.5 hours up; 49°23′17″ N, 123°13′55″ W), 1.5 hours (1.2 km/0.7 mi) from the West Knob turnoff. Through the forest window, spot Bowen Island—known as ċəw̓ċəw̓ʔiqən̓ in the hən̓q̓əmin̓əm̓ language to the Musqueam Nation; Ne<u>x</u>wlélex̱wem in Sḵwx̱wú7mesh. Catch B.C. Ferries' *Queen of Capilano* docking at Snug Cove, next to Mannion Bay (Kwíl'aḵm in Sḵwx̱wú7mesh). Whyte Islet, off Whytecliff Park (St'éx̱w't'eḵw's, "sheared off"), is just visible over the treetops.

Retrace your steps to the trailhead, taking extra care on the steepest parts. It's also possible to continue up the Donut Rock Trail to intersect the B-P Trail. A right turn on the B-P leads to Eagle Bluff, through boulder fields, and back to the Whyte Lake Trail.

GETTING THERE

Transit: From downtown Vancouver or Park Royal, take TransLink Bus 250 (Horseshoe Bay) to the 6300 block of Marine Drive. Walk north to the roundabout and cross the highway overpass. Turn right on Horseshoe Bay Drive and find the Black Mountain trailhead and parking area on the left (49°22′01″ N, 123°16′29″ W). Hike up the Baden-Powell Trail, merging with the Whyte Lake approach in 2 km (1.2 mi).

Vehicle: On Trans-Canada Highway 1 in West Vancouver, take Exit 4. On the north side of the highway, turn left on Westport Road. In 1.8 km (1.1 mi), go under the highway and turn right into the busy Whyte Lake parking lot.

15

KEN'S BLUFFS

Distance: 9 km (5.6 mi)
Time: 5 hours (lollipop)
Elevation gain: 400 m (1,310 ft)
High point: 610 m (2,000 ft)
Season: March to November

Quality: ★★★
Difficulty: ■
Maps: NTS 92-G/6 North Vancouver; Trail Ventures BC North Shore
Trailhead: 49°27′22″ N, 123°13′50″ W

TREAD THE lower slopes of Unnecessary Mountain to find big trees and towering bluffs with super necessary views. Perch above the bustle of Highway 99 and bask in the beauty of Howe Sound—known as Átl'k̲a7tsem in Sk̲wx̲wú7mesh Sníchim, the language of the Squamish Nation (Sk̲wx̲wú7mesh Úxwumixw). Take extra care at the bluffs—one slip could be your last.

From the cul-de-sac atop Oceanview Road (210 m/690 ft), head up the gated access road into the Harvey Creek Community Watershed. In 400 m (0.2 mi), find the signed start of the Mount Unnecessary Trail on the right. Tackle the steep, rocky path. Keep left at two junctions (signed and unsigned) with the lower section of the Erin Moore Trail.

Reach a junction with wooden signs in 45 minutes. Left eventually leads to the Howe Sound Crest Trail atop Unnecessary Mountain (1,548 m/5,080 ft; Hike 11), 5 km (3.1 mi) from Oceanview Road. However, go right (south) on the upper section of the Erin Moore Trail. Pass the inconspicuous turnoff for the Grass Grind (save it for later). Cross two branches of Lone Tree Creek (P'ap'k̲') on logs.

Traverse a broad boulder slope. Spot pink tapes and descend switchbacks. Bear right on the remains of a logging road (passing the north end of the

The Sea to Sky Highway and Átl'ḵa7tsem from the Erin Moore lookout.

rough Mountain Abyss Traverse Trail and then left on a path. Follow the trail to an unmarked junction in the salal.

Take the left spur to the Erin Moore Trail's destination lookout (455 m/1,490 ft; 49°26′21″ N, 123°13′53″ W), 2 hours (4.3 km/2.7 mi) from the trailhead.

Leave the lookout and continue north on the lower section of the Erin Moore Trail. Descend the rough, slippery path to Lone Tree Creek. At a signed junction, 1 hour past the bluff, turn right on the Grass Grind. Switchback up to the next three-way intersection.

Go right for Ken's Bluffs, quickly coming to a fork (560 m/1,840 ft; 49°26′45″ N, 123°13′36″ W), 1.5 hours (2.4 km/1.5 mi) from the Erin Moore lookout. Take your pick of viewpoints to the south and north.

Saying bye to Ken's Bluffs, quickly finish off the top of the Grass Grind, emerging on the upper section of the Erin Moore Trail. Turn left (north) and retrace your steps to the trailhead, 1 hour (2.3 km/1.4 mi) away.

Located in the territories of the Musqueam (xʷməθkʷəy̓əm) and Squamish (Sḵwx̱wú7mesh) First Nations, the Totally Unnecessary Trail was renamed in memory of Erin Kate Moore (2007–2014) after the young hiker died in a rockslide on the trail.

GETTING THERE

Transit: Take TransLink Bus 262 (Lions Bay–Brunswick) from Caulfeild Village or Horseshoe Bay to Crosscreek Road at Oceanview Road in Lions Bay. Walk back to Oceanview, turn left, and continue 1 km (0.6 mi) to the top.
Vehicle: On Highway 99 (Sea to Sky Highway), 12 km (7.5 mi) north of its junction with Trans-Canada Highway 1 at Horseshoe Bay, take the Lions Bay Avenue exit. From the northbound off-ramp, keep right to merge with Oceanview Road. Keep right at Crosscreek Road and drive to the top of Oceanview, where a few parallel parking spots are available. Alternatively, find a legal parking spot lower down on Oceanview or at Lions Bay Beach Park. Pay parking is in effect—use the Flowbird app for street parking.

16

MOUNT HARVEY

Distance: 12.5 km (7.8 mi)
Time: 7.5 hours (out and back)
Elevation gain: 1,420 m (4,660 ft)
High point: 1,652 m (5,420 ft)
Season: July to October

Quality: ★★
Difficulty: ◆
Maps: NTS 92-G/6 North Vancouver; Trail Ventures BC North Shore
Trailhead: 49°28′15″ N, 123°14′05″ W

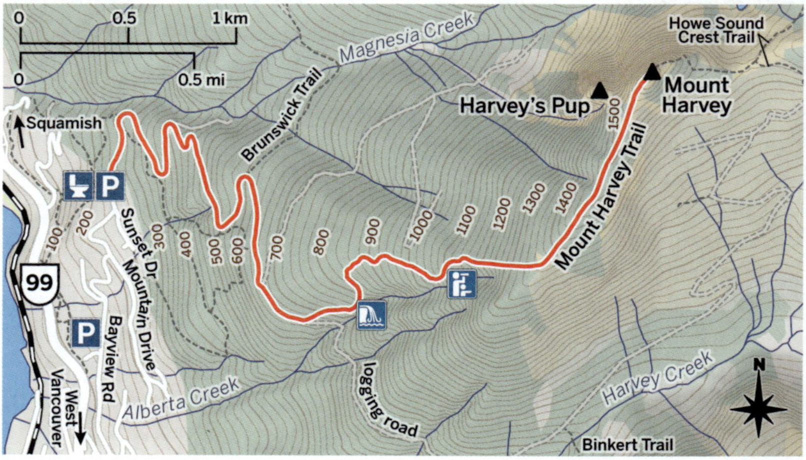

MOUNT HARVEY is the lofty destination of one of the cartoonishly steep trails that snake skyward from the village of Lions Bay. The reward for your considerable efforts is a back-side view of the Twin Sisters—a sacred mountain known as Ch'ich'iyúy in Sḵwx̱wú7mesh Sníchim, the language of the Squamish Nation (Sḵwx̱wú7mesh Úxwumixw)—that most people never get to see.

From the Sunset Drive North gate (230 m/755 ft), head up the logging road, which climbs relentlessly into the Magnesia Creek Community Watershed. Pass a water treatment plant. Keep right at two turnoffs—the first for Tunnel Bluff (Hike 17) and Brunswick Mountain (Hike 18).

In 45 minutes, an orange marker on the left signifies the start of the Mount Harvey Trail (before the road crosses Alberta Creek en route to the Binkert Trail for the Twin Sisters, a.k.a. The Lions). Early on, a waterfall vantage lies off to the right. Two Howe Sound (Átl'ḵa7tsem) viewpoints interrupt the sweaty ascent.

Breaking out of the forest, an eye-popping view of the West Sister (West Lion) provides ample motivation for the ridge walk ahead. Ascending the south ridge, you'll notice a rock tower, called Harvey's Pup by climbers, on

Ch'ich'iyúy (far right) and the North Shore mountains from the summit.

the west ridge. Some simple scrambling earns you Mount Harvey's summit (4 hours up; 49°28′31″ N, 123°12′01″ W). In snow, be sure to stay well away from (overhanging) cornices, as they can collapse suddenly.

From the panoramic peak, the middle ground includes the Twin Sisters, across the Harvey Creek watershed to the south, and Hat Mountain, wearing a radio repeater, with Brunswick Mountain, the North Shore's highest summit, to the north. To the northeast, a red emergency hut catches the eye in Magnesia Meadows, a stop on the 29 km (18 mi) Howe Sound Crest Trail. Under a clear sky, you can perceive Mamquam Mountain (Smánit tl'a Mámxwem), Golden Ears (Hike 56), and Mount Baker (Xwsa7k̲) in the distance.

Heat exhaustion is a significant risk on Mount Harvey, so take lots of water.

GETTING THERE

Transit: Take TransLink Bus 262 (Lions Bay–Brunswick) from Caulfeild Village or Horseshoe Bay to Crosscreek Road at Oceanview Road in Lions Bay. Walk 1.6 km (1 mi) to the Sunset Drive North trailhead.

Vehicle: On Highway 99 (Sea to Sky Highway), 12 km (7.5 mi) north of its junction with Trans-Canada Highway 1 at Horseshoe Bay, take the Lions Bay Avenue exit. From the northbound off-ramp, keep right to merge with Oceanview Road. (From the southbound off-ramp, keep left at Isleview Place, turn left on Lions Bay Avenue, and continue onto Oceanview.) Immediately make a left on Crosscreek Road. On the far side of Harvey Creek, go right on Centre Road, left on Bayview Road, left on Mountain Drive, and left on Sunset Drive. Use the pay parking lot at Sunset's north end (toilet available). Alternatively, find a legal parking spot lower down on Mountain Drive. Pay parking is in effect—use the Flowbird app for street parking. Free parking is available at Lions Bay Elementary School (250 Bayview Road) on weekends and in summer.

17

TUNNEL BLUFF

Distance: 11 km (6.8 mi)
Time: 4 hours (out and back)
Elevation gain: 470 m (1,540 ft)
High point: 700 m (2,300 ft)
Season: March to November

Quality: ★★★★
Difficulty: ●
Maps: NTS 92-G/6 North Vancouver; Trail Ventures BC North Shore
Trailhead: 49°28′15″ N, 123°14′05″ W

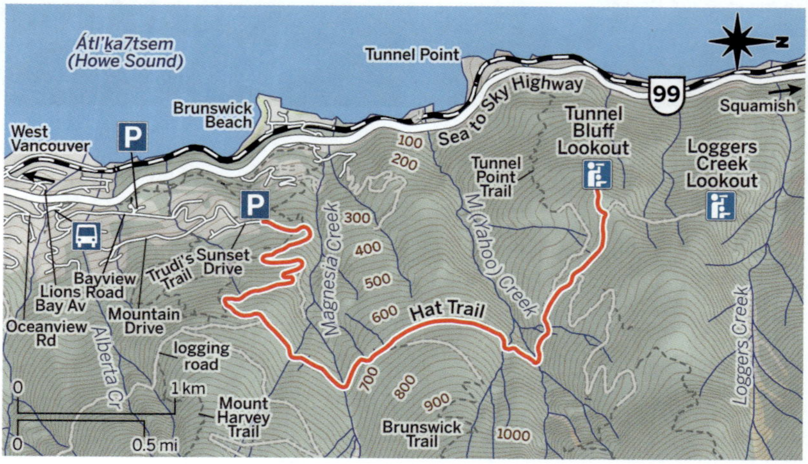

SWEEPING VIEWS of Howe Sound are the raison d'être for this popular hike in Sḵwx̱wú7meshulh Aysáỷch, the territory of the Squamish Nation (Sḵwx̱wú7mesh Úxwumixw). With parking at the Sea to Sky Highway's Tunnel Point rest area sadly limited to 30 minutes, Tunnel Bluff is now best hiked from Lions Bay.

From the Sunset Drive North gate (230 m/755 ft), enter the Magnesia Creek Community Watershed and trudge up the rocky logging road. Pass the Missing Link Trail, Upper Harrison Trail, and water treatment plant. Just beyond the 2 km (1.2 mi) marker, go left at a road junction (49°28′16″ N, 123°13′34″ W), signed for Brunswick. Head north on a gentle road and cross Magnesia Creek—which flows into Howe Sound (Átl'ḵa7tsem in Sḵwx̱wú7mesh Sníchim, the Squamish language) at Brunswick Beach (Ḵéletstn)—on a makeshift log bridge.

Fork left onto the Hat Trail, 1 hour (3.2 km/2 mi) in, diverging from the challenging Brunswick Mountain (Hike 18) route. Take a log bridge over M (Yahoo) Creek (Ḵw'pel). After 30 minutes (1.5 km/0.9 mi) on the Hat Trail, continue straight at the Tunnel Point Trail junction. Shortly thereafter, take

Lháḵw'tich (left) and Nex̱wlélex̱wem in Átl'ḵa7tsem from Tunnel Bluff Lookout.

the left fork. (Right goes to Hat Mountain, northwest of Brunswick Mountain.) In 15 minutes, a faded "Lookout" sign directs you left again.

Tunnel Bluff Lookout (2 hours up; 49°29′24″ N, 123°14′15″ W) overlooks several Átl'ḵa7tsem landforms contextualized by the Sḵwx̱wú7mesh Líl̓wat7úl Cultural Centre's Cultural Journey kiosk at Tunnel Point. Take a long lunch and savour the magnificent scene: Horseshoe Bay (Ch'ax̱áy); Bowyer Island (Lháḵw'tich); Bowen Island (Nex̱wlélex̱wem); Gambier Island (Chá7elḵwnech); Seagull Rocks (Kwiyitkm), a.k.a. Pam Rocks; and Anvil Island (Lhax̱wm). Mind the precipice. Don't roll rocks or feed the ravens. Return the way you came.

Loggers Creek Lookout (15 minutes one way) is an optional extension to your hike. At the "Lookout" sign, go straight ahead for the rough route, featuring lots of deadfall, to the bonus viewpoint (49°29′46″ N, 123°14′11″ W), south of Loggers Creek (Nínich Ḵw'litḵm).

GETTING THERE

Transit: Take TransLink Bus 262 (Lions Bay–Brunswick) from Caulfeild Village or Horseshoe Bay to Crosscreek Road at Oceanview Road in Lions Bay. Walk 1.6 km (1 mi) to the Sunset Drive North trailhead.

Vehicle: On Highway 99 (Sea to Sky Highway), 12 km (7.5 mi) north of its junction with Trans-Canada Highway 1 at Horseshoe Bay, take the Lions Bay Avenue exit. From the northbound off-ramp, keep right to merge with Oceanview Road. (From the southbound off-ramp, keep left at Isleview Place, turn left on Lions Bay Avenue, and continue onto Oceanview.) Immediately make a left on Crosscreek Road. On the far side of Harvey Creek, go right on Centre Road, left on Bayview Road, left on Mountain Drive, and left on Sunset Drive. Use the pay parking lot at Sunset's north end (toilet available). Alternatively, find a legal parking spot lower down on Mountain Drive. Pay parking is in effect—use the Flowbird app for street parking. Free parking is available at Lions Bay Elementary School (250 Bayview Road) on weekends and in summer.

18

BRUNSWICK MOUNTAIN

Distance: 14.5 km (9 mi)
Time: 8.5 hours (out and back)
Elevation gain: 1,560 m (5,120 ft)
High point: 1,788 m (5,870 ft)
Season: July to October

Quality: ★★★
Difficulty: ◆◆
Maps: NTS 92-G/6 North Vancouver; Trail Ventures BC North Shore
Trailhead: 49°28′15″ N, 123°14′05″ W

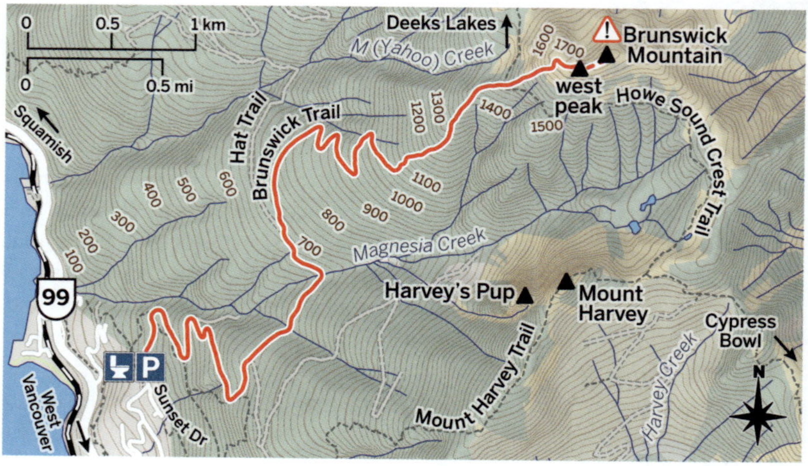

NAMED AFTER a late-1700s British naval warship turned prison boat, Brunswick Mountain is the highest of the North Shore peaks. It shares the same trailhead as Mount Harvey (Hike 16), which commemorates the gunship's captain, and the Twin Sisters. Like those objectives, Brunswick Mountain watches over Sḵwx̱wú7meshulh Aysáy̓ch, the territory of the Squamish Nation (Sḵwx̱wú7mesh Úxwumixw), and calls for a diabolically arduous ascent.

From the Sunset Drive North gate (230 m/755 ft), enter the Magnesia Creek Community Watershed and trudge up the rocky logging road. Just past the 2 km (1.2 mi) marker, go left at a road junction (49°28′16″ N, 123°13′34″ W), signed for Brunswick. Head north on a gentle road and cross Magnesia Creek—which flows into Howe Sound (Átl'ḵa7tsem in Sḵwx̱wú7mesh Sníchim, the Squamish language) at Brunswick Beach (Ḵél̓etstn)—on a makeshift log bridge. It's likely your last chance to refill water bottles.

After 1 hour (3.2 km/2 mi), keep right at a junction for the Hat Trail and Tunnel Bluff (Hike 17), and stick with the Brunswick Trail. The old logging spur rises stiffly, giving way to a path and then dispensing with switchbacks.

Eventually, reach a four-way junction (1,520 m/4,990 ft) with the Howe Sound Crest Trail—in the middle of its 29 km (18 mi) journey between Cypress

Deeks Lakes and Mount Hanover from the west summit.

Bowl and the Sea to Sky Highway, south of Porteau Cove (Xwáw̓chayay). (Left goes to Hat Pass; right leads to Magnesia Meadows.) Don't break out the (melted) chocolate-covered blueberries yet. Your path, straight ahead, is rocky, absurdly steeper, and sometimes faint.

Finally, gain a saddle on Brunswick Mountain's west ridge and the fringe of Cypress Provincial Park. Go right for the straightforward (without rain, snow, or ice, that is) scramble to the west summit. Most hikers are content to stop there. Admire Davidson's penstemon blooming from cracks in the rock.

Only experienced scramblers should consider going any farther. To claim the true summit, continue east, keeping to the south side of the arête. Drop down to a loose gully. Traverse and scramble over the next bump, finding the remains of a mountaintop helipad. Continue to the summit cairn (4.5 hours up; 49°29′15″ N, 123°11′50″ W). Mind the precipice.

Return the way you came.

GETTING THERE

Transit: Take TransLink Bus 262 (Lions Bay–Brunswick) from Caulfeild Village or Horseshoe Bay to Crosscreek Road at Oceanview Road in Lions Bay. Walk 1.6 km (1 mi) to the Sunset Drive North trailhead.

Vehicle: On Highway 99 (Sea to Sky Highway), 12 km (7.5 mi) north of its junction with Trans-Canada Highway 1 at Horseshoe Bay, take the Lions Bay Avenue exit. From the northbound off-ramp, keep right to merge with Oceanview Road. (From the southbound off-ramp, keep left at Isleview Place, turn left on Lions Bay Avenue, and continue onto Oceanview.) Immediately make a left on Crosscreek Road. On the far side of Harvey Creek, go right on Centre Road, left on Bayview Road, left on Mountain Drive, and left on Sunset Drive. Use the pay parking lot at Sunset's north end (toilet available). Alternatively, find a legal parking spot lower down on Mountain Drive. Pay parking is in effect—use the Flowbird app for street parking. Free parking is available at Lions Bay Elementary School (250 Bayview Road) on weekends and in summer.

19

DEEKS BLUFF

Distance: 7.5 km (4.7 mi)
Time: 4 hours (out and back)
Elevation gain: 410 m (1,345 ft)
High point: 470 m (1,540 ft)
Season: Most of the year

Quality: ★★
Difficulty: ■
Maps: NTS 92-G/11 Squamish
Trailhead: 49°32′42″ N, 123°14′25″ W

NO LONGER overgrown, Deeks Bluff is just the ticket for shoulder season. A re-established trail leads to a lovely overlook of Howe Sound—known as Átl'ḵa7tsem in Sḵwx̱wú7mesh Sníchim, the language of the Squamish Nation (Sḵwx̱wú7mesh Úxwumixw).

From the B.C. Parks kiosk at the parking lot, walk 400 m (0.2 mi) south along the shoulder of Highway 99's northbound off-ramp. Find the start of the Deeks Lake Trail section of the Howe Sound Crest Trail (HSCT), lined by a wooden fence (60 m/200 ft). Mining activity necessitated the reactivation of this initial section, previously abandoned, through private property. Follow orange diamonds along a cascading creek and into a power-line corridor.

The base of an H-frame transmission structure doubles as a viewpoint featuring Anvil Island (Lhax̱wm), the Tantalus Range (Tsewílx̱), and The Black Tusk (T'aḵ't'aḵ'múy̓in̓ tl'a In̓inyáx̱a7n; Hike 29). Back in the trees, the highway noise recedes. Cross a creek on a bridge. Hit a logging road and turn right, after 45 minutes (1.3 km/0.8 mi) on foot. (Left provides access to the mining area and a trail up Kallahne Creek to Lost Lake.)

Head south on the eroded road for 30 minutes (1.7 km/1.1 mi). Pass below the Lumberjack Wall climbing crag, Short Stories Boulders, and a waterfall.

The view of Átl'ḵa7tsem from Deeks Bluff.

Reach a major junction (390 m/1,280 ft; 49°31′40″ N, 123°14′36″ W). To the left, the HSCT continues to Deeks Lake (Stl'álḵem Staḵw; Hike 20) in Cypress Provincial Park and its southern terminus in Cypress Bowl.

However, head right on the Deeks Bluff Trail. At a muddy fork, go right, skirting a bog. Pass an inconspicuous cairn and veer north to ascend Deeks Bluff. Follow the path through salal and rocks sprayed with pink paint. Arrive at the blufftop viewpoint (2 hours up; 49°31′40″ N, 123°14′59″ W), with its stained-glass panel and wooden bench, 30 minutes (800 m/0.5 mi) from the HSCT.

Over the shore pines, take a gander at Mount Gardner on Bowen Island (Neẖwlélex̱wem), Mount Artaban on Gambier Island (Chá7elḵwnech), and Vancouver Island. Átl'ḵa7tsem (pronounced "at-KAT-sum") is one of three Sḵwx̱wú7mesh toponyms for Howe Sound; the others are Nexwnéwu7ts and Txwnéwu7ts. In 2021, the United Nations Educational, Scientific and Cultural Organization (UNESCO) designated the basin as the Átl'ḵa7tsem/Howe Sound Biosphere Region. Head back to the HSCT and down (or continue up to Deeks Lake to camp).

From the easy-to-miss cairn, the Deeks Bluff Trail actually continues south to a couple of mossy bluff viewpoints. However, the route has fallen out of use, so it's rough, badly overgrown, irregularly marked, and littered with deadfall. In 2 km (1.2 mi), it meets the old Deeks Creek trail, coming up from Highway 99. Go hard left to loop back to the HSCT, 400 m (0.2 mi) south of the Deeks Bluff junction, in another 2 km (1.2 mi).

GETTING THERE

Vehicle: On Highway 99 (Sea to Sky Highway), 23 km (14 mi) north of its junction with Trans-Canada Highway 1 at Horseshoe Bay, take the Porteau Road exit. From the off-ramp, go west to immediately find the Deeks Lake Trail parking lot.

20

STL'ÁLḴEM STAḴW (DEEKS LAKE)

Distance: 13.5 km (8.4 mi)
Time: 7.5 hours (out and back)
Elevation gain: 980 m (3,215 ft)
High point: 1,040 m (3,410 ft)
Season: May to November

Quality: ★★
Difficulty: ■
Maps: NTS 92-G/11 Squamish; Trail Ventures BC North Shore
Trailhead: 49°32′42″ N, 123°14′25″ W

THE WATERS of Stl'álḵem Staḵw, also known as Deeks Lake and Deeks Creek, are sacred to the Squamish Nation (Sḵwx̱wú7mesh Úxwumixw). Nestled in the Britannia Range, Deeks Lake is the northernmost campsite on the Howe Sound Crest Trail (HSCT), a 29 km (18 mi) backpacking trip that deserves two to four days. This day hike to the lake makes a fine early-season outing.

From the parking lot (a stargazing spot), walk 400 m (0.2 mi) south along the shoulder of Highway 99's northbound off-ramp. Find the start of the Deeks Lake Trail section of the HSCT, lined by a wooden fence (60 m/200 ft). Follow orange diamonds into a power-line corridor.

The base of an H-frame transmission structure doubles as a viewpoint featuring Anvil Island (Lhax̱wm). Back in the trees, the highway noise recedes. Cross a creek on a bridge. Hit an old logging road and turn right, after 45 minutes (1.3 km/0.8 mi) on foot.

Head south on the eroded road for 30 minutes (1.7 km/1.1 mi). Pass below a waterfall. Reach a major junction (390 m/1,280 ft; 49°31′40″ N, 123°14′36″ W).

Low cloud over Deeks Lake.

To the right is the Deeks Bluff Trail (Hike 19). However, continue left, sticking with the HSCT. Deeks Lake is 2.5 hours (3.8 km/2.4 mi) distant.

Keep left at three junctions. In 900 m (0.6 mi), exit the logging road to the left and enter Cypress Provincial Park. Tackle the steep, rocky path, with 2.9 km (1.8 mi) to go. Visit Trailblazer Lookout, off to the right, where a sign memorializes long-time North Shore Hikers member Mary Tainsh (1947–2016).

After taking in the vista of Bowen Island (Nex̱wlélex̱wem) and Gambier Island (Chá7elk̲wnech) in Howe Sound (Átl'k̲a7tsem), continue up the trail and onto an old road. The sound of Deeks Creek grows louder. Steps to the right, Phi Alpha Falls roars down a steep canyon. Enter an old-growth grove, tread below cliffs, scamper up a patch of rock, and reach an upper waterfall. Cross a disturbed area with salmonberries.

Pass tent sites (off to the left, no facilities) before arriving at Deeks Lake (4 hours up; 49°30′59″ N, 123°12′43″ W). From the lakeshore rise Deeks Peak, Mount Windsor, Gotha Peak, and Wettin Peak. To the right, the HSCT continues across the logjammed outlet, up to Hanover Lake and Brunswick Lake (the next campsite) to complete the Deeks Lakes chain, through the Twin Sisters (Ch'ich'iyúy, a.k.a. The Lions), and on to its southern terminus in Cypress Bowl. For a day hike, though, it's best to turn around at Deeks Lake.

Stl'álk̲em Stak̲w is said to be home to supernatural beings. Respect these waters. (Food for thought: Encroachment by hikers and outdoor recreationists is rendering a growing number of First Nations' sacred places unsuitable for spiritual bathing, vision questing, and other cultural practices.) No fires, guns, littering, motorized vehicles, smoking, or vaping. Dogs must be leashed.

GETTING THERE

Vehicle: On Highway 99 (Sea to Sky Highway), 23 km (14 mi) north of its junction with Trans-Canada Highway 1 at Horseshoe Bay, take the Porteau Road exit. From the off-ramp, go west to immediately find the Deeks Lake Trail parking lot.

21

BETH LAKE

Distance: 18 km (11.2 mi)
Time: 7 hours (out and back)
Elevation gain: 1,010 m (3,310 ft)
High point: 1,060 m (3,480 ft)
Season: May to November

Quality: ★★
Difficulty: ■
Maps: NTS 92-G/11 Squamish
Trailhead: 49°35′06″ N, 123°13′11″ W

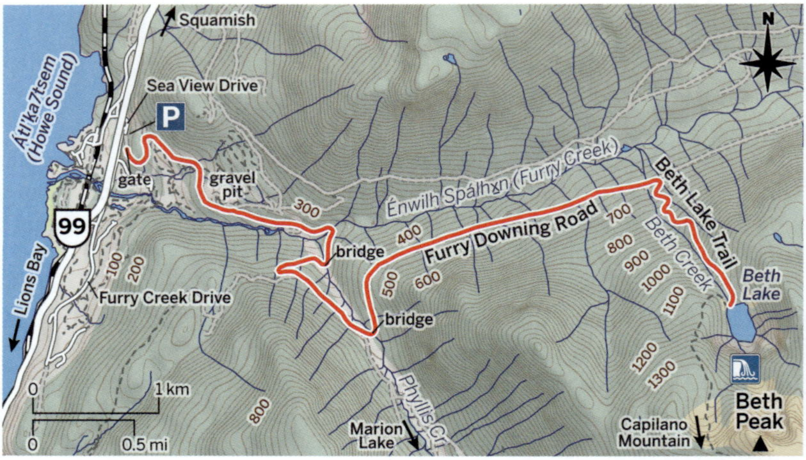

THE BETH LAKE TRAIL climbs through mossy forest to its namesake, which boasts a dramatic mountain backdrop with ramparts and a waterfall. Access requires plodding up logging roads from the community of Furry Creek, located in the Squamish-Lillooet Regional District and Sḵwx̱wú7meshulh Aysáy̓ch, the territory of the Squamish Nation (Sḵwx̱wú7mesh Úxwumixw).

Find the yellow gate (50 m/160 ft), 100 m (110 yd) up the gravel road. Follow the private road as it curves right under the power lines, and ignore a rightward spur. Go right at a triple fork by a gravel pit. Keep left where a gate bars a spur to the powerhouse of a run-of-river hydro power facility, which began operating in 2004.

Head over the penstock and across the concrete bridge spanning the diversion reach of Furry Creek (Énwilh Spálhx̱n in Sḵwx̱wú7mesh Sníchim, the language of the Squamish Nation), after 40 minutes on foot. Rise to cross Phyllis Creek on a bridge and transfer from private to provincial land. Go under two power lines, keep left at a fork, and head upstream in a B.C. Hydro right-of-way.

Orange tapes mark a fork, 1 hour in. Go left on the old and narrow Furry-Downing Road and over a bridge to river right, leaving Phyllis Creek behind.

Thin ice on Beth Lake, with Beth Peak in the background.

(Staying on the Phyllis Creek road leads to Marion Lake and Phyllis Lake.) Negotiate landslides, picking up the deteriorating road on the other side. Step over several small creeks and rock-hop a stream.

Cross boulder-choked Beth Creek, if safe to do so. Quickly follow pink tapes and orange diamonds right off the road and start up the Beth Lake Trail (640 m/2,100 ft; 49°34′58″ N, 123°09′43″ W), almost 2.5 hours (7.3 km/4.5 mi) from the Sea View Drive gate. The rustic path weaves uphill before committing to the fall-line and getting rootier. Enjoy the burble of brooks and the sight of tall cedars and firs.

The path crests before arriving at the logjammed outlet of Beth Lake (3.5 hours up; 49°34′26″ N, 123°09′11″ W), 1.6 km (1 mi) from Furry-Downing Road. Beth Peak stands across the lake, hiding Capilano Mountain (1,692 m/5,550 ft) to the southeast. Find a spot on the shore to lunch, before returning to Sea View Drive. (Peak baggers aiming for Capilano continue across the lake's outflow, bypass Beth Peak and Gordan Lake to the west, and scramble to the summit.)

Spot Mount Sedgwick across Howe Sound (Átl'k̲a7tsem) on the way down. No fires or shooting.

GETTING THERE

Vehicle: On Highway 99 (Sea to Sky Highway), 27 km (17 mi) north of its junction with Trans-Canada Highway 1 at Horseshoe Bay, take the Furry Creek Drive exit. From the northbound off-ramp, turn left on Furry Creek Drive. In 800 m (0.5 mi), go right on Sea View Drive, which immediately becomes gravel. (From the southbound off-ramp, continue onto Howe Sound Drive. Turn left on Sea View Drive and go under the highway.) Park on the shoulder below the gate. Don't block the road.

22

SEA TO SUMMIT TRAIL

Distance: 6.5 km (4 mi)
Time: 4 hours (ascent)
Elevation gain: 850 m (2,790 ft)
High point: 885 m (2,900 ft)
Season: April to November

Quality: ★★
Difficulty: ■
Maps: NTS 92-G/11 Squamish; Carter & Stevens Sea to Sky Backcountry
Trailhead: 49°40′31″ N, 123°09′22″ W

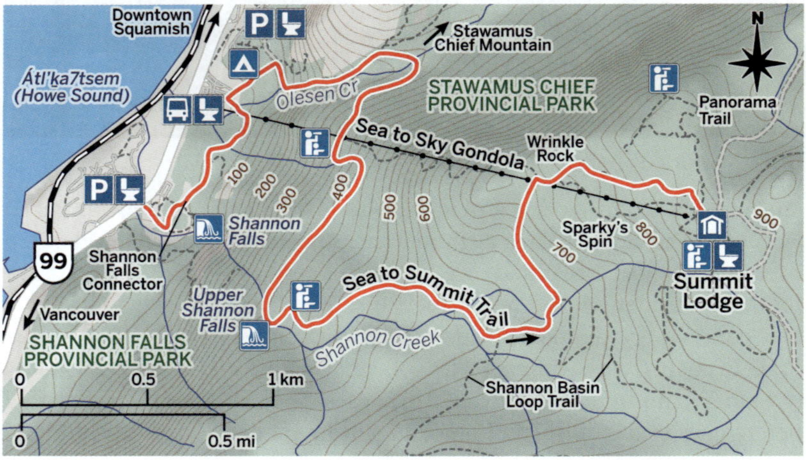

THE SEA TO SUMMIT TRAIL is Squamish's more scenic answer to North Vancouver's Grouse Grind (see Hike 7). Hikers flock to this ascent trail, and pay for a ride down on the privately operated Sea to Sky Gondola.

To access the trailhead (35 m/115 ft) from Shannon Falls Provincial Park, follow signs for the gondola. The base is a 10-minute walk on the Shannon Falls Connector (900 m/0.6 mi). From there, the Sea to Summit Trail strikes off north and enters Stawamus Chief Provincial Park. The trail is marked by 128 numbered green diamonds. In short order, go right, merging with the bustling Chief Peaks Trail, coming up the stairs from the B.C. Parks campground.

At marker 20, part ways with summit seekers heading for Stawamus Chief Mountain (Hike 24)—known as Siỷám̓ Smánit in Sḵwx̱wú7mesh Sníchim, the language of the Squamish Nation (Sḵwx̱wú7mesh Úxwumixw). Turn right and cross a bridge over Olesen Creek.

Follow the diamonds across the gondola corridor, which was removed from the park and redesignated as the Stawamus Chief Protected Area in 2012. In acts of sabotage, the gondola cable was severed in 2019 and 2020.

Stop by two viewpoints, and ascend steep and slippery bits to Upper Shannon Falls, the prelude to the roadside attraction below. Be extra careful on wet

Átl'ḵa7tsem from a bluff on the Sea to Summit Trail.

rock around Shannon Creek. Admire Howe Sound (Átl'ḵa7tsem) and Siy̓ám̓ Smánit from a granodiorite bluff, 15 minutes past the falls.

The Sea to Summit presses on through pleasant forest. Go left at two junctions with the Shannon Basin Loop, the latter at marker 96. Sticking with the Sea to Summit, duck under the gondola again. With aptly named Wrinkle Rock looking on, keep left where the trail meets Sparky's Spin. Celebrate your arrival at the upper terminal (49°40′17″ N, 123°07′49″ W).

To aim higher, continue onto Al's Habrich Ridge Trail and visit Neverland Falls (Hike 23). The Skyline Ridge Trail, a round trip of 24 km (15 mi), is another worthy hike on offer. Make sure to check the gondola's closing time.

Before you depart, check out the suspension bridge and viewing platforms for postcard perspectives on Sky Pilot Mountain, Goat Ridge (Ntsewásus), volcanic Watts Point (Sts'íts'a7ḵin), and Átl'ḵa7tsem. Download tickets are for sale in the Summit Lodge. Downhill hiking on the Sea to Summit Trail is discouraged. Back at the base, consider a quick visit to Shannon Falls (Kwékwetxwm, "rumbling noise").

Dogs must be leashed in the upper terminal area and are only permitted to download on the gondola (dog ticket required).

GETTING THERE

Transit: In summer, Squamish Transit Bus 5 (South Parks) provides service from downtown Squamish to the Sea to Sky Gondola (toilet available). (Squamish Connector offers daily shuttle service from Vancouver's Waterfront Station to the Sea to Sky Gondola.)

Vehicle: On Highway 99 (Sea to Sky Highway), 4.2 km (2.6 mi) south of downtown Squamish, turn east at Darrell Bay Road/Shannon Falls Road to enter the parking lot at Shannon Falls Provincial Park (toilet available). Alternatively, use the overflow parking lot on the west side of the highway. (Unfortunately, parking at the gondola base is limited to 3 hours.)

23
NEVERLAND FALLS

Distance: 9 km (5.6 mi)
Time: 5.5 hours (lollipop)
Elevation gain: 420 m (1,380 ft)
High point: 1,290 m (4,230 ft)
Season: June to October

Quality: ★★★
Difficulty: ■
Maps: NTS 92-G/11 Squamish
Trailhead: 49°40′17″ N, 123°07′49″ W

ONCE UPON A TIME, J.M. Barrie's Peter Pan gave Wendy cryptic directions to the faraway island of Neverland: "Second to the right, and straight on till morning." Fortunately, the trails to Neverland Lake and Neverland Falls on Habrich Ridge, in Squamish Nation (Sḵwx̱wú7mesh Úxwumixw) territory, are clearly indicated with numbered diamonds.

Habrich Ridge is the destination of the Sea to Sky Gondola. A hike on Al's Habrich Ridge Trail and the Neverland Loop must be preceded by either a gondola ride (ticket required) or an ascent of the Sea to Summit Trail (Hike 22) in Stawamus Chief Provincial Park. To access the gondola base (35 m/115 ft) via Shannon Falls Provincial Park, walk the Shannon Falls Connector for 10 minutes (900 m/0.6 mi).

From the map board at the upper terminal (885 m/2,900 ft), briefly go east on a backcountry access road. Follow the summer route of Al's Habrich Ridge Trail (red diamonds) left and pass below Whirring Wall. Rejoin the winter (snowshoeing) route and boulder-hop the south fork of Olesen Creek.

At a fork, the main path goes left and Al's Habrich Ridge Trail Connector goes right; they quickly reunite. Gain height on rocky ground to earn a

The silt-laden Sḵwx̱wú7mesh Staḵw enters Átl'ḵa7tsem.

bird's-eye view of Stawamus Chief Mountain (Siỳám̓ Smánit in Sḵwx̱wú7mesh Sníchim, the language of the Squamish Nation; Hike 24). Keep right to spurn the RC Connector in the trees and emerge on an open bluff overlooking Howe Sound (Átl'ḵa7tsem) and the Squamish River (Sḵwx̱wú7mesh Staḵw).

Al's Habrich Ridge Trail loses a bit of elevation, keeping right at junctions with the Neverland Loop Trail at markers 58 and 63, before officially ending at Neverland Lake. Carefully step over the pond's outlet waterfall to find a path to a viewpoint (1,170 m/3,840 ft; 49°40′22″ N, 123°06′48″ W), 2.5 hours (4 km/2.5 mi) from the upper terminal. Peer across Skwelwílem, the Squamish River estuary, at Castle Rock (St'et'e7ímin) and Echo Falls (Naḵwáach).

Backtrack to marker 63 and tackle the Neverland Loop (purple diamonds) counterclockwise. Take a right spur to visit Neverland Falls, turning around at the base of the upper plunge (3 hours up; 49°40′12″ N, 123°06′33″ W), 30 minutes (900 m/0.6 mi) from the previous viewpoint.

Completing the loop, traverse north and then drop east (with the help of a fixed rope) to return to Al's Habrich Ridge Trail in another 30 minutes (900 m/0.6 mi). Back on familiar ground, retrace your steps for 1.5 hours (3.3 km/2.1 mi) to the upper terminal.

GETTING THERE

Transit: In summer, Squamish Transit Bus 5 (South Parks) provides service from downtown Squamish to the Sea to Sky Gondola. (Squamish Connector offers daily shuttle service from Vancouver's Waterfront Station to the Sea to Sky Gondola.)

Vehicle: On Highway 99 (Sea to Sky Highway), 4.2 km (2.6 mi) south of downtown Squamish, turn east at Darrell Bay Road/Shannon Falls Road to enter the parking lot at Shannon Falls Provincial Park (toilet available). Alternatively, use the overflow parking lot on the west side of the highway. (Unfortunately, parking at the gondola base is limited to 3 hours.)

24

SIỶÁM̓ SMÁNIT (STAWAMUS CHIEF MOUNTAIN)

Distance: 14 km (8.7 mi)
Time: 5 hours (circuit)
Elevation gain: 625 m (2,050 ft)
High point: 702 m (2,300 ft)
Season: March to November
Quality: ★★★★
Difficulty: ■
Maps: NTS 92-G/11 Squamish; Carter & Stevens Sea to Sky Backcountry
Trailhead: 49°40′43″ N, 123°09′16″ W

A SACRED landmark to the Squamish Nation (Sḵwx̱wú7mesh Úxwumixw), Stawamus Chief Mountain goes by the toponym Siỷám̓ Smánit (Highly Respected Mountain) in Sḵwx̱wú7mesh Sníchim, the Squamish language. The Ice Age–sculpted granodiorite monolith is an international rock-climbing destination. For hikers, its back side offers a leg-burning stair climb, fun scrambling (with mild exposure), three summits, and soaring views.

Stroll through the walk-in campground (stays require a reservation from May to October) to start up the steep Chief Peaks Trail. Climb the stairs. In short order, merge with the Sea to Summit Trail (Hike 22), coming from the Sea to Sky Gondola base off to the right. After the Sea to Summit leaves to the right, arrive at a major fork.

Choose the left-hand trail, signed for the First Peak and Second Peak. Past a viewpoint with a big boulder, the trail splits again. Go left and ascend well-worn switchbacks to the bare rock (slippery when wet) of the bustling First Peak (610 m/2,000 ft). According to Sḵwx̱wú7mesh sx̱wex̱wiỷám̓ (ancient stories), the Stawamus Chief is a giant longhouse turned into stone by X̱aays

The First Peak and Átl'k̲a7tsem from the Second Peak.

(Transformer Brothers). Look southwest at Shannon Falls (Kwékwetxwm), The Papoose, and Howe Sound (Átl'k̲a7tsem).

Backtrack to the previous junction, and take the other fork to the top of the South Gully. Ascend a ledge with a fixed chain, traverse a cleft covered by logs, and climb a short ladder (expect a traffic jam). The Second Peak (655 m/2,150 ft) is arguably the prettiest of the three summits. Peer down at Skwelwíl̓em, the estuary of the Squamish River (Sk̲wx̲wú7mesh Stak̲w).

Follow markers east to the top of the North Gully. Keep left to eschew the East Trail for now. Skirt the great precipice, go through the trees, and carry on to a ledge. A U-turn leads to a narrow ridge of rock and the quieter summit of the Third Peak (3 hours up; 49°41′10″ N, 123°08′06″ W). In Sk̲wx̲wú7mesh, the Stawamus Chief is also known as Smánit tl'a St'á7mes (Mountain of St'á7mes). Pick out Cloudburst Mountain (Saw̓pa) and Nch'k̲ay̓ (Mount Garibaldi) to the north.

For a fast, challenging descent, go back to the last junction and plunge down the rough East Trail. Upon meeting the trail from Slhánay̓ (pronounced "sss-thlah-nigh" and meaning "woman"), the Chief's northeastern companion, turn right and head southwest to the trailhead.

If you have to pick one summit, make it the Second Peak. The middle summit offers the most impressive views and enjoyable scrambling. The clockwise lollipop takes 3 hours or so.

GETTING THERE

Transit: In summer, Squamish Transit Bus 5 (South Parks) provides service from downtown Squamish to Stawamus Chief Provincial Park. (Squamish Connector offers daily shuttle service from Vancouver's Waterfront Station to the Sea to Sky Gondola. Hike up the Sea to Summit Trail to quickly join the Chief Peaks Trail.)

Vehicle: On Highway 99 (Sea to Sky Highway) in Squamish, just north of the Sea to Sky Gondola, turn east to enter Stawamus Chief Provincial Park. Keep right to find the day-use parking area (toilet available).

25

WATERSPRITE LAKE

Distance: 17 km (10.6 mi)
Time: 7 hours (out and back)
Elevation gain: 650 m (2,130 ft)
High point: 1,450 m (4,760 ft)
Season: July to October

Quality: ★★★★★
Difficulty: ■
Maps: NTS 92-G/10 Pitt River, 92-G/15 Mamquam Mountain
Trailhead: 49°45′08″ N, 122°56′03″ W

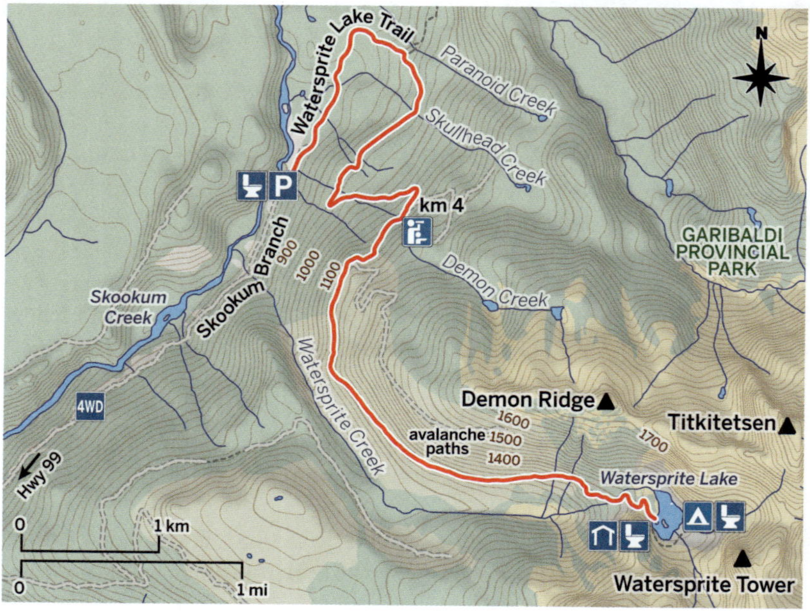

WATERSPRITE LAKE is a stunning turquoise tarn guarded by rugged peaks in Sḵwx̱wú7meshulh Aysáy̓ch, the territory of the Squamish Nation (Sḵwx̱wú7mesh Úxwumixw). The B.C. Mountaineering Club (BCMC) built the trail in 2016 and operates a backcountry cabin and campground at the lake.

From the gate (800 m/2,625 ft), head up to the Watersprite Lake Trail kiosk. Hike north over a debris field and onto a logging road. Cross Demon Creek and Skullhead Creek on a boardwalk and bridge installed by BCMC volunteers. Follow the trail right and uphill to a junction with another road, 1.8 km (1.1 mi) in. Turn right, chasing the orange diamonds. (Left goes to a ford on Paranoid Creek and provides unmaintained access to Darling Lake.)

Travel south and east in a regenerating clear-cut. Swing back south and pass the 4 km (2.5 mi) marker (1,074 m/3,520 ft). A landslide zone offers the best vantage yet of Nch'ḵay̓ (Mount Garibaldi) and Mamquam Mountain (Smánit tl'a Mámxwem in Sḵwx̱wú7mesh Sníchim, the Squamish language).

Watersprite Tower (right) looms over Watersprite Lake.

In 1.5 hours, pass the turnoff (49°44′51″ N, 122°55′39″ W) for the Demon Ridge route, which leads left to Demon Peak on the edge of Garibaldi Provincial Park (no dogs). Negotiate a rockslide. The trail curves east through fireweed—with views of Sky Pilot Mountain; Skookum Creek, a Mamquam River (Mámxwem Sta<u>k</u>w) tributary; and the Tantalus Range (Tsewílx̱)—to head up the Watersprite Creek valley. Make an ascending traverse of the big boulder-strewn avalanche paths below Demon Ridge.

Just after the 8 km (5 mi) mark, switch to river left on a bridge over Watersprite Creek. Go steeply up a boulder field. Spy the eight-bed Watersprite Lake Cabin, built in 2017, atop a bluff. It's locked and not for day use—only for prepaid overnight guests.

Pass the hut turnoff (3.5 hours up; 49°43′53″ N, 122°53′50″ W) and outhouse to reach Watersprite Lake. Titkitetsen and Watersprite Tower (1,810 m/5,940 ft) loom over the enchanting cirque. Return the way you came.

Camping is allowed only in the designated tenting area (open from July to October) on the far side of the lake. Cabin and camping reservations must be booked via the BCMC website.

Dogs are highly discouraged due to the sensitive environment. In any event, dogs must be leashed and are not allowed in the cabin.

GETTING THERE

Vehicle: On Highway 99 (Sea to Sky Highway) in Squamish, just north of Stawamus Chief Provincial Park, turn east on potholed Mamquam River Forest Service Road. Stay left at the Stawamus/Indian River FSR fork. Turn left, 13 km (8.1 mi) up, and go over the Mamquam River bridge. Keep right at the Ring Creek Main fork and cross the Skookum Creek bridge. In short order, turn left on Skookum Branch (4WD with high clearance required) and pass a run-of-river powerhouse. Drive the steep and water-barred road, keeping left at a junction, to arrive at the parking area (toilet available) by the intake dam, 20 km (12.4 mi) from the highway.

26

ELFIN LAKES

Distance: 20 km (12.4 mi)
Time: 6.5 hours (out and back)
Elevation gain: 620 m (2,030 ft)
High point: 1,590 m (5,220 ft)
Season: July to October
Quality: ★★★★
Difficulty: ■
Maps: NTS 92-G/14, 92-G/15; Clark Geomatics 102 Garibaldi Provincial Park
Trailhead: 49°45′01″ N, 123°03′11″ W

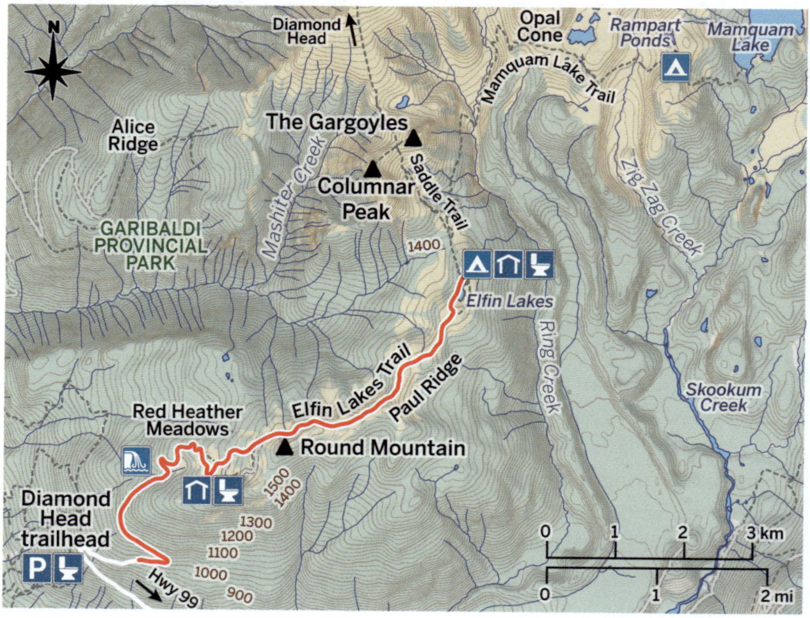

GARIBALDI PROVINCIAL PARK'S Elfin Lakes Trail gets off to a rocky-road start. But everything changes at Red Heather Meadows. Douglas squirrels chatter and whisky-jacks eye your snacks. (Don't feed the wildlife.) Higher on Paul Ridge, in the territory of the Squamish Nation (Sḵwx̱wú7mesh Úxwumixw), the Coast Mountains scenery is simply sublime.

From the trailhead (970 m/3,180 ft), this classic Squamish hike mostly follows the old road to the historical Diamond Head Chalet. A somewhat overgrown vista of Howe Sound (Átl'ḵa7tsem in Sḵwx̱wú7mesh Sníchim, the Squamish language) and Brandvold Falls are welcome interruptions.

In 4.6 km (2.9 mi), breach timberline to find the Red Heather day-use shelter (49°45′45″ N, 123°02′17″ W) and outhouse. At a fork, hikers go left and mountain bikers right, only to rejoin a bit farther uphill.

Tread the old road across the north-slope meadows below Round Mountain (1,644 m/5,390 ft), the lava-dome summit of Paul Ridge. (Marked with

The Moon over Smánit tl'a Mámxwem from Paul Ridge.

orange poles, the winter route for snowshoers and ski tourers sticks to the crest and just south to avoid cornices and avalanche paths.) Atwell Peak, the formidable south summit of stratovolcano Nch'ḵay̓ (pronounced "in-ch-KAY" and meaning "dirty place" or "grimy one" in Sḵwx̱wú7mesh), a.k.a. Mount Garibaldi, commands the northern scene.

Finally, descend to Elfin Lakes—the first lake for swimming, the second for drinking water. Find a 35-site campground, 33-bed hut, and day-use shelter (3 hours up; 1,470 m/4,820 ft; 49°47′18″ N, 122°59′16″ W), 10 km (6.2 mi) from the trailhead. Overnighting at the Elfin Lakes Shelter or any campground in the park requires a reservation year-round.

The sumptuous views of the Garibaldi Névé, Pyramid Mountain, and glaciated Mamquam Mountain (Smánit tl'a Mámxwem) are stone soup for the soul. Sḵwx̱wú7mesh oral history situates sacred Nch'ḵay̓ as a place of refuge during a great flood. Retrace your steps to the trailhead.

Elfin Lakes campers wishing to see more of the dramatic fire-and-ice landscape have very attractive options at a junction past the hut. The Saddle Trail (left) leads northwest to the pass between Columnar Peak and The Gargoyles, facilitating access to both as well as (Little) Diamond Head (7 km/4.3 mi). The Mamquam Lake Trail (right) strikes east, crossing the Ring Creek bridge en route to a water crossing, the remote Rampart Ponds campground, and the lake itself (11 km/6.8 mi). A branch climbs Opal Cone (6.5 km/4 mi).

GETTING THERE

Vehicle: On Highway 99 (Sea to Sky Highway), 3.9 km (2.4 mi) north of downtown Squamish, turn east on Mamquam Road. In 800 m (0.5 mi), turn left on Highlands Way South and right on The Boulevard. Go straight at a roundabout and continue onto University Boulevard. Turn right on Village Drive and left on Mamquam Road, which turns to gravel (2WD). Pass Ring Creek North Forest Service Road. Turn left on Garibaldi Park Road, 9.5 km (5.9 mi) from the highway. Arrive at the busy Diamond Head parking lot (toilet available) at 14 km (8.7 mi). Day-use pass required from June to October (book online). Carrying tire chains is mandatory from October to May.

27

TANTALUS VIEW LOOKOUT

Distance: 12 km (7.5 mi)
Time: 5 hours (double lollipop)
Elevation gain: 170 m (560 ft)
High point: 400 m (1,310 ft)
Season: Most of the year

Quality: ★★★
Difficulty: ●
Maps: NTS 92-G/14 Cheakamus River; SORCA Trails of Squamish
Trailhead: 49°49′20″ N, 123°08′01″ W

EVEN IF you make frequent trips to Whistler, there's a good chance you've blown by Brohm Lake Interpretive Forest numerous times without giving it a second thought. However, Brohm Lake, in Squamish Nation (Sḵwx̱wú7mesh Úxwumixw) territory, is definitely worth a stop, especially for an easy hike in spring or fall, or a refreshing dip in summer.

The provincial recreation site surrounds the lake, which is an expansion of Brohm Creek, the west fork of the Brohm River (Syexwáy̓aḵalh in Sḵwx̱wú7mesh Sníchim, the Squamish language), a tributary of the Cheekye River (Ch'ḵay̓ Staḵw, "dirty water"). For the Sḵwx̱wú7mesh, this is a traditional area for plant food and medicine gathering, trout fishing, deer hunting, and spiritual practices. Stay on trails and respect this land.

From the kiosk at the north end of the parking lot (280 m/920 ft), set off on the Brohm Lake Trail. (The rotten bridge south of the lake is closed indefinitely.) Keep right twice to bypass the Rock Bluff Loop. A fence guards a drop-off before a sublime bluff viewpoint off to the left. Climb beautiful wooden staircases fronting a rock face.

Keep left at junctions with the Powerline Trail, Brohm Creek Trail, and Thompson Trail (which goes to the Tenderfoot Creek Hatchery) to round the

Tsewílx̱ and Ch'iyáḵmesh Staḵw from a clifftop viewpoint.

lakehead and aim south. Exit the Brohm Lake Trail on the Connector Trail to the right.

In 2.6 km (1.6 mi), go left at the High Trail junction to begin a clockwise loop. Pass the Alder Trail. Find the Cheakamus Loop Trail on the other side of a horse road.

Two delightful viewpoints (off to the left) on this 2 km (1.2 mi) scenic byway reward your mild efforts. The second, atop a cliff high above the Cheakamus River (Ch'iyáḵmesh Staḵw), is particularly impressive. Gaze upon the jagged peaks of the Tantalus Range (Tsewílx̱), including Omega Mountain (Nexwyúx̱wm), Alpha Mountain (Ḵiyáy̓aḵep), and Mount Tantalus.

Go left on the High Trail and left again on the short and steep Tantalus View Trail. Arrive at Tantalus View Lookout (2.5 hours up; 49°49′10″ N, 123°08′21″ W), the day's high point, 7.2 km (4.5 mi) from the start. Visit the old fire lookout and take lunch with a view.

Head back down to the High Trail and continue north. Take two more lefts to close the loop and retread part of the Brohm Lake Trail. In 1.8 km (1.1 mi), turn left on the Brohm Creek Trail (before the bridge).

Keep right to continue onto the Powerline Trail. Although the B.C. Hydro pylons aren't exactly gorgeous, the wide-angle vantages from the right-of-way are worth it. Stay left to take the Brohm Lake Trail back to the parking lot.

GETTING THERE

Vehicle: On Highway 99 (Sea to Sky Highway), 14.5 km (9 mi) north of downtown Squamish, turn west into the Brohm Lake Interpretive Forest parking lot (toilet available). On hot days, arrive early before the lot fills up. No shoulder parking on Highway 99.

28

GARIBALDI LAKE AND BLACK TUSK MEADOWS

Distance: 21 km (13 mi)
Time: 6.5 hours (lollipop)
Elevation gain: 1,080 m (3,540 ft)
High point: 1,650 m (5,410 ft)
Season: July to October
Quality: ★★★★★
Difficulty: ■
Maps: NTS 92-G/14 Cheakamus River; Clark Geomatics 102 Garibaldi Provincial Park
Trailhead: 49°57′27″ N, 123°07′12″ W

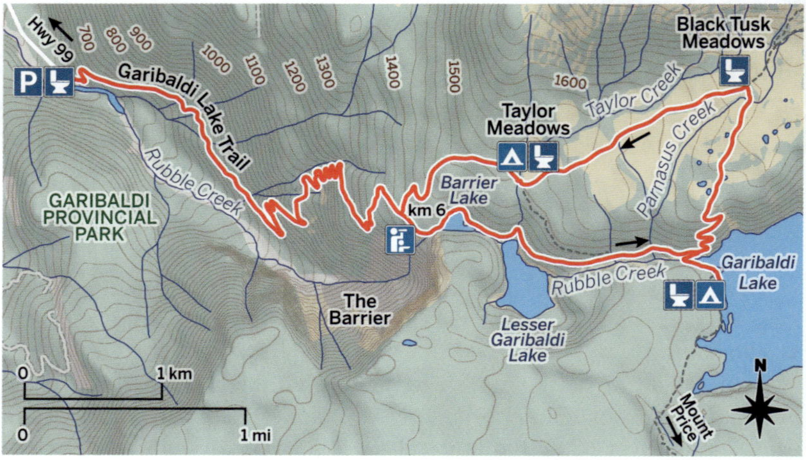

DURING THE Pleistocene epoch, a volcano that would be named Clinker Peak erupted in what is now Garibaldi Provincial Park. Dacite lava flowed north, creating an ice-contact dam across a glaciated valley. Water ponded behind The Barrier, as the 450 m (1,480 ft) lava cliff became known, forming beautiful Garibaldi Lake—a favoured destination of Lower Mainland hikers.

From the trailhead (570 m/1,870 ft) at Rubble Creek (Spú7ets' in Sḵwx̱wú7mesh Sníchim to the Squamish Nation [Sḵwx̱wú7mesh Úxwumixw]; Spó7ez in Ucwalmícwts to the Lílwat Nation), the Garibaldi Lake Trail climbs 800 m (2,625 ft) and switchbacks more than 20 times. In 2 hours, reach a junction (49°56′ 55″ N, 123°05′14″ W) at 6 km (3.7 mi). Take the right fork for Garibaldi Lake, starting a counterclockwise loop.

The Barrier viewpoint, shortly off to the right, is worth a stop. Admire the Tantalus Range (Tsewílx̱) and, of course, The Barrier. Geologists predict the rockfall-prone lava dam will eventually suffer a catastrophic failure. Accordingly, camping is prohibited in the Rubble Creek Landslide Hazard Area below The Barrier.

Castle Towers Mountain (centre) and Phyllis's Engine across Garibaldi Lake.

Continue on the Garibaldi Lake Trail for 3 km (1.9 mi), passing Barrier Lake and Lesser Garibaldi Lake. Keep right to arrive at Garibaldi Lake (1,472 m/ 4,830 ft) itself. For now, go right, cross the outlet bridge, and follow the shore to the Garibaldi Lake campground (3 hours up; 49°56′41″ N, 123°03′18″ W). Facilities include 50 tent sites, 4 day-use shelters, and outhouses.

The Battleship Islands are close at hand. The Black Tusk (T'aḵ't'aḵ'múy̓íṅ tl'a Iṅinyáx̱a7n, "Landing Place of the Thunderbird," in Sḵwx̱wú7mesh; Q'elqámtensa ti Skenknápa, "Place Where the Thunder Rests," in Ucwalmícwts; Hike 29), Panorama Ridge (Hike 30), Castle Towers Mountain, The Sphinx, and Guard Mountain rise across the turquoise water.

Backtrack to the outlet and head north on the path to Black Tusk Meadows, where the colourful wildflowers hit peak bloom in July and August. Stay on the main trail; don't trample the subalpine meadows.

In 2 km (1.2 mi), reach Outhouse Junction. Turn left, tread the boardwalk through the Taylor Meadows campground (40 tent sites, 2 day-use shelters, and outhouses), and return to the day's first junction in 4 km (2.5 mi). Descend the switchbacks to the parking lot.

Dogs are prohibited in Garibaldi Provincial Park. Camp only at designated sites (reservation required year-round).

GETTING THERE

Transit: Parkbus offers coach service on select summer weekends to the Garibaldi Lake parking lot from Burrard Station in Vancouver.

Vehicle: Turn east off Highway 99 (Sea to Sky Highway) between Rubble Creek and Daisy Lake, 33 km (21 mi) north of downtown Squamish and 25 km (15.5 mi) south of Whistler Village. Follow Daisy Lake Road for 2.5 km (1.6 mi) to the Garibaldi Lake parking lot (toilet available). Day-use pass required from June to October (book online). (In winter, the paved road is intermittently plowed; **4WD** and tire chains are recommended.) Warning: Vehicle break-ins have been reported here.

29

T'AḴ'T'AḴ'MÚÝÍŃ TL'A IṅINÝÁX̱A7N (THE BLACK TUSK)

Distance: 27 km (16.8 mi)
Time: 10.5 hours (out and back)
Elevation gain: 1,745 m (5,725 ft)
High point: 2,315 m (7,595 ft)
Season: July to October

Quality: ★★★★★
Difficulty: ◆◆
Maps: NTS 92-G/14 Cheakamus River; Clark Geomatics 102 Garibaldi Provincial Park
Trailhead: 49°57′27″ N, 123°07′12″ W

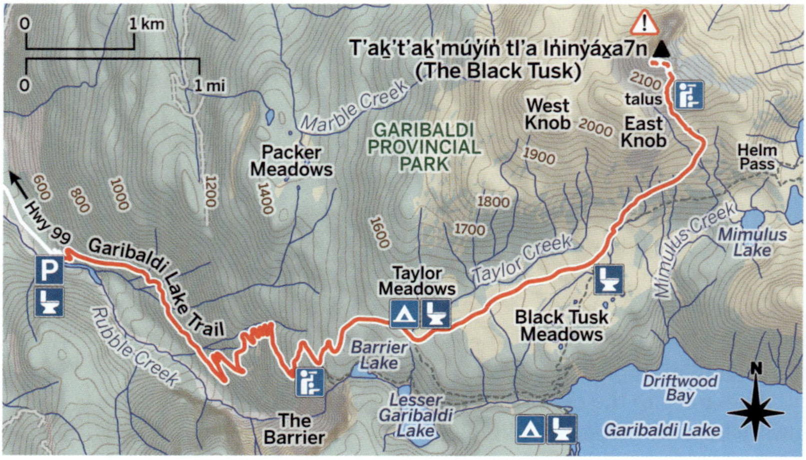

MEMBERS OF the B.C. Mountaineering Club gave The Black Tusk its name in 1912, but the striking remnant of an ancient stratovolcano has long borne storied toponyms. In Sḵwx̱wú7mesh Sníchim, the language of the Squamish Nation (Sḵwx̱wú7mesh Úxwumixw), the hypersthene andesite plug dome is known as T'aḵ't'aḵ'múýíń tl'a Iṅinýáx̱a7n ("Landing Place of the Thunderbird"). The Lílwat Nation refers to the sacred mountain as Q'elqámtensa ti Skenknápa ("Place Where the Thunder Rests") in Ucwalmícwts.

Located in Garibaldi Provincial Park, Black Tusk is a strenuous hike and scramble that earns you breathtaking views of the glaciovolcanic wonderland surrounding turquoise Garibaldi Lake (Hike 28). From the trailhead (570 m/1,870 ft) at Rubble Creek (Spú7ets' in Sḵwx̱wú7mesh; Spó7ez in Ucwalmícwts), the Garibaldi Lake Trail switchbacks more than 20 times as it climbs to a junction (1,380 m/4,530 ft) at 6 km (3.7 mi).

After 2 hours on foot, take the left fork and tread the boardwalk through the Taylor Meadows campground. (The right fork offers a tad longer route

T'aḵ't'aḵ'múy̓íṅ tl'a Iṅiny̓áx̱a7n from Black Tusk Meadows.

via Garibaldi Lake.) In 4 km (2.5 mi), meet the path coming up from the lake at Outhouse Junction.

Continue east in paradisiacal Black Tusk Meadows.

Arrive at the Black Tusk junction. Turn left and ascend the trail and talus for 3 km (1.9 mi) to the Black Tusk viewpoint. (Hikers unprepared for scrambling, stop here.) Press on to the saddle above, then traverse west below the columnar-jointed wall to the final wide chimney (helmet advised). Many hikers are satisfied with seeing the base of the chimney, which is lined with loose rock, foolhardy to climb when wet, and prone to traffic jams.

To tackle the Class 3 route, climb up the chimney crux (one person at a time!) and keep right to find a narrow gully. Emerge from the gully, which ends precipitously, higher up. Follow a boot-beaten path right, then left, up the talus to the south summit (6 hours up; 49°58′30″ N, 123°02′35″ W).

The north summit, marginally higher and rarely climbed, taunts you across a formidable gap. Survey the splendiferous scene: Castle Towers Mountain, Panorama Ridge (Hike 30), and Mount Price around Garibaldi Lake, and majestic Nch'ḵay̓, a.k.a. Mount Garibaldi, farther south.

Take extra care not to stray from your ascent route on the descent. Retrace your steps to Taylor Meadows and the parking lot.

GETTING THERE

Transit: Parkbus offers coach service on select summer weekends to the Garibaldi Lake parking lot from Burrard Station in Vancouver.

Vehicle: Turn east off Highway 99 (Sea to Sky Highway) between Rubble Creek and Daisy Lake, 33 km (21 mi) north of downtown Squamish and 25 km (15.5 mi) south of Whistler Village. Follow Daisy Lake Road for 2.5 km (1.6 mi) to the Garibaldi Lake parking lot (toilet available). Day-use pass required from June to October (book online). (In winter, the paved road is intermittently plowed; 4WD and tire chains are recommended.)

30

PANORAMA RIDGE

Distance: 30 km (18.6 mi)
Time: 10.5 hours (out and back)
Elevation gain: 1,560 m (5,120 ft)
High point: 2,133 m (7,000 ft)
Season: July to October

Quality: ★★★★★
Difficulty: ◆
Maps: NTS 92-G/14 Cheakamus River; Clark Geomatics 102 Garibaldi Provincial Park
Trailhead: 49°57′27″ N, 123°07′12″ W

PANORAMA RIDGE isn't misnamed, that's for sure. From the mountaintop, overlooking Garibaldi Lake in the territories of the Líl̓wat and Squamish (Sḵwx̱wú7mesh) First Nations, the 360-degree view is out of this world. Panorama Ridge is also surrounded by stratovolcanoes, being situated amid the Garibaldi Lake Volcanic Field, part of the larger Cascade Volcanic Arc.

From the trailhead (570 m/1,870 ft) at Rubble Creek (Spú7ets' in Sḵwx̱wú7mesh Sníchim, the Squamish language; Spó7ez in Ucwalmícwts to the Líl̓wat Nation), the Garibaldi Lake Trail (Hike 28) switchbacks more than 20 times as it climbs to a junction (1,380 m/4,530 ft) at 6 km (3.7 mi). After 2 hours on foot, take the left fork and tread the boardwalk through the Taylor Meadows campground (40 tent sites, 2 day-use shelters, and water from Taylor Creek). (The right fork offers a tad longer route via Garibaldi Lake.)

In 4 km (2.5 mi), meet the path coming up from the lake at Outhouse Junction. Continue east in dreamy Black Tusk Meadows for 2 km (1.2 mi).

Pass the leftward turnoff for The Black Tusk (T'aḵ't'aḵ'múy̓ín̓ tl'a In̓iny̓áx̱a7n, "Landing Place of the Thunderbird" in Sḵwx̱wú7mesh; Q'elqámtensa ti Skenknápa, "Place Where the Thunder Rests" in Ucwalmícwts; Hike 29).

Helm Peak (top), the Cinder Cone, and Cinder Flats from Helm Pass.

Keep going to the junction at Helm Pass (1,780 m/5,840 ft; 49°57′52″ N, 123°01′41″ W). For a shorter, wildflower-centric hike, turn around here. Regardless, contemplate the desolate landscape ahead, featuring Helm Lake.

With Panorama Ridge as your goal, turn right and head south. Enjoying the elevated perspective of Black Tusk Lake and Mimulus Lake, as well as outcrops of 100-million-year-old seabed strata, ascend scree and snow. Reach the viewpoint atop Panorama Ridge in 3 km (1.9 mi) and admire beautiful, blue Garibaldi Lake. The summit (6 hours up; 49°57′15″ N, 123°00′50″ W) is nearby to the east.

The volcanic rock stars in the vicinity include: Black Tusk, Cinder Cone, Sphinx Moraine, Glacier Pikes, Nch'ḵay̓ (Mount Garibaldi), The Table, Mount Price, and Clinker Peak. The Table is a hornblende andesite tuya, a kind of volcanic mesa that geologists attribute to lava flooding a hole in an ice sheet. The geological term *tuya* comes from Tuya Butte, named after neighbouring Tuya Lake, in Tāłtān Nation territory, northwestern B.C. In Tāłtān ẕāk'eh, the Tāłtān language, the place name Tūyah refers to "a river running between two bluffs." Retrace your steps to Taylor Meadows and the parking lot.

GETTING THERE

Transit: Parkbus offers coach service on select summer weekends to the Garibaldi Lake parking lot from Burrard Station in Vancouver.

Vehicle: Turn east off Highway 99 (Sea to Sky Highway) between Rubble Creek and Daisy Lake, 33 km (21 mi) north of downtown Squamish and 25 km (15.5 mi) south of Whistler Village. Follow Daisy Lake Road for 2.5 km (1.6 mi) to the Garibaldi Lake parking lot (toilet available). Day-use pass required from June to October (book online). (In winter, the paved road is intermittently plowed; **4WD** and tire chains are recommended.)

31

BRANDYWINE MOUNTAIN

Distance: 10 km (6.2 mi)
Time: 5.5 hours (out and back)
Elevation gain: 860 m (2,820 ft)
High point: 2,213 m (7,260 ft)
Season: July to October

Quality: ★★★★★
Difficulty: ◆◆
Maps: NTS 92-J/3 Brandywine Falls; Clark Geomatics 103 Callaghan Valley Area
Trailhead: 50°05′22″ N, 123°10′51″ W

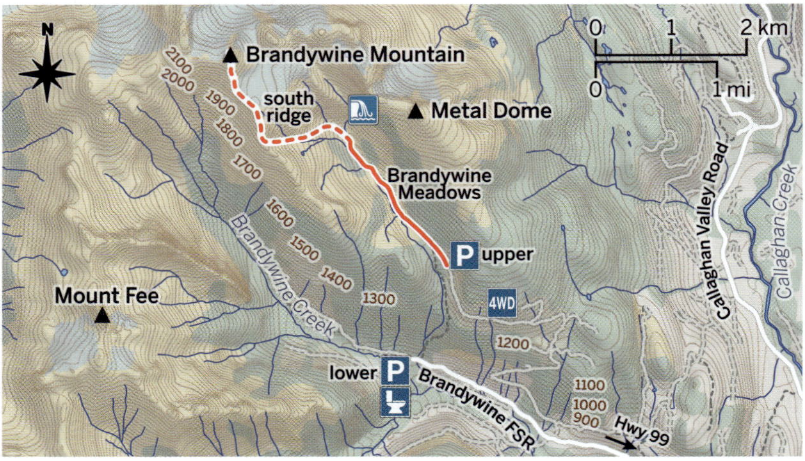

EVERYWHERE YOU LOOK, there's evidence of glaciation in the Pacific Ranges of the Coast Mountains. Arêtes, cirques, fjords, horns, paternoster lakes, tarns, and U-shaped valleys are landforms shaped by glacial erosion, while moraines arise from sediment deposited by glacial ice. At Brandywine Meadows, in the territories of the Lílwat and Squamish (Sḵwx̱wú7mesh) First Nations, you'll explore a hanging valley, once home to a tributary glacier.

From the upper trailhead (1,350 m/4,430 ft), the Brandywine Meadows Trail switchbacks and crosses a few small creeks. After just 15 minutes, arrive at a junction (1,440 m/4,720 ft; 50°05′39″ N, 123°11′15″ W) in the colourful but often buggy meadows, where the old trail from the lower trailhead joins from the left. Protect the subalpine flora by keeping to the raised gravel path.

Eventually, the gravel ends and the provincial recreation trail merges with an old path. A kaleidoscope of wildflowers, big boulders, and a headwall waterfall catch the eye. Looking back, the hanging valley beautifully frames a trio of postcard peaks in Garibaldi Provincial Park: Castle Towers Mountain, The Black Tusk (T'aḵ't'aḵ'múýíń tl'a Iṅinýáx̱a7n in Sḵwx̱wú7mesh Sníchim; Q'elqámtensa ti Skenknápa in Ucwalmícwts, the language of the Lílwat Nation; Hike 29), and Nch'ḵaý (Mount Garibaldi).

Descending Brandywine Mountain, with Mount Fee in the background.

For a quick and easy wildflower stroll, turn around at a creek crossing at the head of the valley. Scramblers bear left, and climb west up steepening heather, talus, and snow (ice axe advised). After a challenging ascent, gain the shoulder at the end of the south ridge of Brandywine Mountain. A dirt track and a sequence of snow and boulders lead north to the top. Stay off the glacier and cornices to the right.

From the summit cairn (3 hours up; 50°06′52″ N, 123°13′16″ W), on the southern edge of the Squamish Nation's Páyakéntsut Wild Spirit Place, drink up the glaciovolcanic views: Black Tusk, Nch'ḵaỷ, Mount Fee's ominous twin towers, Pyroclastic Peak, Mount Cayley, and Ring Mountain. Also prominent are Icecap Peak (Sxel'tskwu7 in Sḵwx̱wú7mesh) to the west and Wedge Mountain to the east. Head back the way you came.

Brandywine Mountain is not recommended for dogs, due to the difficult terrain. In the meadows, keep dogs on the trail and out of creeks, and pack out dog poop. No fires in the subalpine!

GETTING THERE

Vehicle: Turn west off Highway 99 (Sea to Sky Highway) on Callaghan Valley Road, 3.1 km (1.9 mi) north of Brandywine Falls Provincial Park and 14 km (8.7 mi) south of Whistler Village. In 900 m (0.6 mi), turn left on Brandywine Creek Forest Service Road. Drive the bumpy gravel main for 4.5 km (2.8 mi) to a signed junction. With high-clearance **4WD**, take the right fork (extremely rough). Follow signs for the Brandywine Meadows Trail for 5 km (3.1 mi)—negotiating big rocks, potholes, and water bars—to reach the upper trailhead. (With high-clearance 2WD, take the left fork, which reaches the lower parking area [toilet available; 50°04′41″ N, 123°11′08″W] in 2 km/1.2 mi. The final hill requires 4WD; park at the bottom. Hike up the steep lower trail for 4 km/2.5 mi to join the upper trail [add 2 hours or so to the round trip].)

32

CONFLICT LAKE

Distance: 12 km (7.5 mi)
Time: 4 hours (lollipop)
Elevation gain: 180 m (590 ft)
High point: 1,370 m (4,495 ft)
Season: July to October

Quality: ★★★★
Difficulty: ■
Maps: NTS 92-J/3 Brandywine Falls; Clark Geomatics 103 Callaghan Valley Area
Trailhead: 50°11′27″ N, 123°10′56″ W

THE SQUAMISH NATION (Sḵwx̱wú7mesh Úxwumixw) has designated five Wild Spirit Places (Ḵw'áyḵw'ay̓ex̱ Kw'elh7aynexw ta Sḵwx̱wú7mesh Temíxw). These areas of cultural, spiritual, and ecological importance are meant to be protected as wilderness and be off limits to industrial development. One is Páyakéntsut Wild Spirit Place, which is home to lovely Conflict Lake and also lies in Líl̓wat Nation territory. It covers the west side of the Callaghan Creek (Scwálem in Ucwalmícwts, the language of the Líl̓wat) watershed.

From its unsigned trailhead (1,200 m/3,940 ft) in Callaghan Lake Provincial Park, the Conflict Lake Trail goes west into Páyakéntsut and the Callaghan Conservancy and up the Solitude Valley. To begin, follow the Parkway cross-country track (part of the Callaghan Country Nordic ski area) over a log bridge in the woods. Flagging tape leads hikers right on a rooty path with planks over brooks and muddy sections.

A half-hour (1.8 km/1.1 mi) in, after a pond with lily pads, find a signed fork (50°11′07″ N, 123°12′06″ W). Right is for Conflict Lake. (Left goes to a service road connecting Alexander Falls, worth a stop on the drive out, and the Journeyman Lodge.) Skirt thickets at the base of the wooded ridge leading to Hidden Peak, 1 hour from the trailhead.

Wildfire smoke in Páyakéntsut Wild Spirit Place.

Descend to cross a creek and wander through lonely subalpine meadows. Upon reaching Journeyman Lodge (closed in summer), turn right and follow the path (Meadows Loop) down to Conflict Lake. Arrive at its west shore (2 hours up; 1,350 m/4,430 ft; 50°11′39″ N, 123°14′38″ W), after hiking for 6 km (3.7 mi).

Ring Lake, nestled in a cirque 4 km (2.5 mi) northwest of Conflict Lake and 300 m (985 ft) higher, offers the option of a longer, more challenging hike. Find the trail leaving from the left side of the Meadows Loop, 300 m (330 yd) north. Ring Mountain and Mount Callaghan (Sts'áḵ'ay̓s in Sḵwx̱wú7mesh Sníchim, the Squamish language) loom above the tarn.

From Conflict Lake, retracing your steps is surely the more scenic return route. However, a quicker way back is to head east from the lodge on the service road. Leave the road 3.7 km (2.3 mi) from the lake and go left on a trail signed for Callaghan Lake. Moments later, rejoin the Conflict Lake Trail at the initial fork and continue to the trailhead.

Páyakéntsut is pronounced "pie-a-cun-sote" and means "to train oneself physically as a warrior." Camping is prohibited in the conservancy, and dogs should be left at home.

GETTING THERE

Vehicle: Turn west off Highway 99 (Sea to Sky Highway) on Callaghan Valley Road, 3 km (1.9 mi) north of Brandywine Falls Provincial Park and 14 km (8.7 mi) south of Whistler Village. In 8 km (5 mi), pass the Alexander Falls Recreation Site and go left on rough Callaghan Creek Forest Service Road (possible with 2WD and high clearance, but **4WD** recommended), which has cross-ditches and is closed to motorized vehicles November to May. Take a left fork, enter Callaghan Lake Provincial Park, and find the trailhead on the left, just before Callaghan Lake campground (toilet available), 16 km (9.9 mi) from the highway.

33
CIRQUE LAKE

Distance: 4 km (2.5 mi)
Time: 3 hours (out and back)
Elevation gain: 330 m (1,080 ft)
High point: 1,530 m (5,020 ft)
Season: July to October

Quality: ★★★★★
Difficulty: ◆
Maps: NTS 92-J/3 Brandywine Falls; Clark Geomatics 103 Callaghan Valley Area
Trailhead: 50°12′26″ N, 123°11′57″ W

THE HIKE to Cirque Lake is short but incredibly gratifying. It also requires a canoe, kayak, or stand-up paddleboard to accomplish. To set off on this land and water adventure, head to Callaghan Lake Provincial Park in the territories of the Lílwat and Squamish (Sḵwx̱wú7mesh) First Nations.

Find the put-in (50°11′35″ N, 123°10′58″ W) past the kiosk at the end of the campground. Don a life vest and paddle the length of Callaghan Lake (2 km/1.2 mi or 30 minutes one way), aiming for the tall waterfall, Cirque Falls, at its head. The takeout is between channels on the right side (as seen from the lake) of the mouth of the upper course of Callaghan Creek (Scwálem in Ucwalmícwts, the language of the Lílwat Nation).

Stash your watercraft in a clearing—with no-camping and no-fires signs—that serves as the trailhead (1,200 m/3,940 ft). Set off on a muddy path through the heather, crossing a distributary on small logs and staying on river left of the main channel.

In 20 minutes, start up a rockslide. Look back to see Castle Towers Mountain, The Black Tusk (T'aḵ't'aḵ'múýíń tl'a Iṅiny̓áx̱a7n, "Landing Place of the Thunderbird," in Sḵwx̱wú7mesh Sníchim; Q'elqámtensa ti Skenknápa,

Subalpine meadows at Cirque Lake.

"Place Where the Thunder Rests," in Ucwalmícwts; Hike 29), and Nch'k̲aỷ ("dirty place" or "grimy one" in Sḵwx̱wú7mesh), a.k.a. Mount Garibaldi. Exit to the left in a scrambly fashion, just below the gap between the cliffs at the rockslide's head. Head up through the berries and past slabs.

See Callaghan Creek below to the left, then scramble up and away to reach a viewpoint (1,480 m/4,860 ft) atop a rock and heather mound. Stick to the main path to preserve the meadows of mountain arnica and subalpine daisy. Finally, spy Cirque Lake over the lip. Drop down boulders to the left and make for a wondrous rocky viewpoint (1.5 hours up; 50°13′01″ N, 123°12′30″ W) overlooking the clear blue tarn. Survey the ramparts and waterfalls of Hidden Peak and the lush meadows around the lake. Retrace your steps to Callaghan Lake and paddle back to the campground.

No drones, fires (except in pits at the first-come, first-served campground), littering, mushroom or plant harvesting, snowmobiling, smoking, or vaping in Callaghan Lake Provincial Park. Camping is prohibited at Cirque Lake and outside of the campground. Dogs must be leashed; however, B.C. Parks doesn't recommend taking dogs into the backcountry due to the potential for conflict with grizzly bears and other wildlife.

GETTING THERE

Vehicle: Turn west off Highway 99 (Sea to Sky Highway) on Callaghan Valley Road, 3 km (1.9 mi) north of Brandywine Falls Provincial Park and 14 km (8.7 mi) south of Whistler Village. In 8 km (5 mi), pass the Alexander Falls Recreation Site and go left on rough Callaghan Creek Forest Service Road (possible with 2WD and high clearance, but **4WD** recommended), which has cross-ditches and is closed to motorized vehicles from November to May. Take a left fork, enter Callaghan Lake Provincial Park, and arrive at the Callaghan Lake campground (toilet available), 16 km (9.9 mi) from the highway.

34
CRATER RIM TRAIL

Distance: 11.5 km (7.1 mi)
Time: 5.5 hours (loop)
Elevation gain: 320 m (1,050 ft)
High point: 920 m (3,020 ft)
Season: April to November

Quality: ★★★
Difficulty: ■
Maps: NTS 92-J/3 Brandywine Falls; Green Trails 92J1S Whistler
Trailhead: 50°05′11″ N, 123°02′08″ W

YOU CAN travel to Oregon to circumambulate Crater Lake in the caldera of Mount Mazama. Or, just make a day trip to Whistler Interpretive Forest and visit a much smaller, but no less intriguing, volcanic crater lake.

The interpretive forest is home to the Crater Rim Trail and part of the larger Cheakamus Community Forest, jointly managed by the Lí̓lwat Nation, Squamish Nation (Sḵwx̱wú7mesh Úxwumixw), and Resort Municipality of Whistler. A loop allows you to survey Loggers Lake, which sits in a 10,000-year-old crater, from all sides.

Opposite the parking-lot outhouse (600 m/1,970 ft), head south on the Riverside Trail. Keep right to reach Eastside Main. Find the continuation of Riverside across the forestry road and to the left. Go right at the Farside junction. Keep left to cross the Westside Main bridge over the Cheakamus River (Ch'iyáḵmesh Staḵw in Sḵwx̱wú7mesh; Ntsítsugwten in Ucwalmícwts), then exit left on Riverside.

Keep left at the House Rock day-use site. Continue upstream, briefly running alongside Westside Main twice and ignoring trails from the right. Follow Riverside until it bends right to meet a kiosk beside Westside Main, after 1 hour (2.5 km/1.6 mi). Take a trail, Ridge Connector, across the road

The Crater Rim Trail overlooks Loggers Lake.

and to the right. (Housing development may alter trail connections.) Go left, then quickly right on the Ridge Trail.

Turn right at the signed start of the Crater Rim Trail (50°04′06″ N, 123°02′35″ W). The trail switchbacks up to a lookout.

Earn your first vista of Loggers Lake, before crossing paths with the Ridge Trail again. Go left and then right to stay on the Crater Rim. Enjoy two up-valley vantage points and keep right at the second.

Arrive at the viewpoint overlooking Loggers Lake (3 hours up; 770 m/2,530 ft; 50°03′50″ N, 123°02′08″ W), 4 km (2.5 mi) after leaving Riverside.

Just past the viewpoint, drop down on a steep path to the lakeshore. Go right on the shoreline path. Turn right on a gravel road and descend to Westside Main. Cross to the Loggers Lake parking lot and rejoin the Riverside Trail, heading downstream. Take the MacLaurin's Crossing suspension bridge over the Cheakamus River. Turn right on the Farside Trail, keeping left at Far Out to hit Eastside Main.

Head up the Highline Trail opposite. At the end of Highline, go left on the microwave tower access road. Admire Mount Fee from a viewpoint off to the left. Continue down the 4×4 road. At a four-way junction, turn left on the Valley Trail. Tread the paved path to the trailhead, 2 hours (5 km/3.1 mi) from Loggers Lake.

GETTING THERE

Transit: From Whistler Village, take Whistler Transit Bus 10 (Valley Express), 20 (Cheakamus), or 20X (Cheakamus Express, winter only) to Cheakamus Lake Road.

Vehicle: Northbound on Highway 99 (Sea to Sky Highway), turn right (south) on Cheakamus Lake Road at Cheakamus Crossing (opposite Function Junction), 7.6 km (4.7 mi) south of Whistler Village. Immediately turn left to enter the Whistler Interpretive Forest parking lot (toilet available).

35
FLUTE SUMMIT

Distance: 9 km (5.6 mi)
Time: 4 hours (descent)
Elevation loss: 455 m (1,490 ft)
High point: 2,182 m (7,160 ft)
Season: July to September

Quality: ★★★★
Difficulty: ■
Maps: NTS 92-J/2 Whistler; Clark Geomatics 102 Garibaldi Provincial Park
Trailhead: 50°03′31″ N, 122°57′26″ W

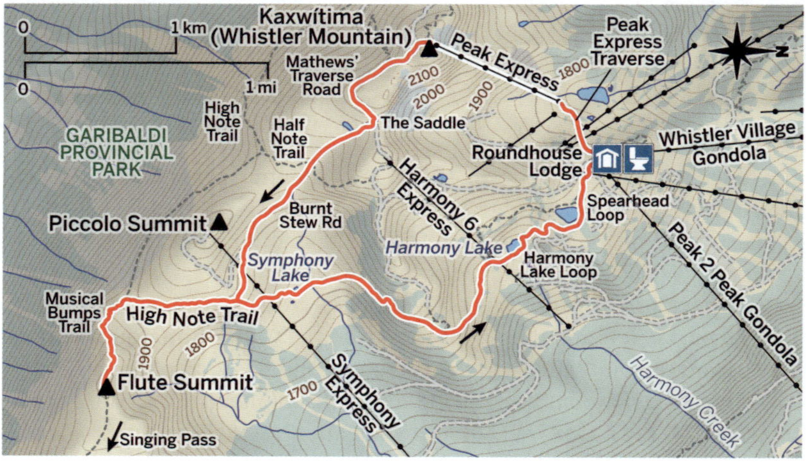

THE ALPINE scenery reaches a crescendo atop the Musical Bumps in the territories of the Lílwat and Squamish (Sḵwx̱wú7mesh) First Nations. With vehicle access to the old Singing Pass trailhead cut off since the 1990s, many hikers opt to pay for lift-serviced admission.

To reach Flute Summit the Whistler Blackcomb way, ride the Whistler Village Gondola (ticket required) to the Roundhouse Lodge (1,850 m/6,070 ft). Walk down the Peak Express Traverse (600 m/0.4 mi). Board the Peak Express to the top of Whistler Mountain (Kaxwítima in Ucwalmícwts, the language of the Lílwat), briefly known as London Mountain.

Just down from the chairlift terminal, take the left fork for Mathews' Traverse Road. At The Saddle, before Little Whistler Peak, turn right on the steep and loose—or snow-buried—Burnt Stew Road. Cross the Half Note Trail and take the right fork to contour below Piccolo Summit.

Bear left on a path through the boulders (50°02′54″ N, 122°56′19″ W) and go under the Symphony Express above Tower 19. Arrive at a T-junction with the High Note Trail, after 50 minutes of hiking. Go right (south) and follow the mellow path through rock and heather terrain to the Piccolo-Flute col.

Flute Summit from the High Note Trail on Kaxwítima.

Leave High Note, and head left (east) and up the Musical Bumps Trail to tick off Flute Summit (2,015 m/6,610 ft; 50°02′23″ N, 122°55′34″ W), 1.5 hours in. Beware of cornices.

To return to the Roundhouse Lodge, retrace your steps to the junction with the Burnt Stew connector. This time, stick with High Note. Where High Note ends, bear right for the Harmony Lake Loop. Keep left on the lakeside boardwalk and take the left side of the Spearhead Loop. Arrive at the Roundhouse for your gondola ride down.

Day hikers wanting to explore beyond Flute may continue to Singing Pass (4.5 km/2.8 mi)—choosing to return to the Roundhouse or descend the Singing Pass Trail (11.5 km/7.1 mi) to Whistler Village afterward. Backpackers keep going east to the Kees and Claire Hut, built by the Spearhead Huts Society in 2019, or to the Russet Lake campground (both require reservations).

Take note of the gondola's closing time.

In recent years, the Federation of Mountain Clubs of B.C. has sought a new trailhead and parking lot on the Blackcomb side of Fitzsimmons Creek (S7i'tem) to restore public access to Singing Pass.

GETTING THERE

Transit: Take Whistler Transit Bus 4, 5, 6, 7, 8, 20, 20X, 21, 25, 30, 31, or 33, or Pemberton Valley Transit Bus 99 to Gondola Transit Exchange. (Epic Rides offers daily shuttle service from Vancouver's Burrard Station to Whistler's Gateway Loop.)

Vehicle: On Highway 99 (Sea to Sky Highway) at Whistler Village, 58 km (36 mi) north of downtown Squamish, turn east on Village Gate Boulevard. Go left on Blackcomb Way and turn right to enter the Whistler Village day lots (electric-vehicle charging available). Park in Lot 1, 2, or 3. Designated overnight parking spots for Garibaldi Provincial Park are in Day Lot 4.

36
BLACKCOMB BURN

Distance: 6.2 km (3.9 mi)
Time: 3 hours (ascent)
Elevation gain: 1,165 m (3,820 ft)
High point: 1,850 m (6,070 ft)
Season: July to September

Quality: ★★★
Difficulty: ◆
Maps: NTS 92-J/2 Whistler
Trailhead: 50°06′55″ N, 122°56′51″ W

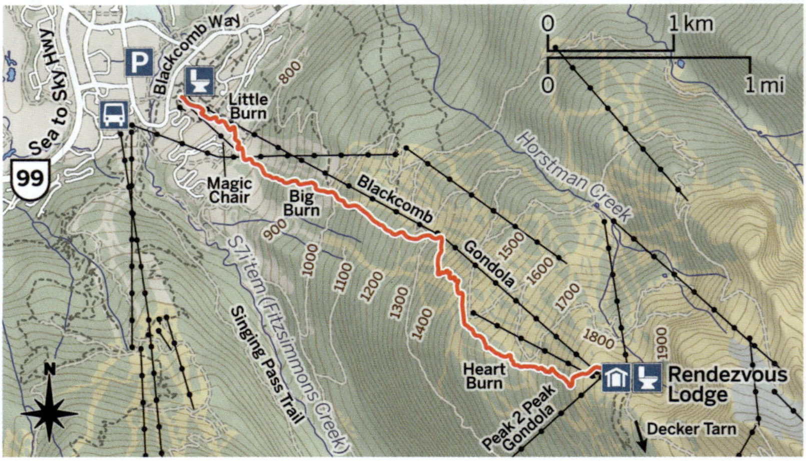

THE BLACKCOMB BURN boasts more elevation gain than any other lift-serviced ascent trail in southwestern B.C. Throw in the fact that Whistler Blackcomb engineered the Burn, opened in 2017, to provide a virtually continuous uphill climb, and you have an appealing summer workout for hikers, trail runners, and fitness freaks. The trail lies in the territories of the Lílwat and Squamish (Sḵwx̱wú7mesh) First Nations.

The first section, Little Burn, starts between the Blackcomb Gondola and Magic Chair lifts (685 m/2,250 ft). The mellow gravel path leads into pleasant woods between ski runs, emerging in 800 m (0.5 mi) at Base 2.

Big Burn, covering 2 km (1.2 mi), is the most scenic section. It steepens, following a riparian zone and transitioning from montane to alpine snow forest with Douglas-fir, western hemlock, western red cedar, and yellow cedar trees that are hundreds of years old. Wildlife sightings include Douglas squirrels and pileated woodpeckers. Going up and across the Upper Mainline ski run, take a breather to savour the valley view and colourful wildflowers, including arctic lupine, red paintbrush, subalpine daisy, and tiger lily. Look east to Mount Sproatt and the 21 Mile Creek (Stsátscwam in Ucwalmícwts, the language of the Lílwat Nation) basin.

Heart Burn is the third leg of the Blackcomb Burn.

Heart Burn begins at the Blackcomb Gondola mid-station, visits the Magic Castle kids' play area, and switchbacks up the Bark Sandwich glade run. Stairs are scarce on the Burn. Fixed chains and ropes help with potentially slippery bits. After 3.4 km (2.1 mi), the trail terminates at the Rendezvous Lodge (50°05′45″ N, 122°54′05″ W), where you can enjoy the views before riding the Blackcomb Gondola back to the base. (Downhill hiking on the Burn is discouraged. Make sure to buy a download ticket in advance.)

Enjoying the burn too much to stop? Check the lift system's posted hours. Then aim your boots at the 7th Heaven zone below Blackcomb Peak (Tsíqten, "fish spear"). Hike the Overlord Trail to Blackcomb Lake or Decker Tarn (Hike 37), cutting across the Sunburn ski run on the way there and back.

Dogs are not allowed on Whistler Blackcomb lifts or trails, which occupy a controlled recreation area on provincial land. No camping, drones, fires, or smoking.

For an après-hike activity, consider visiting the Sḵwx̱wú7mesh Líl̓wat7úl Cultural Centre (4584 Blackcomb Way) to learn about the Indigenous Peoples of this land. Opened in 2008, the museum, art gallery, and gift shop is located in the Upper Village, close to Blackcomb base.

GETTING THERE

Transit: Take Whistler Transit Bus 4, 5, 6, 7, 8, 20, 20X, 21, 25, 30, 31, or 33, or Pemberton Valley Transit Bus 99 to Gondola Transit Exchange. Walk east on Blackcomb Way to Blackcomb base. (Epic Rides offers daily shuttle service from Vancouver's Burrard Station to Whistler's Gateway Loop.)

Vehicle: On Highway 99 (Sea to Sky Highway) at Whistler Village, 58 km (36 mi) north of downtown Squamish, turn east on Village Gate Boulevard. Go left on Blackcomb Way and turn right to enter the Whistler Village day lots (electric-vehicle charging available). Park in Lot 1, 2, or 3. Walk east on the Valley Trail to Blackcomb base.

37

DECKER TARN

Distance: 9 km (5.6 mi)
Time: 4 hours (double lollipop)
Elevation gain: 240 m (790 ft)
High point: 2,050 m (6,730 ft)
Season: July to September

Quality: ★★★★
Difficulty: ■
Maps: NTS 92-J/2 Whistler; John Baldwin Backcountry Whistler
Trailhead: 50°05′45″ N, 122°53′59″ W

LISTEN FOR the whistles of hoary marmots, stop and smell the colourful wildflowers, and marvel at the glory of the Coast Mountains. A hike to Decker Tarn takes full advantage of Whistler Blackcomb's superb summer trails in the 7th Heaven zone below Blackcomb Peak, in the territories of the Líl̓wat and Squamish (Sḵwx̱wú7mesh) First Nations. Access entails booting it up the Blackcomb Burn (Hike 36) and/or coughing up for a lift ticket.

The trailhead lies near the Rendezvous Lodge (1,850 m/6,070 ft)—by the Blackcomb Gondola and Peak 2 Peak Gondola terminals. With Blackcomb Lake, Decker Tarn, or both as your goal, follow selfie-seeking sightseers up and immediately right on the gravel Alpine Loop. In 10 minutes, the Fitzsimmons Lookout grants a beautiful view of the Musical Bumps (see Hike 35) and Whistler Mountain (Kaxwítima in Ucwalmícwts, the language of the Líl̓wat Nation).

At the next right, leave the tourist loop and head southeast on the Overlord Trail, traversing bouldery meadows, losing some elevation, and passing the Marmot Trail. Under the 7th Heaven Express chairlift, bear left for the Lakeside Loop (1.3 km/0.8 mi), which quickly ascends to Blackcomb Lake

The Lakeside Loop takes aim at the Musical Bumps.

(1,918 m/6,290 ft) in its cirque (Lakeside Bowl) at the foot of Blackcomb Peak (Tsíqten, "fish spear"). Cross the outflow, descend the muddy path, and turn left to rejoin the Overlord Trail. Enter Garibaldi Provincial Park.

Several minutes later (50°04′40″ N, 122°53′07″ W), take the left fork for the more challenging Decker Loop (1.8 km/1.1 mi). Switchback up a ridge—avoiding a cornice to your left—to the windy Overlord Glacier Lookout, the day's high point. After crossing a snowy boulder field, the trail plunges to your ultimate destination.

After 2 hours of hiking, reach milky Decker Tarn (1,925 m/6,320 ft; 50°04′05″ N, 122°52′20″ W). Decker Mountain, rising to the east, is a potential off-trail objective for peak baggers.

Cross the tarn's boulder dam and recross the outflow creek to begin the mellow return via the Overlord Trail (3.7 km/2.3 mi). At the Alpine Loop, head right to complete the tourist stroll.

Return to the base via the Blackcomb Gondola. Take note of the gondola's closing time.

GETTING THERE

Transit: Take Whistler Transit Bus 4, 5, 6, 7, 8, 20, 20X, 21, 25, 30, 31, or 33, or Pemberton Valley Transit Bus 99 to Gondola Transit Exchange. Walk east on Blackcomb Way to Blackcomb base. (Epic Rides offers daily shuttle service from Vancouver's Burrard Station to Whistler's Gateway Loop.)
Vehicle: On Highway 99 (Sea to Sky Highway) at Whistler Village, 58 km (36 mi) north of downtown Squamish, turn east on Village Gate Boulevard. Go left on Blackcomb Way and turn right to enter the Whistler Village day lots (electric-vehicle charging available). Park in Lot 1, 2, or 3. Walk east on the Valley Trail to Blackcomb base.

38
RAINBOW PASS

Distance: 18 km (11.2 mi)
Time: 7 hours (out and back)
Elevation gain: 840 m (2,760 ft)
High point: 1,510 m (4,950 ft)
Season: July to October

Quality: ★★★★
Difficulty: ■
Maps: NTS 92-J/2 Whistler, 92-J/3 Brandywine Falls; Green Trails 92J1S Whistler
Trailhead: 50°07′49″ N, 122°59′09″ W

THE RAINBOW-MADELEY TRAIL is an overnight backpacking route linking Whistler and the Callaghan Valley, in the territories of the Lílwat and Squamish (Sḵwx̱wú7mesh) First Nations. Day hiking the Rainbow Lake Trail section is popular, especially during wildflower season.

This trip enters the Rainbow Mountain Wildland Area and the municipal watershed that supplies almost half of Whistler's drinking water. Accordingly, camping, fires, fishing, and swimming are prohibited at Rainbow Lake, and the 21 Mile Creek (Stsátscwam in Ucwalmícwts, the language of the Lílwat Nation) water supply area is a no-go zone for dogs, horses, mountain bikes, and snowmobiles. Hikers are asked to poop in the outhouses along the trail.

From the west end of the parking area (670 m/2,200 ft), head into the woods with 21 Mile Creek to your right. Keep right on the Rainbow Falls Loop where it joins an access road at a bend. Visit the Rainbow Falls viewpoint, then continue to a four-way junction overlooked by a building. Go straight ahead onto a gravel road. Keep right on the road, spurning leftward exits for Whip Me Snip Me and the Rainbow-Sproatt Flank Trail, the latter by an outhouse.

Trade road for path. Cross an A-frame bridge, with an outhouse before and a waterfall view after. Steadily gain elevation in montane forest, with

A stream crossing on the Rainbow Lake Trail.

Mount Sproatt to the south. Take a nifty suspension bridge over Gin and Tonic Creek; the decking is removed for winter. Delight in the subalpine meadows ahead. Green false hellebore, leatherleaf saxifrage, and pink monkey-flower contribute to the floral rainbow.

Finally, arrive at Rainbow Lake and cross the bridge over the outlet. Find a kiosk (50°09′16″ N, 123°03′41″ W) with an outhouse nearby, 7.7 km (4.8 mi) from the trailhead. Go ahead and admire the pretty tarn sitting in its bowl between Gin Peak and Rainbow Mountain, but don't call it quits here.

Keep going 1.5 km (0.9 mi) west to Rainbow Pass (3.5 hours up; 50°09′09″ N, 123°04′35″ W) for superlative views of Metal Dome, Brandywine Mountain (Hike 31), Mount Cayley, and Powder Mountain to the west—and a satisfying look back at its namesake mountain and lake. The Rainbow Meadows Trail branches off to the right before the pass; Pot of Gold and the Ninja Lakes Loop intersect your path on the divide.

If you wish to cool off with a swim, Hanging Lake lies 700 m (0.4 mi) farther—and outside the municipal watershed—down the Madeley Lake Trail. You can camp there too. (The west trailhead at Madeley Lake is 14.6 km/9.1 mi distant.) Otherwise, turn around at the pass and retrace your steps to the east trailhead on Alta Lake Road.

GETTING THERE

Vehicle: Northbound on Highway 99 (Sea to Sky Highway), 5.2 km (3.2 mi) south of Whistler Village, turn left (north) on Alta Lake Road. In 6.1 km (3.8 mi), find the parking area (toilet available) by the Rainbow Trail sign on the left.

39
SKYWALK SOUTH

Distance: 18 km (11.2 mi)
Time: 6.5 hours (lollipop)
Elevation gain: 1,050 m (3,445 ft)
High point: 1,790 m (5,870 ft)
Season: July to October
Quality: ★★★★
Difficulty: ◆
Maps: NTS 92-J/3 Brandywine Falls
Trailhead: 50°08′40″ N, 122°58′23″ W

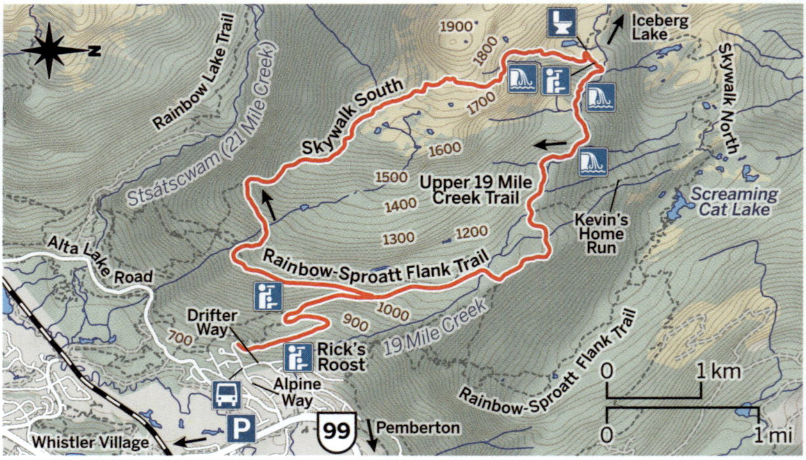

MAY THE FORCE be with you, Skywalk hiker. The Force was certainly strong with the Alpine Club of Canada's Whistler section in 2014, when volunteers completed the stellar Skywalk trail network on the east side of Rainbow Mountain. It's best explored in two loops—Skywalk South and Skywalk North (Hike 40)—in the territories of the Líl̓wat and Squamish (Sḵwx̱wú7mesh) First Nations. Skywalk South offers the more challenging terrain.

From the yellow gate (740 m/2,430 ft) at the top of Alpine Way in Alpine Meadows, ascend the gravel road, ignoring two leftward spurs. At the Rick's Roost sign, sidetrack right for the first viewpoint of the day. After 45 minutes, turn left on the multi-use Rainbow-Sproatt Flank Trail. Score a big view of Whistler (Sḵwiḵw in Sḵwx̱wú7mesh Sníchim, the Squamish language; Cwítima in Ucwalmícwts to the Líl̓wat) at a paragliding launch site.

Shortly thereafter, Skywalk South begins on the right (50°08′37″ N, 122°59′13″ W). Your path merges with the Rainbow's End bike trail to head skyward. The superbly built trail climbs northwest, steepening as it passes over rocky outcrops. After 1 hour on Skywalk South, the forest thins and snags are abundant. Soon, colourful meadows are predominant, and the glaciated

Cairns mark Skywalk South in wildfire smoke.

crown of Rainbow Mountain comes into view. Passing a pond and crossing a brook, the trail gains elevation over rocky terrain.

Beside a gorgeous tarn, 4 km (2.5 mi) up Skywalk South, the trail takes a right turn behind Rainbow's End. Reach the high point, and follow cairns and orange squares through the wild, boulder-covered landscape.

Up next is the most difficult section of the clockwise loop: the thrilling descent to the 19 Mile Creek basin. After crossing creeks above two waterfalls, the path eases up somewhat, following a smooth ridge with tarns to an outhouse junction with Skywalk North and the Upper 19 Mile Creek Trail (50°10′39″ N, 123°01′01″ W), after 3 hours on Skywalk South.

Go right to descend the latter trail for 3.7 km (2.3 mi). (Optionally, head 900 m/0.6 mi up Skywalk North to visit Iceberg Lake before doing so.) On the way down, check out a viewpoint bench (off right) and a couple of waterfalls (off left). Turn right on the Flank Trail, cross the 19 Mile Creek bridge, and make a left on the Rick's Roost road to return to the trailhead.

No dogs, helicopter access, horses, littering, mountain biking, or shooting. Carry bear spray and be wary of grizzly bears.

GETTING THERE

Transit: From Whistler Village, take Whistler Transit Bus 31 or 33 (Alpine) to Drifter Way at Alpine Way. Walk west for 350 m (0.2 mi) to the top of Alpine.

Vehicle: On Highway 99 (Sea to Sky Highway), 3.9 km (2.4 mi) north of Whistler Village, turn west on Alpine Way. It's best to use the parking lot at Meadow Park (toilet available); go left on Rainbow Drive and left on Camino Drive. (Walk 1 km/0.6 mi, via Matterhorn Drive and Drifter Way, to the top of Alpine Way.) Alternatively, continue up Alpine Way, and look for scarce legal street parking. No parking at the top of Alpine Way or on the odd-numbered side of the streets.

40

SKYWALK NORTH

Distance: 18 km (11.2 mi)
Time: 8 hours (lollipop)
Elevation gain: 1,050 m (3,445 ft)
High point: 1,790 m (5,870 ft)
Season: July to October

Quality: ★★★★★
Difficulty: ■
Maps: NTS 92-J/2 Whistler, 92-J/3 Brandywine Falls
Trailhead: 50°09′16″ N, 122°58′06″ W

MANY HIKERS venturing onto Whistler's Skywalk trail network make a beeline to Iceberg Lake. However, it's even more rewarding to approach this lacustrine gem via Skywalk North. Taking the scenic loop pays off with quality time in the subalpine meadows of Rainbow Mountain, in the territories of the Líl̓wat and Squamish (Sḵwx̱wú7mesh) First Nations.

From the top of Mountain View Drive (740 m/2,430 ft), start by going left on the Lower 19 Mile Creek Trail, paying attention to signs and orange markers. Head left on a gravel road, then quickly take a trail leaving to the right. Cross another road. A half-hour in, a viewpoint bench overlooks Green Lake. Cross the Howler downhill bike path, and head up a steep road.

Go left on a path, and immediately keep left on Lower 19 Mile, spurning the Screaming Cat Lake Connector. Follow the orange diamonds right at three forks. Then go left at a fork and left at the Prowler junction, after 1 hour on foot. Hit the Rainbow-Sproatt Flank Trail, with a gate to the right. Briefly go left to find the bottom of the Upper 19 Mile Creek Trail on the right.

Iceberg Lake and Rainbow Mountain from Skywalk North.

Follow Upper 19 Mile to a signed fork (1,135 m/3,720 ft; 50°10′20″ N, 122°59′34″ W), after more than 1.5 hours (3.6 km/2.2 mi) of hiking. Go right on Kevin's Home Run, starting a counterclockwise loop. Over 2.5 km (1.6 mi), ascend a wooded ridge, and enter heather meadows.

Arrive at the junction of Kevin's Home Run and Skywalk North (1,565 m/5,135 ft; 50°11′19″ N, 123°00′10″ W), 3 hours in. Head left for Iceberg Lake, 2 hours (4.2 km/2.6 mi) away. Cairns lead the way across rocky slopes.

From the high point, survey the Coast Mountains—Tśzil ("slides on the mountain" in Ucwalmícwts, the language of the Lílwat Nation), a.k.a. Mount Currie, Wedge Mountain, Blackcomb Peak (Tsíqten), and Fissile Peak. The elating descent to Iceberg Lake is muddy and steep. Cross a boulder moraine to arrive at the lakeshore (5 hours up; 1,610 m/5,280 ft).

Look for a large cairn (50°10′46″ N, 123°01′38″ W) near the lake outlet. Drop down, with a big waterfall to your right, to the meadows below. Cross 19 Mile Creek to river right on a bridge. Find an outhouse by the Skywalk South (Hike 39) junction; go left on the Upper 19 Mile Creek Trail. On the way down, check out a viewpoint bench (off right) and waterfalls (off left).

Cross back to river left to close the loop at the bottom of Kevin's Home Run, 1.5 hours (3.8 km/2.4 mi) from the lake. Mountain View Drive is 1 hour away via the Lower 19 Mile Creek Trail.

GETTING THERE

Transit: From Whistler Village, take Whistler Transit Bus 30 (Emerald via Alpine), 31, or 33 (Alpine) to Mountain View Drive at Valley Drive. Walk 700 m (0.4 mi) to the top of Mountain View.

Vehicle: On Highway 99 (Sea to Sky Highway), 3.9 km (2.4 mi) north of Whistler Village, turn west on Alpine Way. It's best to use the parking lot at Meadow Park (toilet available); go left on Rainbow Drive and left on Camino Drive. (Walk 2 km/1.2 mi to the top of Mountain View Drive.) Alternatively, turn right on Valley Drive and left on Mountain View Drive, and look for scarce legal street parking. No parking in the Mountain View cul-de-sac.

41

HÁWINT (TENQUILLE LAKE)

Distance: 13 km (8.1 mi)
Time: 4.5 hours (out and back)
Elevation gain: 445 m (1,460 ft)
High point: 1,710 m (5,610 ft)
Season: July to October

Quality: ★★★★
Difficulty: ■
Maps: NTS 92-J/10 Birkenhead Lake
Trailhead: 50°32′21″ N, 123°00′01″ W

THE LÍL̓WAT NATION'S Qwalímak (Upper Birkenhead) Nt̓ákmen Area is home to legends, rock art, and village and burial sites. Qwalímak includes beautiful Tenquille Lake, which is flanked by enticing mountains.

In Ucwalmícwts, the language of the Líl̓wat, Háwint (meaning "pack rat") is the name for the Tenquille Lake area and nearby Wolverine Creek. For hikers, the Branch 12 Trail is the easiest way in. From the buggy trailhead (1,265 m/4,150 ft), the path climbs and then undulates eastward.

Cross Mowich Creek (Maowets Stswaw̓cw) and steadily gain elevation in the woods above Wolverine Creek to a three-way junction (1,565 m/5,135 ft; 50°32′02″ N, 122°57′10″ W) at 4.3 km (2.7 mi). Entering from the right is the longer, steeper, and overgrown Tenquille Trail, which climbs 1,320 m (4,330 ft) over 7 km (4.3 mi) from the Líl̓wat River (Lilwatátkwa, a.k.a. Lillooet River) bridge. Thus, go left, with 2.1 km (1.3 mi) left to your destination.

Goat Peak (left) and Tenquille Mountain across Tenquille Lake.

A glorious subalpine meadow stroll awaits at Tenquille Pass (warning: high avalanche danger in winter and spring). Descend to Tenquille Lake Cabin (2 hours up; 1,660 m/5,450 ft; 50°32′12″ N, 122°55′47″ W). An outhouse is nearby, and a small day-use beach on the lake.

A 2.6 km (1.6 mi) loop encircles Tenquille Lake; head left to find the nine-site campground. (Camping and cabin stays require reservations, bookable via the Pemberton Wildlife Association website.) Scramblers have no shortage of nearby objectives: Goat Peak, Tenquille Mountain, and Finch Ridge to the north; Copper Mound (Hike 42), Mount McLeod (Hike 43), and Mount Barbour to the south. Beyond the lake, the challenging Owl-Tenquille Traverse (see Hikes 44 and 45) beckons. Retrace your steps on the return.

In 2022, the Lílwat, N'Quatqua First Nation, and B.C. government released a visitor use management strategy for Háwint. The area is monitored by Lílwat Skél7awlh (stewards). This is grizzly bear country. No dogs, drones, fires, hunting, mountain biking, or shooting.

The Lílwat Nation has identified five Nt̓ákmen (Our Way) areas in its territory. These zones are meant to protect old-growth forests and places for Lílwat people to conduct traditional harvesting and cultural practices.

GETTING THERE

Vehicle: From Whistler, head north on Highway 99 (Sea to Sky Highway). In Pemberton, turn left on Portage Road at the traffic lights. Go left at a roundabout onto Birch Street. Turn right on Pemberton Meadows Road. In 23 km (14 mi), head right on (Upper) Lillooet River Forest Service Road. Keep left on the far side of the Lílwat River bridge. (Unless you're hiking the gruelling Tenquille Trail—in that case, find the trailhead just up the road to the right.) After 8.5 km (5.3 mi) on Lillooet River FSR, make a right on Hurley River FSR. Look for Tenquille Branch (Branch 12) on the right at a leftward road bend, 10 km (6.2 mi) up Hurley River FSR. 2WD vehicles may park on the roadside here or, with high clearance, head 1.9 km (1.2 mi) up Branch 12 to a parking lot. With the benefit of **4WD**, continue 3.1 km (1.9 mi) farther, negotiating large water bars, to the trailhead.

42
COPPER MOUND

Distance: 14 km (8.7 mi)
Time: 6 hours (out and back)
Elevation gain: 890 m (2,920 ft)
High point: 2,157 m (7,080 ft)
Season: July to September

Quality: ★★★★
Difficulty: ◆◆
Maps: NTS 92-J/10 Birkenhead Lake
Trailhead: 50°32′21″ N, 123°00′01″ W

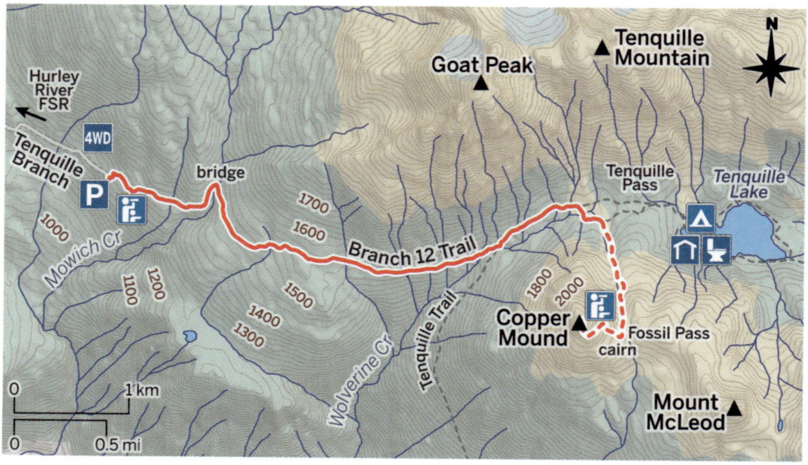

IF YOU LIKE a sprinkle of scrambling and route-finding with your hiking, Copper Mound is a delightful day or overnight trip. From this wide, open summit in Lílwat Nation territory, the panoramic payoff is solid gold.

Set off on the Branch 12 Trail from the kiosk at the end of the road (1,265 m/4,150 ft). Take a bridge over Mowich Creek (Maowets Stswaw̓cw in Ucwalmícwts, the language of the Lílwat) en route to a three-way junction at 4.3 km (2.7 mi). Your path is the left one, which leads to Tenquille Lake (Hike 41). Háwint is the Ucwalmícwts name for Wolverine Creek and the Tenquille Lake area.

The trail enters subalpine meadows and bears right to traverse the south side of Tenquille Pass. Boulder-hop Wolverine Creek. After 1.5 hours of hiking and 1.1 km (0.7 mi) past the junction, take a path leaving to the right (1,690 m/5,545 ft; 50°32′10″ N, 122°56′22″ W) along a south branch of the creek. When this path peters out, cross to river right and ascend to Fossil Pass, the saddle between Mount McLeod (Hike 43) and Copper Mound, following intermittent tracks and cairns through heather and boulders.

Keep right of the summit of Fossil Pass, 1 hour after diverging from the trail. The mound-top is 30 minutes away. Pick up a path indicated by small

Finch Ridge and Háwint from Copper Mound.

cairns. Ascend to a bench with a view of Tenquille Lake, then swing left to traverse boulders and loose rock and rise to a vantage of the Pemberton Valley. Head up through the outcrops to the summit (3 hours up; 50°31′42″ N, 122°56′31″ W), 1.6 km (1 mi) from the Tenquille Lake trail.

Copper Mound, formerly known as Fossil Peak, is capped by volcanic tuff and sedimentary rock. Fossils from the Late Triassic epoch (more than 200 million years ago) have been found here. Since the 1890s, prospectors and miners have sought copper, gold, lead, silver, and zinc around Háwint.

Looking west, spot Mount Pauline (Quleỷsút, "all alone") down by the Lil̓wat River. Ipsoot Mountain, Sugarloaf Mountain (Qw̓exwqw̓ixaltcw), and The Camels Back rise south of the Pemberton Valley.

Be mindful of cliffs on the descent. Back at Tenquille Pass, head left to return to the Branch 12 trailhead. If you are camping at Tenquille Lake, go right for 1 km (0.6 mi).

Camping requires a reservation (book via the Pemberton Wildlife Association website). No dogs.

GETTING THERE

Vehicle: From Whistler, head north on Highway 99 (Sea to Sky Highway). In Pemberton, turn left on Portage Road at the traffic lights. Go left at a roundabout on Birch Street. Turn right on Pemberton Meadows Road. In 23 km (14 mi), head right on (Upper) Lillooet River Forest Service Road. After 8.5 km (5.3 mi) on Lillooet River FSR, make a right on Hurley River FSR. Look for Tenquille Branch (Branch 12) on the right at a leftward road bend, 10 km (6.2 mi) up Hurley River FSR. 2WD vehicles may park on the roadside here or, with high clearance, head 1.9 km (1.2 mi) up Branch 12 to a parking lot. With the benefit of **4WD**, continue 3.1 km (1.9 mi) farther to the trailhead.

43

MOUNT MCLEOD

Distance: 15.5 km (9.6 mi)
Time: 7 hours (out and back)
Elevation gain: 890 m (2,920 ft)
High point: 2,158 m (7,080 ft)
Season: July to September

Quality: ★★★★
Difficulty: ◆
Maps: NTS 92-J/10 Birkenhead Lake
Trailhead: 50°32′21″ N, 123°00′01″ W

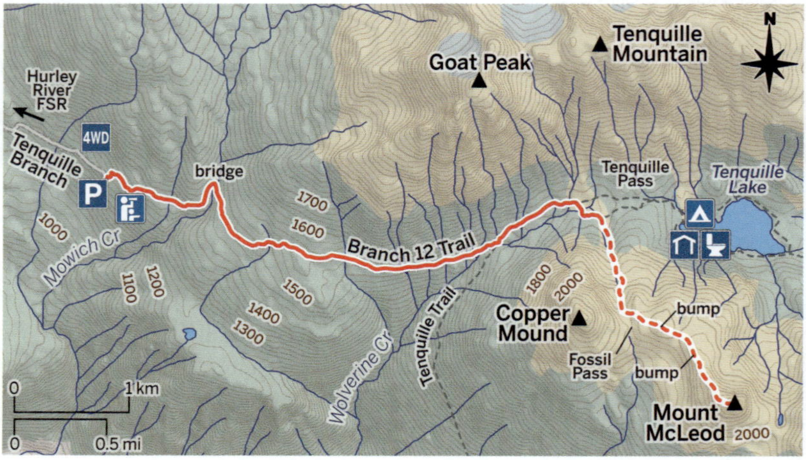

ALSO KNOWN AS Crown Mountain, Mount McLeod stands immediately south of Tenquille Lake in Líl̓wat Nation territory. Reaching the summit has its scenic rewards and requires route-finding as there is no formal trail.

Set off on the Branch 12 Trail (1,265 m/4,150 ft). Take a bridge over Mowich Creek (Maowets Stswaw̓cw in Ucwalmícwts, the language of the Líl̓wat) en route to a three-way junction at 4.3 km (2.7 mi). A right turn would see you cross Wolverine Creek and descend the Tenquille Trail to the Líl̓wat River (Líl̓watátkwa), a.k.a. Lillooet River. However, your path is the left one, which leads to Tenquille Lake (Hike 41). Háwint is the Ucwalmícwts name for Wolverine Creek and the Tenquille Lake area.

The trail enters subalpine meadows and bears right to traverse the south side of Tenquille Pass. Boulder-hop Wolverine Creek. After 1.5 hours of hiking and 1.1 km (0.7 mi) past the junction, take a path leaving to the right (1,690 m/5,545 ft; 50°32′10″ N, 122°56′22″ W) along a south branch of the creek. When this path peters out, cross to river right and head toward Fossil Pass, the saddle between Mount McLeod and Copper Mound (Hike 42), following intermittent tracks and cairns through heather and boulders.

Copper Mound (left), Goat Peak (centre), and Tenquille Mountain from Mount McLeod.

As you near Fossil Pass, look for a path leading up the slope to the left. In the open alpine, follow occasional cairns and tracks southeast over a bump and gain the easygoing ridge leading to Mount McLeod. Pass over another bump and make your way through a rock field. Keep back from cliffs on both sides. Reach the broad summit plateau, a cairn marks the highest outcrop (3.5 hours up; 50°31′17″ N, 122°55′23″ W), 2 hours (2.3 km/1.4 mi) from the Tenquille Lake trail.

Peer down at gorgeous Tenquille Lake, which lies along N'chat-quil-nash (In-cha-Qual-nash), a route used by Lil̓wat and N'Quatqua people to travel between the valleys of the Lil̓wat and Birkenhead (Qwalímak) Rivers. To the east, spy Sun God Mountain and Mount Barbour beyond Gingerbread Peak.

Retrace your steps to Tenquille Pass. Head left to return to the Branch 12 trailhead. If you are camping at Tenquille Lake, go right for 1 km (0.6 mi). Camping requires a reservation (book via the Pemberton Wildlife Association website).

For the Lil̓wat, Háwint is an important area for hunting, gathering, and cultural practices. This is grizzly bear and mountain goat country.

GETTING THERE

Vehicle: From Whistler, head north on Highway 99 (Sea to Sky Highway). In Pemberton, turn left on Portage Road at the traffic lights. Go left at a roundabout onto Birch Street. Turn right on Pemberton Meadows Road. In 23 km (14 mi), head right on (Upper) Lillooet River Forest Service Road. After 8.5 km (5.3 mi) on Lillooet River FSR, make a right on Hurley River FSR. Look for Tenquille Branch (Branch 12) on the right at a leftward road bend, 10 km (6.2 mi) up Hurley River FSR. 2WD vehicles may park on the roadside here or, with high clearance, head 1.9 km (1.2 mi) up Branch 12 to a parking lot. With the benefit of **4WD**, continue 3.1 km (1.9 mi) farther to the trailhead.

44

ONE DUCK LAKE

Distance: 25 km (15.5 mi)
Time: 11.5 hours (out and back)
Elevation gain: 775 m (2,540 ft)
High point: 2,040 m (6,690 ft)
Season: July to September

Quality: ★★★★★
Difficulty: ◆◆
Maps: NTS 92-J/10 Birkenhead Lake
Trailhead: 50°32′21″ N, 123°00′01″ W

ONE DUCK LAKE is a vivid turquoise jewel, located northeast of Mount Barbour in the vicinity of Tenquille Lake and the territory of the Lí̓lwat Nation. It's encountered on the northern leg of the multi-day Owl-Tenquille Traverse (see Hike 45). However, a long day trip or, preferably, a hike from a base camp at Tenquille Lake will suffice too.

Set off on the Branch 12 Trail from the kiosk at the end of the road (1,265 m/4,150 ft). At a three-way junction, take the left path, signed for Tenquille Lake (Hike 41). Travel through subalpine meadows at the headwaters of Wolverine Creek and Tenquille Pass. Háwint is the name for Wolverine Creek and the Tenquille Lake area in Ucwalmícwts, the language of the Lí̓lwat.

Arrive at Tenquille Lake Cabin (1,660 m/5,450 ft; 50°32′12″ N, 122°55′47″ W), after 2 hours (6.4 km/4 mi) of hiking. A 2.6 km (1.6 mi) loop encircles Tenquille Lake. Right is the quickest way to the far side; left offers access to the campground. (Camping and cabin stays at Tenquille Lake require reservations, bookable via the Pemberton Wildlife Association website.)

At the unsigned three-way junction by the lake outlet, head east on the Mount Barbour Trail, now on the Owl-Tenquille Traverse proper. In 10 minutes,

One Duck Lake with Sun God Mountain in the background.

fork right. (Left is the closed Tenquille Creek Trail.) Gradually gain elevation, crossing rockslides and creeks. Leave the trees and pass a tall cascade.

Enter a broad meadow and reach an unsigned fork. Go left on the Barbour Valley route. Soon your path bears right to avoid a cliff, where a viewpoint overlooks two tarns. Cross a rockslide, switchback up a steep incline, and find a cairn atop the rise (1,970 m/6,460 ft; 50°31′06″ N, 122°53′26″ W) with Dora Lake ahead. Solid route-finding skills are required beyond this point.

Some cairns lead down to the lakehead, but follow other cairns slightly leftward toward the foot of the lake. Step over the outlet of a little tarn immediately downstream of Dora Lake, 3.5 km (2.2 mi) from Tenquille Lake Cabin, and bear right. Pursue cairns and intermittent paths up and away from the lake, outflanking the headwall. Tread on rocky ground and beaten paths as much as possible to protect the meadows. Gain the alpine saddle south of Dora Peak (2,093 m/6,870 ft), on the ridge north of Mount Barbour.

Over the saddle, cairns lead down to Dead Duck Wall. Get a good look at One Duck Lake (with a backdrop of Sun God Mountain) and the milky upper tarn below Mount Barbour. Zigzag down the loose path to One Duck Lake (6 hours up; 1,830 m/6,000 ft; 50°30′52″ N, 122°52′41″ W), 4 hours (6 km/3.7 mi) from Tenquille Lake Cabin. After a rest, head back to Branch 12.

GETTING THERE

Vehicle: From Whistler, head north on Highway 99 (Sea to Sky Highway). In Pemberton, turn left on Portage Road at the traffic lights. Go left at a roundabout onto Birch Street. Turn right on Pemberton Meadows Road. In 23 km (14 mi), head right on (Upper) Lillooet River Forest Service Road. After 8.5 km (5.3 mi) on Lillooet River FSR, make a right on Hurley River FSR. Look for Tenquille Branch (Branch 12) on the right at a leftward road bend, 10 km (6.2 mi) up Hurley River FSR. 2WD vehicles may park on the roadside here or, with high clearance, head 1.9 km (1.2 mi) up Branch 12 to a parking lot. With the benefit of **4WD**, continue 3.1 km (1.9 mi) farther to the trailhead.

45

UPPER FOWL LAKE

Distance: 15 km (9.3 mi)
Time: 7 hours (out and back)
Elevation gain: 510 m (1,670 ft)
High point: 1,730 m (5,680 ft)
Season: July to October

Quality: ★★★★★
Difficulty: ◆
Maps: NTS 92-J/7 Pemberton
Trailhead: 50°24′17″ N, 122°47′46″W

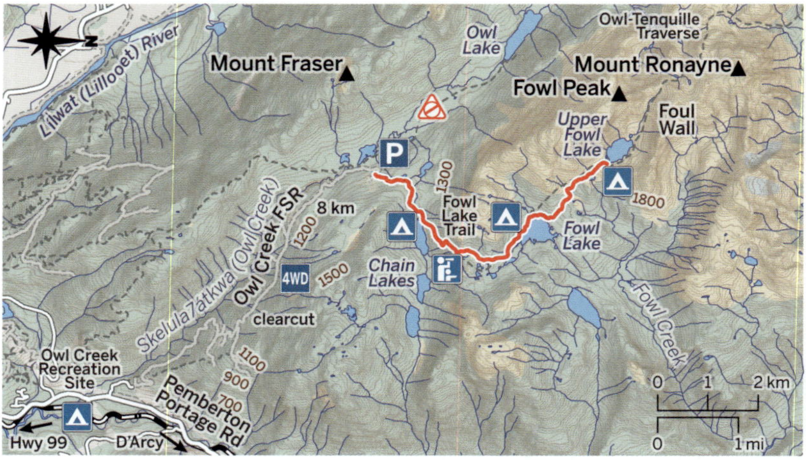

THE OWL-TENQUILLE TRAVERSE is a wonderfully wild alpine route in the Coast Mountains, north of Pemberton, that covers rugged terrain and entails tricky route-finding. For experienced parties, it's worth spending three or four days to backpack the 32 km (20 mi) traverse in Lílwat Nation territory. Another attractive option is a day or overnight hike to Upper Fowl Lake.

From the pullout, head 100 m (110 yd) up Owl Creek Forest Service Road to find the signed trailhead (1,220 m/4,000 ft) on the left, before the next clear-cut. Set off on the Fowl Lake Trail, overcoming deadfall. In 30 minutes (1.7 km/1.1 mi), reach a signed junction (1,280 m/4,200 ft; 50°24′47″ N, 122°47′03″ W). The largest of the (Owl) Chain Lakes, with its small campsite, is a quick visit to the right. The lake drains into Owl Creek, known as Skelula7átkwa in Ucwalmícwts, the language of the Lílwat. Owl Mountain (Skelúla7) rises south of Chain Lakes.

Back at the junction, continue left on the Fowl Lake Trail. Various coloured tapes lead up to a viewpoint overlooking Chain Lakes. Breach timberline, and weave muddily through several ponds. Gently descend to the south shore of Fowl Lake (1,510 m/4,950 ft; 50°25′50″ N, 122°46′47″ W) and find meadow tent sites, 1.5 hours (3.1 km/1.9 mi) past the Chain Lakes junction.

Looking across Upper Fowl Lake to Foul Wall.

Upper Fowl Lake is 1.5 hours (2.8 km/1.7 mi) farther. From here, the path is difficult to discern at times; cairns and orange flagging assist in some spots. Round the east shore and loosely follow a creek northwest, making upward progress to a lovely cyan tarn. Tread the intermittent path over the final rise to Upper Fowl Lake (3.5 hours up; 50°26′46″ N, 122°47′57″ W). With cerulean waters surrounded by boulder fields, the lake is a stunning sight. Rocky tent sites are found in the vicinity of the lake outlet.

Beyond Upper Fowl Lake, the Owl-Tenquille Traverse becomes a very challenging route, negotiating high mountain passes and awkward boulder fields, and requiring navigation skills. Developed by the Pemberton Wildlife Association in the 1990s, the route pierces Foul Wall, visits Ogre Lake (a designated camping spot), enters the Barbour valley, and passes One Duck Lake (Hike 44) on the way to Háwint (Tenquille Lake, Hike 41; no dogs).

The trail to Upper Fowl Lake lies in the Skelula7átkwa/Owl Creek and Qwalímak/Birkenhead Headwaters Wildland Areas, both culturally and spiritually important places to the Lil̓wat. This is grizzly bear country. Please use designated campsites to minimize environmental damage.

GETTING THERE

Vehicle: From Whistler, head north on Highway 99 (Sea to Sky Highway) past Pemberton. At the Mount Currie intersection, continue straight on Main Street, which becomes Pemberton Portage Road, crossing a Lil̓wat Nation reserve and Canadian National Railway track. Pass the Owl Creek Recreation Site (toilet available) and turn left on Owl Creek Forest Service Road (4WD), 4.9 km (3 mi) from Mount Currie. Cross the power-line corridor. Watch out for logging trucks. After passing the 8 km (5 mi) marker on the mainline, fork right and then ignore a right spur in a clear-cut. Keep right at a fork with a kiosk (at the entrance to the closed Owl Lake Trail). Park in a pullout at the next rightward road bend, 9 km (5.6 mi) from Pemberton Portage Road.

46

VALENTINE LAKE

Distance: 12 km (7.5 mi)
Time: 5.5 hours (out and back)
Elevation gain: 670 m (2,200 ft)
High point: 1,770 m (5,810 ft)
Season: July to October

Quality: ★★★★
Difficulty: ◆
Maps: NTS 92-J/7 Pemberton
Trailhead: 50°23′19″ N, 122°40′09″ W

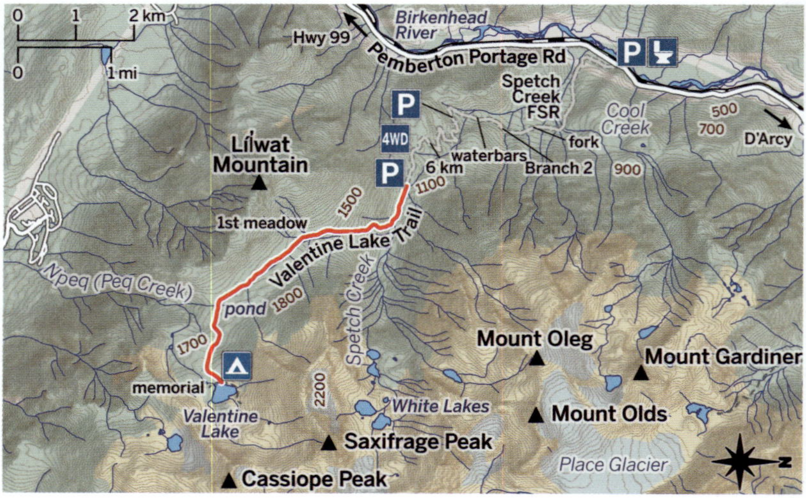

A HEART-SHAPED LAKE nestled in a meadowy bowl flanked by a couple of peaks of scrambling interest—what's not to love? Valentine Lake is certainly a sweetheart destination in Lílwat Nation territory, but getting there means persevering through deadfall, muddy bits, and overgrown sections.

From the trailhead (1,100 m/3,610 ft), follow flagging into the forest. A police-issued sign calls attention to the case of Rachael Bagnall and Jonathan Jetté, who disappeared in 2010. The Valentine Lake Trail runs between Spetch Creek, a.k.a. White Creek (left), and a clear-cut (right), before veering south, steepening, and paralleling Spetch's south fork. This part of the trail is a jumping-off point for the bushwhack southwest to Lílwat Mountain.

Step over brooks in beautiful boggy meadows, where the path is sometimes imperceptible. Saxifrage Peak (2,501 m/8,205 ft) gradually reveals itself to the northeast. Ascend in trees to a meadow studded with boulders. Continue upwards, cross the threshold of the subalpine bowl, and finally see Valentine Lake before you. Arrive at a makeshift memorial for Bagnall and Jetté near the east lakeshore (3 hours up; 50°21′36″ N, 122°37′19″ W), with the outlet to your right and tent sites (and one tent pad) in the vicinity.

Hibachi Ridge and Tśzil rise beyond Valentine Lake.

The main trail continues round the lake's east side before petering out upslope. If time and energy allow, it's rewarding to ascend another 1.5 hours to the ridge connecting Saxifrage Peak and Cassiope Peak (2,284 m/7,490 ft) for five-star views. Both peaks are challenging scrambles. To the east, spot Lower Joffre Lake (see Hike 48), Mount Chief Pascall (Ntaoz'a in Ucwalmícwts, the language of the Lil̓wat), and the Matier Glacier opposite Duffey Lake Road. Look back at Valentine Lake to see Tśzil ("slides on the mountain"), a.k.a. Mount Currie, perfectly framed by the landscape.

When it's time to go, follow the Valentine Lake Trail back to Branch 2. By the way, did you notice leatherleaf saxifrage and western bell heather (*Cassiope mertensiana*) growing in the meadows?

Valentine Lake spills into Peq Creek (Npeq, "white spot on the deer's behind"). Peq Creek is a Lil̓wat community watershed.

GETTING THERE

Vehicle: From Whistler, head north on Highway 99 (Sea to Sky Highway) past Pemberton. At the Mount Currie intersection, continue straight on Main Street, which becomes Pemberton Portage Road, crossing a Lil̓wat Nation reserve and Canadian National Railway track. Go over the Spetch Creek bridge and turn right on Spetch Creek Forest Service Road, 13 km (8.1 mi) from Mount Currie, by a trailhead kiosk for Cool Creek Canyon (a good little hike). After 2.4 km (1.5 mi) on the mainline, including a steep and loose section, take the left fork for Branch 2. (The right fork is Branch 1.) The road becomes rutted and brushed-in, with shallow water bars. 2WD vehicles should park in a pullout (770 m/2,530 ft; 50°23′46″ N, 122°41′07″ W) on the left, 4.3 km (2.7 mi) from Pemberton Portage Road. Beyond this point, sections of the road are severely erosion-damaged. **4WD** vehicles with high clearance may make it 2.8 km (1.7 mi) farther. Pass a right-hand spur to a clear-cut, immediately before finding the trailhead pullout on the right. (If using the lower parking area, add 45 minutes on foot each way.)

47

WETSCÍN'ATKWA (LIZZIE CREEK)

Distance: 27 km (16.8 mi)
Time: 10 hours (out and back)
Elevation gain: 1,220 m (4,000 ft)
High point: 1,610 m (5,280 ft)
Season: July to October

Quality: ★★
Difficulty: ◆
Maps: NTS 92-J/1 Stein Lake; Trail Ventures BC Stein to Joffre
Trailhead: 50°11′53″ N, 122°27′31″ W

THE LIZZIE CREEK Cabin Trail provides access to the sparkling subalpine lakes and meadows of the Lillooet Ranges and constitutes the westernmost leg of the 75 km (47 mi) Stein Traverse. Lizzie Creek is doable as a long day hike but is better as part of a multi-day backpacking trip.

From the outside of the road bend (410 m/1,345 ft), head into the trees on a signed path that bypasses a washout on the old Lizzie Lake Forest Service Road. Cross steep slopes and a wide rockslide with Lizzie Creek below to your right. In the Ucwalmícwts dialect of the Lower St'át'imc people, Lizzie Creek (including Lizzie Lake) is known as Wetscín'atkwa ("lizard water"). After 1 km (0.6 mi) on foot, merge with the old logging road.

Cross the north fork of Lizzie Creek on a felled tree with a rope for aid, 7 km (4.3 mi) from the trailhead. Higher up, the road is washed out; cross the debris channel. Continue ascending the road, which runs precariously atop

A subalpine meadow above Lizzie Creek Cabin.

the landslide that took it out below. On the bright side, this spot affords a vista down the Lizzie Creek valley (Nwuwqwileqs, "going down") to Líl̓wat Lake (Líl̓wat Tselálh), a.k.a. Lillooet Lake.

After 4 hours (11 km/6.8 mi) of hiking, squeeze through boulders to find a B.C. Parks kiosk and a doorless, roofless outhouse at the Lizzie Lake Recreation Site (1,310 m/4,300 ft; 50°08′08″ N, 122°23′33″ W). Step forth to find the rustic campground and muddy lakeshore.

Lizzie Creek Cabin is 1.5 hours (2.5 km/1.6 mi) away. Follow the orange diamonds southeast through the trees. Negotiate deadfall, steep sections, and wasp nests. At the Gates of Shangri-La, quartz cairns show the way through the boulders of the rock-walled entrance to a hanging valley. Make a sharp descent to pull alongside the creek en route to the small log cabin (5.5 hours up; 50°07′48″ N, 122°21′48″ W), A-frame outhouse sans door, and camping area.

Built in 1968, the rustic cabin has a maximum capacity of six people, including four in the loft. Day hikers should turn back here.

Backpackers may follow trails to Arrowhead Lake or Long Lake, where there are tent sites but no facilities—and venture into the Upper Rogers Kó̲lii7 Conservancy and Stein Valley Nlaka'pamux Heritage Park. Tundra Lake and the Stein River (Sti'yen, "hidden place" in Nłeʔkepmxcín, the language of the Nlaka'pamux people; Stegáyn in Ucwalmícwts) beckon over the divide. The Líl̓wat and Nlaka'pamux fought many battles in these highlands.

The Lizzie Creek Cabin Trail lies in the territory of the St'át'imc people, including the Lil̓wat, Samahquam, and Skatin First Nations, who identify Wetscín'atkwa as an important area for cultural practices.

GETTING THERE

Vehicle: From Whistler, head north on Highway 99 (Sea to Sky Highway) past Pemberton. In Mount Currie, turn right to stay on Highway 99 (Lillooet Lake Road) for 10 km (6.2 mi). Go right on In-SHUCK-ch Forest Service Road. In 16 km (9.9 mi), after passing the Lizzie Bay Recreation Site (toilet available) and crossing a bridge, turn left on Lizzie Branch (2WD). Continue 1.6 km (1 mi) on the gravel road to its second leftward bend and park on the roadside.

48

PIPI7ÍYEKW (JOFFRE LAKES)

Distance: 9.5 km (5.9 mi)
Time: 4 hours (out and back)
Elevation gain: 360 m (1,180 ft)
High point: 1,570 m (5,150 ft)
Season: July to October

Quality: ★★★★★
Difficulty: ●
Maps: NTS 92-J/8 Duffey Lake; Trail Ventures BC Stein to Joffre
Trailhead: 50°22′10″ N, 122°29′55″ W

WHILE SOLITUDE is in short supply at picture-perfect Joffre Lakes, alpine splendour is certainly not. Mountains tower over a trio of glacier-floured tarns, wildflowers bloom in technicolour, and smiles are everywhere.

The Joffre Lakes and Cayoosh Pass area is called Pipi7íyekw (pronounced "pippy yook") in Ucwalmícwts, the language of the Líl̓wat Nation. The Ucwalmícwts name for Joffre Creek, which drains the lakes, and its watershed is Nsk'enú7. Joffre Lakes Provincial Park lies in the territories of the Líl̓wat and N'Quatqua peoples, for whom it is part of a larger "banquet place" for hunting, trapping, fishing, gardening, and gathering.

Please respect this place and Líl̓wat and N'Quatqua stewardship. Just south of the trailhead (1,220 m/4,000 ft), come to a fork. The left spur terminates quickly at Lower Joffre Lake. Right continues on to the middle and upper of these paternoster lakes, 3 km (1.9 mi) and 4 km (2.5 mi) up, respectively.

At deep-blue Middle Joffre Lake (1,490 m/4,890 ft), you'll probably see a queue for photo ops on an Instagram-famous log. The last push is more challenging. Holloway Falls, a staircase waterfall, is an impressive sight.

After 1.5 hours (4 km/2.5 mi) on foot, many hikers turn around at the boulder viewpoint on Upper Joffre Lake. Feel free to continue 700 m (0.4 mi) around

Cayoosh Mountain and Upper Joffre Lake.

the west shore to the campground (2 hours up; 50°20′39″ N, 122°28′38″ W), which is overlooked by Mount Matier and the Matier Glacier. Retrace your steps to the trailhead.

Optionally, head up the moraine for 15 minutes to lunch above the Upper Joffre Lake campground. Higher terrain, exposed to icefall, is best left to experienced mountaineers only. This area is particularly prone to avalanches in winter and spring.

In 2021, the Lílwat, N'Quatqua, and B.C. Parks collaborated on the release of a visitor use management strategy for Joffre Lakes. In the strategy, Kúkwpi7 Skalúlmecw Dean Nelson (Lílwat) and Chief Micah Thevarge (N'Quatqua) wrote: "The establishment of Joffre Lakes Park has served to protect this unique and beautiful place from impacts of industrial activities; however, it also disrupted our traditional use and access to these lands."

Visitors must have a day-use pass from May to October (book online). Periodic closures provide opportunities for Lílwat and N'Quatqua people to connect with the land. Dogs are prohibited. Camping is allowed only on designated tent pads (reservation required) between June and November.

GETTING THERE

Transit: Parkbus offers coach service on select summer weekends to Joffre Lakes Provincial Park from Burrard Station in Vancouver.

Vehicle: From Whistler, head north on Highway 99 (Sea to Sky Highway) past Pemberton. In Mount Currie, turn right to stay on Highway 99 (Lillooet Lake Road/Duffey Lake Road) for 23 km (14 mi). Find the Joffre Lakes overflow parking lot on the left before the main parking lot on the right. A 150 m (165 yd) path connects the two lots (toilet available). Parking on the shoulder of Highway 99 is prohibited.

49
MOUNT ROHR

Distance: 12 km (7.5 mi)
Time: 8 hours (out and back)
Elevation gain: 1,030 m (3,380 ft)
High point: 2,423 m (7,950 ft)
Season: July to October

Quality: ★★★★★
Difficulty: ◆◆
Maps: NTS 92-J/8 Duffey Lake; John Baldwin Duffey Lake
Trailhead: 50°24′18″ N, 122°27′44″ W

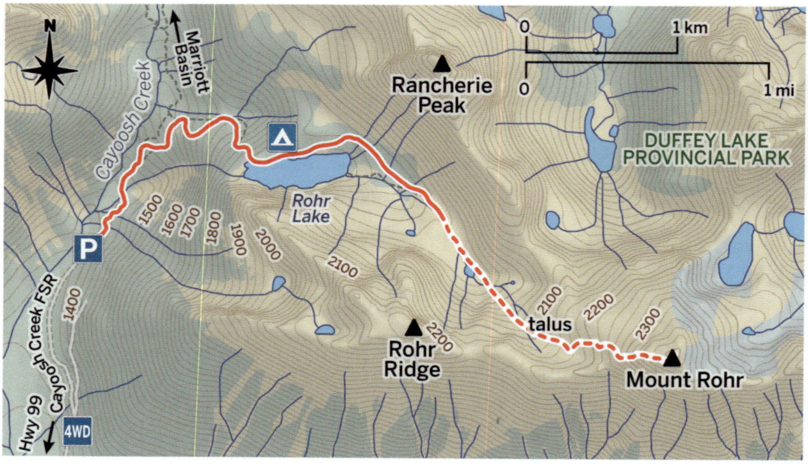

THE ALPINE terrain of the Rohr Lake and Marriott Basin area in the Cayoosh Range is spectacular for summer hiking and scrambling. These glacier-carved valleys, north of Joffre Lakes (Hike 48)—in the territory of the St'át'imc people, including the Lílwat, N'Quatqua, and T'ít'q'et First Nations—are also known for excellent ski touring in winter.

From the avalanche-terrain map at the top of Cayoosh Creek Forest Service Road (1,390 m/4,560 ft), head north on the Marriott Basin Trail under cover of forest. Reach a major junction within 20 minutes (50°24′37″ N, 122°27′30″ W). Left is signed "WTH" (for the Wendy Thompson Hut in the Marriott Basin), so take the right fork for the Rohr Lake Trail.

The steep trail switchbacks east to a lovely subalpine bowl. Follow the muddy path up the right side of a boulder field. Traverse left at a small waterfall, and ascend to the shore of beautiful blue Rohr Lake (1,800 m/5,910 ft; 50°24′35″ N, 122°26′54″ W), 1.5 hours (2 km/1.2 mi) from the trailhead.

On its own, Rohr Lake is ample reward for a 3-hour round trip with 410 m (1,345 ft) of elevation gain. There are lakeside tent sites (no facilities).

Mount Rohr beckons 2.5 hours beyond the lake, requires solid route-finding skills, and should be left to experienced parties. From the lakeshore, follow

Rohr Lake (front), Marriott Lake, and Mount Marriott from Mount Rohr.

meadow paths and cairns up-valley, passing to the left of tarns and picking your way through boulders. At the head of the basin, ascend slopes of talus and fireweed east toward your objective. Stay away from cornices.

Once on the west ridge, a quick bit of easy scrambling leads to a succession of false summits. At last, gain the true summit (4 hours up; 50°23′52″ N, 122°24′32″ W), on the edge of Duffey Lake Provincial Park. The glorious panorama includes Duffey Lake (Teq in Ucwalmícwts, the language of the Lílwat) to the east; the Joffre Group to the south; Ts̓zil (Mount Currie) to the west; and Mount Marriott to the northwest. Skihist Mountain (Skī′-hist in Secwepemctsín, the language of the Secwépemc people) is visible on the southeast horizon. Retrace your route back to the trailhead.

Mount Rohr overlooks Pipi7íyekw, a place that includes Cayoosh Pass and Joffre Lakes and holds importance to Lílwat culture and livelihoods. Rohr Lake lies in the Lílwat's Nlháxten Nt̓ákmen (Our Way) Area—highly valued as a site of culturally modified trees, legends, mineral gathering, rock art, transportation routes, and vision quests.

GETTING THERE

Vehicle: From Whistler, head north on Highway 99 (Sea to Sky Highway) past Pemberton. In Mount Currie, turn right to stay on Highway 99 (Lillooet Lake Road/Duffey Lake Road) for 26 km (16 mi). Past the Cayoosh Creek #1 bridge, turn left on Cayoosh Creek Forest Service Road (unsigned)—before the sand shed. With **4WD** and high clearance, drive north as far as 2.3 km (1.4 mi), keeping left, to the trailhead at road's end. (Drivers with 2WD or concerned about their exterior paint should use the parking area on the right near the bottom of the FSR, or park on the roadside by the sand shed, and walk the rest of the way.)

50

CINNABAR RIDGE

Distance: 14.5 km (9 mi)
Time: 6.5 hours (out and back)
Elevation gain: 1,000 m (3,280 ft)
High point: 2,213 m (7,260 ft)
Season: July to September

Quality: ★★★
Difficulty: ■
Maps: NTS 92-J/15 Bralorne; Trail Ventures BC Southern Chilcotin Mountains
Trailhead: 50°57′46″ N, 122°45′16″ W

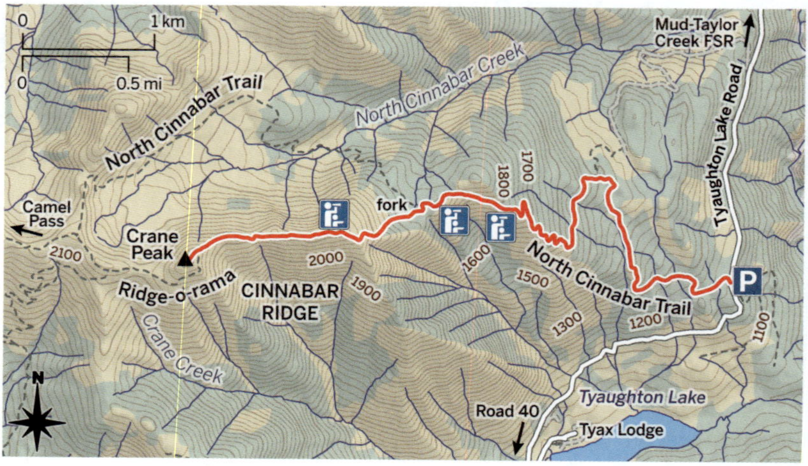

RIDGE WALKING is so sweet on the divide between North Cinnabar Creek and Crane Creek on the periphery of South Chilcotin Mountains Provincial Park. Slow down and savour the colourful rocks, views, and wildflowers of Cinnabar Ridge, located in the territories of the Secwépemc, St'át'imc, and Tŝilhqot'in peoples. Watch out for mountain bikers though.

Find the trailhead (1,210 m/3,970 ft) on the west side of Tyaughton Lake Road, 35 m (40 yd) south of the pullout. Set off on the North Cinnabar Trail and rise steadily in the woods. Pass the remains of a log cabin.

Make a hard left at an unsigned junction, 2.3 km (1.4 mi) in. (The right-hand path goes to a logging road.) Zigzag up to a pair of viewpoints facing Tyaughton Lake, Carpenter Lake, and the Bendor Range.

Arrive at a key fork (1,860 m/6,100 ft; 50°58′05″ N, 122°47′16″ W), 2 hours (4.9 km/3 mi) from the trailhead. The North Cinnabar Trail continues right, into its namesake basin. However, go left for Cinnabar Ridge on the trail known as Ridge-o-rama, which is dreadfully bike-rutted. Enter subalpine meadows and leave the forest behind.

Gain the east end of the ridge and find a cairned viewpoint off to the right, 900 m (0.6 mi) from the fork. Survey the verdant basin of North Cinnabar

Hiking on ore-stained Cinnabar Ridge.

Creek, a tributary of Tyaughton Creek (Gwezɨsh Yeqox in Nenqayni Ch'ih, the Tŝilhqot'in language). Revel in the gently undulating 1.4 km (0.9 mi) ridge walk ahead. Stay left of the crest, minding drop-offs to the right. Tread on cinnamon- and plum-tinted rocks. Ascend the steep and loose path to the summit outcrop of Crane Peak (3.5 hours up; 50°57′50″ N, 122°48′49″ W).

The joyous panorama includes: Eldorado Mountain and the Taylor Creek basin to the north; the Shulaps Range to the east; Mount Truax, the Bridge River (Nxwísten, "the foamy waters after the rapids," in Sť̓át̓imcets, the language of the St'át'imc people), and Gun Lake to the south; and Dickson Peak and Mount Sheba to the west. Once your eyes are satiated, retrace your steps to Tyaughton Lake Road.

Optionally, continue west toward Camel Pass (2,140 m/7,020 ft) to enjoy more of Cinnabar Ridge. Along the way, Ridge-o-rama enters South Chilcotin Mountains Provincial Park (dogs must be leashed) and reunites with the North Cinnabar Trail, making (with a map) a longer lollipop hike possible.

Remember to carry bear spray and plenty of water.

GETTING THERE

Vehicle: From Whistler, head north on Highway 99 (Sea to Sky Highway). In Pemberton, turn left on Portage Road at the traffic lights. Go left on Birch Street and right on Pemberton Meadows Road. Turn right on (Upper) Lillooet River Forest Service Road and right on Hurley River FSR (rough 2WD). Where the Hurley ends at Gold Bridge, head right (northeast) on Carpenter Lake Road (Lillooet-Pioneer Road 40) for 11.5 km (7.1 mi). (Road 40 can also be accessed from the east via Highway 99 at Lillooet.) At Tyax Junction, turn north on Tyaughton Lake Road and continue on gravel (2WD)—passing the Friburg Recreation Site (toilet available) and Tyax Lodge—for 11 km (6.8 mi). Park in a pullout on the right.

51
LITTLE HORN MOUNTAIN

Distance: 18 km (11.2 mi)
Time: 6.5 hours (out and back)
Elevation gain: 350 m (1,150 ft)
High point: 451 m (1,480 ft)
Season: March to November

Quality: ★★
Difficulty: ■
Maps: NTS 92-G/7; Canadian Map Makers Coquitlam; Trail Ventures BC PoMo
Trailhead: 49°20′19″ N, 122°51′23″ W

IN CONTRAST TO bustling Buntzen Lake, Little Horn Mountain is a forest of solitude. Take a hike from one to the other to tour a B.C. Hydro off-stream reservoir and gaze up the scenic fjord known as səlilw̓ət in hən̓q̓əmin̓əm̓, the language of the Tsleil-Waututh (səlilwətaɬ) Nation.

From the northeast corner of the South Beach parking lot (140 m/460 ft), take the gravel path toward the off-leash dog area. Keep right, taking a bridge over Buntzen Creek. Go left and continue north on the easy Buntzen Lake Trail for 1 hour (3.9 km/2.4 mi).

Soon, a left spur to a lakeside viewing platform presents an optional diversion. Stick with the trail until it rises to join Powerhouse Road and go over the diversion tunnel, built in 1905, supplying water from Coquitlam Lake (skʷƛ̓əma:ɬ x̌acaʔ in hən̓q̓əmin̓əm̓ to the Kwikwetlem [kʷikʷəƛ̓əm] First Nation). Follow the trail left and down stairs to North Beach.

Little Horn Mountain is 2 hours (5 km/3.1 mi) away. Don't cross the Buntzen Lake Suspension Bridge; rejoin Powerhouse Road for 1.1 km (0.7 mi), heading north through the rockslide zone on the east side of McCombe (Trout) Lake. (If the slide area is closed, take the bridge and keep right to round McCombe Lake.) Pass the bottom of the Swan Falls Trail and reach the Buntzen Dam, with its huge penstock.

Where a yellow gate bars Powerhouse Road, head right on a gravel road leading to Buntzen Bay. Descend for 1.5 km (0.9 mi), going past two waterfalls. At the day's low point (100 m/330 ft; 49°23′04″ N, 122°51′34″ W), exit right on the Dilly Dally Trail, the north branch of the Halvor Lunden Trail.

Croker Island in səl̓ilw̓ət from Croker Lookout.

Enter Say Nuth Khaw Yum Provincial Park, and head uphill in the trees. Cross a boulder-choked creek above a waterfall. As a saddle nears, reach a signed junction, 2 km (1.2 mi) from the Buntzen Bay road.

The strenuous Dilly Dally Trail continues to 157 Lookout, Dilly Dally Peak (1,272 m/4,170 ft), and the top of the Swan Falls Trail. However, go left for Little Horn Mountain—crossing a creek, and looking for pink tapes. In 300 m (330 yd), arrive at Croker Lookout. Look north to Croker Island and the xʔəl̓íilwətaʔɬ (Indian River) watershed at the head of səl̓ilw̓ət (Indian Arm).

The path continues southwest to Little Horn Mountain's mossy summit (3 hours up; 49°24′00″ N, 122°51′24″ W) and quickly ends at a rocky bluff. Retracing your steps, return to South Beach.

Buntzen Lake lies in the territories of several First Nations, including the Kwikwetlem, Musqueam (xʷməθkʷəy̓əm), Qayqayt (qiqéyt), Squamish (Sḵwx̱wú7mesh), and Tsleil-Waututh.

GETTING THERE

Transit: In summer, TransLink Bus 179 (Buntzen Lake) provides service from Coquitlam Central Station to South Beach. Otherwise, take Bus 182 (Belcarra) from Moody Centre Station to Sunnyside Road at Anmore Grocery Store. Walk north, shortly bearing left on Pumphouse Road, to meet the Buntzen Lake Trail in 1 km (0.6 mi). Cross the floating bridge and follow the trail to South Beach.

Vehicle: From its junction with Highway 7 (Lougheed Highway) in Coquitlam, head west on Barnet Highway (formerly Highway 7A), then quickly north on Johnson Street. Turn left on David Avenue, right on Forest Park Way West in Port Moody, and left on Aspenwood Drive, which becomes East Road in Anmore. Go right on Sunnyside Road. Continue 2.7 km (1.7 mi) to the South Beach parking area (toilet available). Parking reservations required in summer. Note the gate closing time.

52

COQUITLAM LAKE VIEW TRAIL

Distance: 12.5 km (7.8 mi)
Time: 5.5 hours (circuit)
Elevation gain: 600 m (1,970 ft)
High point: 930 m (3,050 ft)
Season: May to November

Quality: ★★
Difficulty: ■
Maps: NTS 92-G/7; Canadian Map Makers Coquitlam; Trail Ventures BC PoMo
Trailhead: 49°18′49″ N, 122°44′56″ W

BURKE MOUNTAIN in Coquitlam offers a menu of delectable forest hikes. Let's call this one the falls bagger's special: Dry Crossing Falls is the appetizer, Sawblade Falls is the entree, and Woodland Walk Falls is the dessert. This triple serving of waterfalls, with a viewpoint side dish, is found in Pinecone Burke Provincial Park and the territory of the Kwikwetlem (kʷikʷəƛ̓əm) First Nation.

From the park gate (330 m/1,080 ft), head east up the gravel road and away from the shooting range (closed Tuesdays). Take the first road on the left, which serves as the Coquitlam Lake View Trail (CLVT). At a fork, 800 m (0.5 mi) from the entrance, go right. Fork right again under the big power lines, then quickly go left at a signpost missing a sign. Take the right fork, where the left branch is signed for Sawblade Falls (save for later).

Follow the CLVT past a left-hand spur and across Coho Creek, where Dry Crossing Falls fans out over a rock incline. Take a right fork, then exit left on a path signed as the "new route." Meet the road again higher up and turn left. Follow signs right for the viewpoint. Tackle the very steep and rough switchbacks to a cramped blufftop (2 hours up; 49°21′04″ N, 122°44′12″ W), overlooking Coquitlam Lake (skʷƛ̓əma:ɬ x̌acaʔ in hən̓q̓əmin̓əm̓, the language of the kʷikʷəƛ̓əm m̓əlstéyəxw), 5.5 km (3.4 mi) from the trailhead.

The view of skʷƛ́əma:ɬ x̌acaʔ from Burke Mountain.

The damming of the reservoir in the early 1900s decimated the sockeye salmon of the Coquitlam River (skʷƛ̓əma:ɬ stáləw̓). The kʷikʷəƛ̓əm have been working to restore them ever since.

Backtrack 1.5 km (0.9 mi) to Dry Crossing Falls. Continue south on the CLVT for 130 m (140 yd) and turn right (west) on a spur (49°20′26″ N, 122°44′28″ W). Follow pink tapes to The Sawblade. Have fun plunging down the mountain-bike single track to the end of the CLVT's Lower West Fork. Dart upstream to devour Sawblade Falls (560 m/1,840 ft; 49°20′28″ N, 122°44′48″ W). Head south on the Lower West Fork momentarily, following tapes off to the right.

In short order, take the right fork to reach a viewpoint. Don't turn around; a steep path drops north to the top of the Woodland Walk. Take a look at Woodland Walk Falls before heading south.

Turn left and then right on the Woodland Walk's Upper Loop. Go left on a power-line road and cross a bridge over Pritchett Creek. (Consider the bonus cascades here the digestif.) Follow the Woodland Walk off the power-line corridor to the right and back to the CLVT. Return to Upper Harper Road.

GETTING THERE

Vehicle: From Highway 7 (Lougheed Highway) in Port Coquitlam, 2 km (1.2 mi) west of the Pitt River Bridge, go north on Lougheed-Meridian Connector. Turn left on Coast Meridian Road and enter Coquitlam. In 5 km (3.1 mi), turn right on Harper Road. Drive 2 km (1.2 mi) farther—turning left on Upper Harper Road and trading pavement for gravel (2WD)—to find the Pinecone Burke Provincial Park gate on the right, outside of the Port Coquitlam and District Hunting and Fishing Club (5000 Upper Harper Road). Park on the shoulder, but not in the club's driveway.

53
ALOUETTE MOUNTAIN

Distance: 22 km (13.7 mi)
Time: 9 hours (circuit)
Elevation gain: 1,110 m (3,640 ft)
High point: 1,361 m (4,465 ft)
Season: July to October

Quality: ★★★
Difficulty: ■
Maps: NTS 92-G/7, 92-G/8; Canadian Map Makers Golden Ears Provincial Park
Trailhead: 49°16′22″ N, 122°32′06″ W

FROM THE WEST, Alouette Mountain appears to be a wooded, viewless ridge of little interest in Golden Ears Provincial Park. Well, don't judge a mountain by its far-off visage. The million-dollar views from the stadium-sized summit plateau, in Katzie (q̓ic̓əy̓) First Nation territory, are a revelation.

Briefly known as Battery Mountain, Alouette sits on the fringe of the Mount Blanshard massif (x̣ɛ'ɛc'ɛnxʷ in hən̓q̓əmin̓əm̓, the language of the Katzie), which is capped by the twin peaks of Golden Ears (Hike 56). Alouette rises south of dramatic Blanshard Peak and west of Evans Peak (Hike 54). Although Alouette can be summited more speedily via the rough Evans Peak route, the classic approach follows its long, mellow south ridge.

From Mike Lake Road (250 m/820 ft), set off north on the steep Incline Trail (1.1 km/0.7 mi), which was historically used by loggers to skyline timber down to the lake. Go right on the winding Alouette Mountain Fire Access Road, an old rail bed, enjoying the pleasant grade and shady second growth.

After the road bends west, take a shortcut trail to the right. Rejoining the road higher up, go right to visit the Stephen Canning memorial viewpoint, then take advantage of another shortcut on the right.

The geodetic survey cairn and Mount Robie Reid behind.

Where the trails rejoin and then redivide, choose right yet again (saving Lake Beautiful for later). After the branches reunite for a final time, continue north, eventually arriving on the wide-open summit, with its large cairn and spectacular vantages (4.5 hours up; 49°20′19″ N, 122°29′47″ W).

To the north, Blanshard Peak and Edge Peak frame Golden Ears. Mount Judge Howay and Mount Robie Reid tower to the northeast. West of Alouette, the Pitt River (sq̓əyc̓əyaʔɬ státləw, "River of the Katzie") drains tidal Pitt Lake (sq̓əyc̓əyaʔɬ x̌acaʔ, "Lake of the Katzie"), the latter obscured by the topography.

On the way back, go right on the scenic byway to visit Lake Beautiful (officially named Beautiful Lake) for some added variety. The lovely old-growth trees and colourful fungi along this stretch are invigorating. The lake is closed to camping, due to the sensitive environment. Once on familiar ground, retrace your steps to the trailhead.

GETTING THERE

Vehicle: Heading east on Highway 7 (Lougheed Highway) in Maple Ridge, turn left onto Dewdney Trunk Road, 5 km (3.1 mi) east of the Pitt River Bridge. (On Trans-Canada Highway 1, take Exit 57 in Surrey or Exit 58 in Langley. Follow signs for the Golden Ears Bridge, take the Maple Ridge exit, and continue onto Dewdney Trunk.) In 6 km (3.7 mi), make a left on 232 Street. At the traffic circle, go right on 132 Avenue/Fern Crescent. Stay on Fern, bear left onto 128 Avenue, and rejoin Fern, which becomes Golden Ears Parkway. Turn left on Mike Lake Road, 4.6 km (2.9 mi) past the park gate. Keep left and find parking at the Incline Trail or Mike Lake (toilet available). No overnight parking. The park gate is closed at night; check the posted hours.

54
EVANS PEAK

Distance: 8 km (5 mi)
Time: 5 hours (out and back)
Elevation gain: 950 m (3,120 ft)
High point: 1,132 m (3,710 ft)
Season: June to November

Quality: ★★★★
Difficulty: ◆
Maps: NTS 92-G/8 Stave Lake; Canadian Map Makers Golden Ears Provincial Park
Trailhead: 49°19′38″ N, 122°27′47″ W

THE SUPER-STEEP trail to Evans Peak lands you on an airy summit ridge. It's not suitable for novices, young kids, or dogs. But it makes an excellent day trip for experienced hikers, including restless ones car camping in Golden Ears Provincial Park, located in the territory of the Katzie (q̓ic̓əy̓) First Nation.

From the parking lot (180 m/590 ft), set off on the well-trafficked West Canyon Trail. In a few minutes (330 m/0.2 mi), make a left turn on the Viewpoint Trail. After 1.4 km (0.9 mi) on this path, a sign on the right identifies the start of the Evans Peak Trail (408 m/1,340 ft; 49°19′41″ N, 122°28′21″ W), which doubles as an alternate route to Alouette Mountain (Hike 53). (The short Viewpoint Trail continues to vistas of Alouette Lake [sa'nəsaʔɬ x̣a'cɛʔ in hən̓q̓əmin̓əm̓, the language of the Katzie] and Viking Creek.)

Now the sweating (and spiderweb eating) begins. Unrelentingly steep, the forest path is rough but well defined and marked, having benefited from the volunteer work of the Ridge Meadows Outdoor Club. A viewpoint, 1.5 hours in, offers peeks at your imposing-looking objective and Alouette Lake.

At 2 hours, reach a signed fork: left for Alouette Mountain, right for Evans Peak. Before the final push, earn a breather following the crest of a wooded

A cloudy day on Evans Peak.

ridge. Then the steepness goes up another level. Exercise caution as the route comes uncomfortably close to drop-offs. A fixed line helps with scrambling up a challenging section.

Evans Peak's rocky summit is crowned by a small tree (2.5 hours up; 49°20′16″ N, 122°28′41″ W). To the southeast, Alouette Lake looms. Waterfalls plunge and snow caves (approached via the Evans Valley Trail) lie at the foot of Edge Peak, a component of Mount Blanshard (x̣ɛ′ɛc’ɛnxʷ), to the northwest. Evans Peak is named for a father and son who vanished in 1966 while on a hike in the valley below.

The going is much quicker on the descent. Hiking poles will save your knees.

GETTING THERE

Transit: Parkbus offers coach service on select summer weekends to the Gold Creek parking lot from Burrard Station in Vancouver. Walk south on Golden Ears Parkway, cross the Gold Creek bridge, and go right on the Menzies Trail to join the West Canyon Trail.

Vehicle: Heading east on Highway 7 (Lougheed Highway) in Maple Ridge, turn left onto Dewdney Trunk Road, 5 km (3.1 mi) east of the Pitt River Bridge. (On Trans-Canada Highway 1, take Exit 57 in Surrey or Exit 58 in Langley. Follow signs for the Golden Ears Bridge, take the Maple Ridge exit, and continue onto Dewdney Trunk.) In 6 km (3.7 mi), make a left on 232 Street. At the traffic circle, go right on 132 Avenue/Fern Crescent. Stay on Fern, bear left onto 128 Avenue, and rejoin Fern, which becomes Golden Ears Parkway. After the road becomes gravel (2WD), turn left for the West Canyon parking lot (toilet available). Day-use pass required until 4 p.m. from June to October (book online). The park gate is closed at night; check the posted hours.

55
GOLD CREEK

Distance: 11.5 km (7.1 mi)
Time: 3.5 hours (loop)
Elevation gain: 210 m (690 ft)
High point: 360 m (1,180 ft)
Season: Most of the year

Quality: ★★
Difficulty: ■
Maps: NTS 92-G/8 Stave Lake; Canadian Map Makers Golden Ears Provincial Park
Trailhead: 49°20′04″ N, 122°27′24″ W

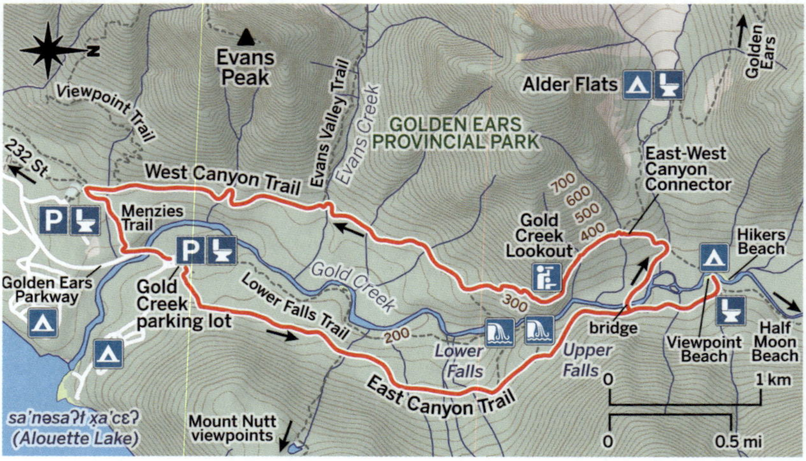

A BRIDGE spanning Gold Creek makes possible an attractive loop for hikers and trail runners in Golden Ears Provincial Park. This outing, as described, visits Viewpoint Beach and is ideal for kids, rainy days, and shoulder season. Take a hike in the territories of the Katzie (q̓ic̓əy̓) and Stó:lō peoples to smell the conifers and hear the streams of the lush temperate rainforest.

The East Canyon Trail starts at the northeast corner of the Gold Creek parking lot (160 m/525 ft). In short order, take the left fork and go left again where the trail merges with an old logging road. Pass turnoffs for the Mount Nutt viewpoints (right) and Lower Falls (left). Descend to intersect the East-West Canyon Connector at 3.8 km (2.4 mi).

Continue on the East Canyon Trail for several minutes to the turnoff for Viewpoint Beach (1 hour up; 49°21′58″ N, 122°27′16″ W), a backcountry campsite, 4.5 km (2.8 mi) from the trailhead. Go left to a gravel point bar on Gold Creek, across the water (sometimes fordable) from Hikers Beach. (The East Canyon Trail continues ruggedly upstream to Half Moon Beach, another campsite.) The double summits of Edge Peak and Golden Ears (1,716 m/5,630 ft; Hike 56) on Mount Blanshard (x̣ɛ'ɛc'ɛnxʷ in hən̓q̓əmin̓əm̓, the language of the Katzie First Nation) loom in the background.

The view upstream from the East-West Canyon Connector bridge.

Backtrack to the East-West Canyon Connector. Cross the Gold Creek bridge, built in 2015 and resting on an old concrete pier that supported a logging bridge until the 1960s. Pass a turnoff for Hikers Beach and rise to a junction with the West Canyon Trail in 15 minutes. Right goes to the Alder Flats campground and Golden Ears. Saving them for a longer day, head left, with 1.5 hours to go. Pause at the Gold Creek Lookout (320 m/1,050 ft).

Ignore the Lower Falls turnoff (unless you have excess energy), cross Evans Creek, and spurn the Evans Valley Trail and Viewpoint Trail. As the West Canyon parking lot nears, turn left on the Menzies Trail. Hit the Golden Ears Parkway, cross the bridge, and return to the Gold Creek parking lot.

Dogs must be leashed on trails, including Menzies, within 1 km (0.6 mi) of the Golden Ears Parkway. Camping is allowed only at designated sites (reservation required year-round).

GETTING THERE

Transit: Parkbus offers coach service on select summer weekends to the Gold Creek parking lot from Burrard Station in Vancouver.

Vehicle: Heading east on Highway 7 (Lougheed Highway) in Maple Ridge, turn left onto Dewdney Trunk Road, 5 km (3.1 mi) east of the Pitt River Bridge. (On Trans-Canada Highway 1, take Exit 57 in Surrey or Exit 58 in Langley. Follow signs for the Golden Ears Bridge, take the Maple Ridge exit, and continue onto Dewdney Trunk.) In 6 km (3.7 mi), make a left on 232 Street. At the traffic circle, go right on 132 Avenue/Fern Crescent. Stay on Fern, bear left onto 128 Avenue, and rejoin Fern, which becomes Golden Ears Parkway. Continue onto gravel (2WD) and find the Gold Creek parking lot (toilet available) on the left at the parkway's end. Day-use pass required until 4 p.m. from June to October (book online). The park gate is closed at night; check the posted hours.

56

X̣Ɛ’ƐC’ƐNXʷ (GOLDEN EARS)

Distance: 24 km (14.9 mi)
Time: 11 hours (out and back)
Elevation gain: 1,540 m (5,050 ft)
High point: 1,716 m (5,630 ft)
Season: July to October

Quality: ★★★★
Difficulty: ◆◆
Maps: NTS 92-G/7, 92-G/8; Canadian Map Makers Golden Ears Provincial Park
Trailhead: 49°19′38″ N, 122°27′47″ W

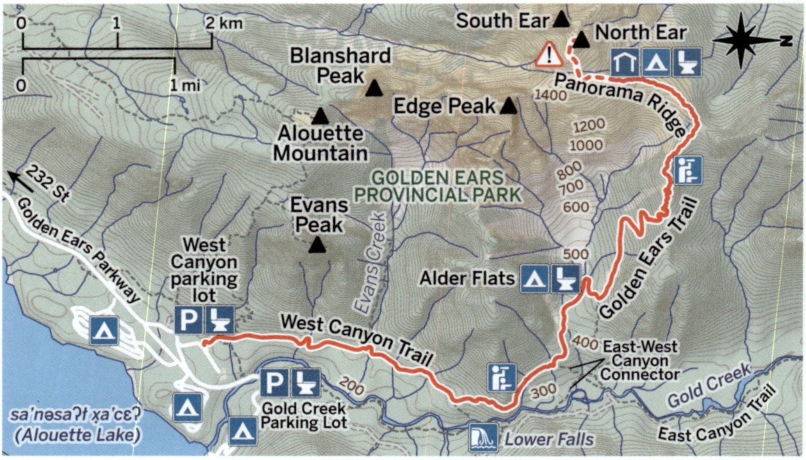

THE GOLDEN EARS are the twin summits of Mount Blanshard. An ascent can be done in a very long day or, more happily, with a night at Alder Flats or Panorama Ridge.

Mount Blanshard rises in the territory of the Katzie (q̓ic̓əy̓) First Nation, whose oral history recalls the sacred mountain serving as a refuge during a great flood. A number of Indigenous toponyms are associated with the mountain, including x̣ɛ’ɛc’ɛnxʷ (Xe’ex’enxw) in hən̓q̓əmin̓əm̓, the language of the Katzie, and Xí:tselexw in Halq’eméylem, spoken by the Stó:lō people.

Set off north on the West Canyon Trail (180 m/590 ft). Stay left at the East-West Canyon Connector junction (merging with the alternate approach via the East Canyon Trail [see Hike 55]) to reach the campground at Alder Flats (480 m/1,575 ft; 49°21′49″ N, 122°28′19″ W) in 5.7 km (3.5 mi). Water can be scarce past this point.

Up next: the merciless switchbacks of the Golden Ears Trail. Climb to the east spur of Panorama Ridge. Once on the main ridge, follow it southwest—with Pitt Lake (sq̓əyc̓əyaʔɬ x̌acaʔ, “Lake of the Katzie”) below to your right.

At 5 km (3.1 mi) past Alder Flats, arrive at the Golden Ears Emergency Shelter (1,400 m/4,590 ft; 49°22′00″ N, 122°30′06″ W, plus a camping area).

Edge Peak (left) and Golden Ears from Mount Nutt.

The final 1 km (0.6 mi) lies before you. Backcountry experience, avalanche awareness, and route-finding skills are essential, and an ice axe is advisable. Ascend steep snow to a dip on the east ridge of the North Ear. Once on the ridge, turn west for the Class 2 scramble to the summit (6 hours up; 49°21′46″ N, 122°30′27″ W).

Soak in the Pacific Ranges panorama (or fog). Optionally, the lower, less-visited South Ear (1,701 m/5,580 ft) is a straightforward scramble from the North Ear. Descend to the trailhead, reversing your ascent route.

The Kwantlen (q̓ʷɑ:n̓ƛ̓ən̓) First Nation's hən̓q̓əmin̓əm̓ name for the area between Mount Blanshard and the Fraser River (staləw̓)—now known as Maple Ridge—is q'wa?acstan ("the place where the golden eagles are").

Camping is allowed only at designated sites (reservation required year-round).

GETTING THERE

Transit: Parkbus offers coach service on select summer weekends to the Gold Creek parking lot from Burrard Station in Vancouver. Walk south on Golden Ears Parkway, cross the Gold Creek bridge, and go right on the Menzies Trail to join the West Canyon Trail.

Vehicle: Heading east on Highway 7 (Lougheed Highway) in Maple Ridge, turn left onto Dewdney Trunk Road, 5 km (3.1 mi) east of the Pitt River Bridge. (On Trans-Canada Highway 1, take Exit 57 in Surrey or Exit 58 in Langley. Follow signs for the Golden Ears Bridge, take the Maple Ridge exit, and continue onto Dewdney Trunk.) In 6 km (3.7 mi), make a left on 232 Street. At the traffic circle, go right on 132 Avenue/Fern Crescent. Stay on Fern, bear left onto 128 Avenue, and rejoin Fern, which becomes Golden Ears Parkway. After the road becomes gravel (2WD), turn left for the West Canyon parking lot (toilet available). Day-use pass required until 4 p.m. from June to October (book online). The park gate is closed at night.

57

79 GRIND

Distance: 6.5 km (4 mi)
Time: 4 hours (out and back)
Elevation gain: 530 m (1,740 ft)
High point: 700 m (2,300 ft)
Season: March to November

Quality: ★★
Difficulty: ■
Maps: NTS 92-G/8 Stave Lake
Trailhead: 49°16′53″ N, 122°21′54″ W

MOSSY FOREST, a waterfall, and vistas make Mission's 79 Grind, which climbs to a lookout on Rockwell Knob, worth the sweat. With an average grade of 17 per cent, it's less arduous than the North Shore's infamous Grouse Grind (see Hike 7), which clocks in at 32 per cent, but still a workout. Opened in 2022, the 79 Grind is found in the Stave West Forest and Recreation Area—also named Mekw̓ wa't a'xwest ikw̓elo' ("everyone shares here") in Halq'eméylem, the language of the Stó:lō people.

From the trailhead (170 m/560 ft) on the west side of Florence Lake Forest Service Road, head up the steps and immediately bear left, following orange diamonds and flagging tape into the second-growth woods. In 15 minutes, take a plunging side path to the right to see Fiddlehead Falls in the ravine of 79 Creek. Return to the main trail and continue up.

Briefly join the S100 logging road at a bend, and re-enter the woods to the right. Follow orange diamonds left and cross a wooden bridge amid large stumps. Cross S100 higher up. The trail rises with a clear-cut to the right, passes a big hollow stump, traverses left, and bends right with another cutblock ahead. Where the trail reapproaches the cutblock, a makeshift bench

The Rockwell Knob viewpoint overlooks Stave Lake.

at the end of the R250 branch of Rockwell Road, off to the left, invites a rest stop. Peer down at Devils Lake, which has a trail around it. Continue up the stiff switchbacks, earning a few peekaboo views.

Finally, a big arrow sends you left on the R200 road to a good-sized viewing platform (2 hours up; 49°16′26″ N, 122°22′42″ W) on a bluff atop a clear-cut, with an outhouse standing by. It's a fabulous prospect. Survey the teal waters of big Stave Lake, impounded by B.C. Hydro's Stave Falls Dam, and the logging-scarred forests of the Stave River watershed. The river is known as šxʷeẏəqʷs in hən̓q̓əmin̓əm̓, the language of the Kwantlen (q̓ʷɑ:n̓ƛ̓ən̓) First Nation. Hoover Bluff (Hike 58) rises across Stave Lake from Devils Lake.

There is no trail access to the summit of Rockwell Knob, which lies in an old-growth management area. A sign asks hikers to "keep out and do not disturb." Head back the way you came. Remember to keep right at the Fiddlehead Falls junction.

Established in 2011 as Mission Interpretive Forest, Stave West is part of Mission Municipal Forest (Tree Farm Licence 26). The forest lies in the territories of the Kwantlen, Semiahmoo (se'mya'me), and Stó:lō peoples, including the Leq'á:mel and Matsqui (Máthxwi) First Nations. No camping, fires, littering, or target shooting. Dogs must be leashed.

GETTING THERE

Vehicle: From Highway 7 (Lougheed Highway) in Maple Ridge, go north on 287 Street, just west of the Stave River and Silvermere Lake. Continue onto Wilson Street and enter Mission. Turn right on Dewdney Trunk Road, 6 km (3.7 mi) from the highway. In 4 km (2.5 mi), just before the Stave Falls Dam, go left on Burma Street, which becomes Florence Lake Forest Service Road (2WD). Find the parking area (no overnight use) on the right in 6.6 km (4.1 mi), south of the 79 Creek bridge.

58
HOOVER BLUFF

Distance: 11 km (6.8 mi)
Time: 4.5 hours (out and back)
Elevation gain: 300 m (980 ft)
High point: 490 m (1,610 ft)
Season: Most of the year

Quality: ★★
Difficulty: ■
Maps: NTS 92-G/1 Mission, 92-G/8 Stave Lake
Trailhead: 49°13′45″ N, 122°20′14″ W

WHILE THE hike starts inauspiciously by a garbage dump, Hoover Bluff pays off historically and scenically and is definitely worth the effort.

From the gate (190 m/620 ft), head north on Hoover Road (HL 1000) into Mission Municipal Forest. Follow the main stem left, where a right spur goes to private property, and steadily uphill, keeping Brown Creek to your left. Cross a power-line corridor and road (LH 300). Fork left at the 1 km (0.6 mi) marker, where the right branch is HE 100. Keep right where HL 100 exits left. Pass a clear-cut at 2 km (1.2 mi). Spurn HL 200 and HL 300.

After 3.1 km (1.9 mi) on Hoover Road, spot the signed start of the Hoover Lake Trail (470 m/1,540 ft; 49°15′12″ N, 122°19′53″ W) on the left. Ahead lies 700 m (0.4 mi) of wonderful, rooty single track (hiking only). The trail pulls alongside an old corduroy logging road made of cedar planks. Help preserve this historical remnant by not straying off the designated path. Keep right at forks with orange diamonds in both directions. A boardwalk carries you over a pond. After crossing the corduroy road, the trail descends. Notice rusted logging relics in the woods. (Leave No Trace principles discourage removing or disturbing cultural artifacts and natural objects.)

Stave Lake from Hoover Bluff.

Pass a rightward exit to Upper Hoover Road and arrive at an inconspicuous junction, just shy of Hoover Lake in its forested bowl, after 1 hour on foot. Ahead lies the south shore and a boardwalk to a peninsula. For Hoover Bluff (1.8 km/1.1 mi away), though, turn left and follow pink tapes and the muddy, undulating path around the lake's west side. The trail curves left as it nears the outflow creek to meet a logging road, with a bridge to your right.

Turn left and head to the top of the road, which offers a view up Stave Lake. Dammed for hydroelectricity since 1911, the Stave River is known as šxʷeỷəqʷs in hən̓q̓əmin̓əm̓, the language of the Kwantlen (q̓ʷɑ:n̓ƛ̓ən̓) First Nation. Look for a path ahead to the right. Take the lovely single track through moss and salal to two clifftop viewpoints on Hoover Bluff. Spy Rockwell Knob (see Hike 57) across the water. Keep away from the edge.

Follow tapes through the trees and to the right for the somewhat precarious final viewpoint (2 hours up; 49°15′40″ N, 122°20′01″ W). Fixed ropes aid the mildly exposed descent to a downsloping rock ledge ideal for lunch. Best to skip it in wet weather. Mission accomplished—head back the way you came.

Established in 1958, Mission Municipal Forest (Tree Farm Licence 26) is managed by the City of Mission. The forest lies in the territories of the Kwantlen, Semiahmoo (se'mya'me), and Stó:lō peoples, including the Leq'á:mel and Matsqui (Máthxwi) First Nations. No camping, fires, littering, or target shooting. Dogs must be leashed.

GETTING THERE

Vehicle: From Highway 7 (Lougheed Highway) in Maple Ridge, go north on 287 Street, just west of the Stave River and Silvermere Lake. Continue onto Wilson Street and enter Mission. Turn right on Dewdney Trunk Road, 6 km (3.7 mi) from the highway. Cross the Stave Falls Dam and Blind Slough Dam; continue 2 km (1.2 mi) east. Find the parking area on the north shoulder, opposite the Mission Landfill, a.k.a. Minnie's Pit. Don't block the gate.

59

LEQ'Á:MEL (NICOMEN MOUNTAIN)

Distance: 16 km (9.9 mi)
Time: 8 hours (out and back)
Elevation gain: 1,210 m (3,970 ft)
High point: 1,221 m (4,010 ft)
Season: June to October
Quality: ★★
Difficulty: ◆
Maps: NTS 92-G/1 Mission
Trailhead: 49°10′33″ N, 122°08′57″ W

IN HALQ'EMÉYLEM, the language of the Stó:lō people, Leq'á:mel is the name for Nicomen Mountain, Nicomen Slough, and a trading hub near Deroche, east of Mission, that was home to many longhouses. Pronounced "la-cam-el," Leq'á:mel means "the level place where people meet." The demanding trail to the mountaintop pays off with solitude and hard-won views.

From the yellow gate, walk east on Hawkins Pickle Road to find the unmarked trailhead on the far side of the Norrish Creek (Tsa-ho-mass) bridge (10 m/30 ft). Take the upstream path on the left, stepping over concrete blocks and railroad tracks. Go right at three forks; the second is marked by a red diamond on a log. Hike uphill in the mixed woods.

Find four numbered bluff viewpoints of varying quality en route to a major fork at 2.1 km (1.3 mi). Left goes to Little Nicomen Mountain (464 m/1,520 ft), but your path is the right one to Raven Bluffs. The fifth viewpoint is close at hand. Your reward is a sweeping perspective of the Fraser Valley—including Sumas Mountain (Kw'ekw'e'i:qw; Hike 61) to the south.

Follow the path through wildflowers to a junction (330 m/1,080 ft; 49°11′02″ N, 122°08′36″ W), 200 m (220 yd) from the previous fork, where a wooden sign directs summit seekers left. (A short-and-sweet, moderate

The Stó:lō, Nicomen Island, and Nicomen Slough from Raven Bluffs.

option is to go right, descend to the sixth viewpoint, and head back to the trailhead.) Take the overgrown path onto a mellow, old logging road.

With signs showing the way, bear left to avoid a vegetated spur, turn right on a 4×4 road, and then make a hard right at a junction. Cross and recross a creek, then ascend to a road bend atop a clear-cut. Peer across the Norrish Creek valley at Dewdney Peak (Xelxé:yles; 930 m/3,050 ft), a.k.a. Hatzic Mountain. Up the road, enter a shady tunnel of trees.

Just before the road ends, a steep and rough path strikes off left into a thorny, regenerating clear-cut, a little more than 1 hour (3.8 km/2.4 mi) from Raven Bluffs. Pause to enjoy the Fraser Valley view atop the clear-cut, before following ribbons uphill in the dappled light of the forest. Highlights include another viewpoint and a humongous conk known as The Wizard.

As you near the mountaintop, the grade relents but the path becomes indistinct and route-finding is required. Gain the wooded west ridge and bear right, negotiating a dip before the final knoll. Arrive at the summit outcrop (49°12′18″ N, 122°07′13″ W), 1.8 km (1.1 mi) from the road.

Push on 250 m (270 yd) farther, following tapes left and through the berry bushes to a better viewpoint (4.5 hours up; 49°12′18″ N, 122°07′02″ W). Survey the North Cascades from across the Fraser Valley: Slesse Mountain (Selísi), Tomyhoi Peak, Mount Shuksan, and Mount Baker (Kwelxá:lxw). Retrace your steps to Hawkins Pickle Road.

Nicomen Mountain lies in S'ólh Téméxw, the territory of the Stó:lō people, including the Leq'á:mel First Nation.

GETTING THERE

Vehicle: In Mission, head east for 10.6 km (6.6 mi) on Highway 7 (Lougheed Highway) from its junction with Highway 11 (Abbotsford-Mission Highway). Where Highway 7 turns right to cross the Dewdney Bridge, use the left lane to continue straight onto Hawkins Pickle Road. In 2.3 km (1.4 mi), turn right and cross the Canadian Pacific Railway tracks to stick with Hawkins Pickle for another 1.2 km (0.7 mi). (If you miss the turn and end up on Norrish Creek Forest Service Road, backtrack via Bell Road.) Park on the roadside before the yellow gate (whether open or closed), minding any no-parking signs.

60
CAMPBELL LAKE

Distance: 10 km (6.2 mi)
Time: 6 hours (out and back)
Elevation gain: 675 m (2,215 ft)
High point: 690 m (2,260 ft)
Season: April to November

Quality: ★
Difficulty: ■
Maps: NTS 92-H/5 Harrison Lake
Trailhead: 49°17′46″ N, 121°47′06″ W

THE CELEBRITY of the Grouse Grind (see Hike 7) has spawned a number of decent copycats around the region: the Abby Grind, Dewdney Grind, 79 Grind (Hike 57), and so on. The Campbell Lake Trail is Harrison Hot Springs' version of a steep and satisfying workout trail, in the territories of the Stó:lō and Sts'ailes peoples. Also known as the Harrison Grind, the path snakes up the northeast flank of Mount Agassiz.

After consulting the map board at the trailhead (15 m/50 ft), go west through the gate. Immediately turn right on a gravel road, which climbs steeply to the village water reservoir. Head south into the woods on the now mossy, cobbly, water-bearing road, with the hum of Highway 9 to your left and the sight of numerous outcrops among the cedars on your right.

After switchbacking, you follow a power-line right-of-way north. Returning to tree cover after 1 hour of hiking, the pleasant trail switchbacks westward, indicated by orange diamonds and arrows, pink flagging tape, and rotting wooden stairs. There's a creek crossing, the 2 km (1.2 mi) marker, and then a sketchy log bridge, 2 hours in. The rooty, muddy path ascends slopes littered with moss-covered boulders and deadfall.

Campbell Lake on Mount Agassiz.

Pass the 3 km (1.9 mi) sign en route to the lookout (680 m/2,230 ft; 49°17′41″ N, 121°48′25″ W) at the top of the Harrison Grind—and the scenic climax of the hike. After 3 hours (4 km/2.5 mi) on the trail, you earn a fine view of 10 Mile Point, Long Island (Híkw Tl'tsás in Halq'eméylem, the language of the Stó:lō), and Echo Island (Xweqw'eyíqw) on Harrison Lake (Peqwpa:qotel, "splashing down off the mountain, water joining"). Some hikers turn around here.

Backtrack a few steps to continue on the undulating trail to your ultimate destination. Cross a boulder-filled gully, descend slippery steps, and follow an old, puddly road to the east shore of Campbell Lake (640 m/2,100 ft; 49°17′17″ N, 121°48′59″ W), 30 minutes beyond the lookout.

As you retrace your steps to the trailhead, keep your eyes peeled for white trillium, a perennial herb with a distinctive three-petalled flower.

Qweqwatchem is a Halq'eméylem name associated with Mount Agassiz and neighbouring Mount Woodside. In 2006, the Sts'ailes First Nation put in place the Kweh-Kwuch-Hum spiritually sensitive designated area on Mount Woodside to protect the sacred mountain.

GETTING THERE

Transit: From Lougheed Town Centre Station in Burnaby or Carvolth Exchange in Langley, take Fraser Valley Regional Transit Bus 66 FVX (Fraser Valley Express) to downtown Chilliwack. Ride Agassiz-Harrison Transit Bus 71 (Agassiz-Harrison) from downtown Chilliwack to Hot Springs Road at Balsam Avenue.

Vehicle: From Trans-Canada Highway 1 (Exit 135), east of Chilliwack—or Highway 7 (Lougheed Highway), west of Agassiz—head north on Highway 9 (Rosedale-Agassiz Bypass Highway/Hot Springs Road) to Harrison Hot Springs. At Balsam Avenue, 5.5 km (3.4 mi) north of Highway 7, turn left into the trailhead parking area or find street parking nearby.

61 KW'EKW'E'I:QW (SUMAS MOUNTAIN)

Distance: 14.5 km (9 mi)
Time: 6.5 hours (out and back)
Elevation gain: 750 m (2,460 ft)
High point: 910 m (2,990 ft)
Season: May to November
Quality: ★★★
Difficulty: ■
Maps: NTS 92-G/1 Mission
Trailhead: 49°07′20″ N, 122°11′18″ W

RISING FROM the floor of the Fraser Valley, Sumas Mountain is a sacred place to the Stó:lō people, particularly the Sumas (Semá:th) First Nation. In Halq'eméylem, the language of the Stó:lō, the mountain and an associated ancestral village site are known as Kw'ekw'e'i:qw (Kw-ewkweeuwkw), meaning "sticking up."

For hikers, Kw'ekw'e'i:qw offers plenty of pleasant forest walking on the way to dynamite views from the top. From the trailhead (180 m/590 ft), enter the mixed woods on the Centennial Trail. Head up a ravine and cross Wades Creek (Yeeh-hyl). Ascend an old roadbed, pursuing red rectangles. Keep left where a rightward path goes over a bridge to private property.

Approach a logged area, and go right on a gravel road, after 1 hour on foot. In short order, turn left at a trail entrance (49°07′06″ N, 122°10′14″ W), signed for Chadsey Lake. Hike up between clear-cuts. From the forest edge, earn views of Sumas Mountain's knolls. The trail levels out. There are vistas of Fraser Valley farmland through the trees. Sidehill across steep wooded slopes to reach the 4.5 km (2.8 mi) marker.

The Stó:lō (left), Qwemí:líts, and Semá:th Stótelō from the Eastern Lookout.

Cross the south fork of Chadsey Creek (Tsah-mohlt) on a log bridge above a waterfall. Head upstream and descend into the basin of Chadsey Lake (Xwexwóstel). Hit the 5 km (3.1 mi) marker and a junction, after 2.5 hours on foot. Turn left to go clockwise around the north shore. (The trail on the south shore is rough and littered with blowdowns.) Stick with the lake loop where the Centennial Trail leaves to the left at a junction signed for Quadling Road (section closed due to trail damage).

With the Eastern Lookout as your goal, make a hard left at a junction (650 m/2,130 ft; 49°07′23″ N, 122°08′30″ W) on the east side of the lake. Don't head toward microwave towers. Keep left at a mountaintop junction to surmount Sumas Peak (49°07′14″ N, 122°07′39″ W). Just before the summit, a trail drops left, headed for the Eastern Lookout (3.5 hours up). In short order, burst into the open atop a cliff.

Feast your eyes on Nicomen Mountain (Leq'á:mel; Hike 59), the Fraser River (Stó:lō), Chilliwack Mountain (Qwemí:líts), Sumas River (Semá:th Stótelō), Cheam Peak (Lhílheqey; Hike 65), Mount McGuire (T'amiyehó:y), and Mount Baker (Kwelxá:lxw). Until it was drained in 1924, Sumas Lake (Semá:th X̱ótsa) covered the prairie between Kw'ekw'e'i:qw and Vedder Mountain (Qoqó:lem; Hike 62). Return the way you came.

Kw'ekw'e'i:qw lies in the territories of the Kwantlen (q̓ʷɑ:n̓ƛ̓ən̓) and Stó:lō peoples.

GETTING THERE

Vehicle: On Trans-Canada Highway 1 in Abbotsford, take Exit 95. Head north on Whatcom Road. Quickly turn right on North Parallel Road. In 2.3 km (1.4 mi), go left on Sumas Mountain Road and drive through the Sumas First Nation reserve. Keep left at Atkinson Road and Carlyle Road to stay on Sumas Mountain Road for 9 km (5.6 mi). Hit gravel (2WD) and continue 400 m (0.2 mi) to an S-bend, where the trailhead is on the right. Park on the shoulder, 12 km (7.5 mi) from Exit 95.

62

QOQÓ:LEM (VEDDER MOUNTAIN)

Distance: 11.5 km (7.1 mi)
Time: 5 hours (out and back)
Elevation gain: 365 m (1,200 ft)
High point: 925 m (3,035 ft)
Season: May to October

Quality: ★★
Difficulty: ■
Maps: NTS 92-G/1 Mission; Trail Ventures BC Chilliwack West
Trailhead: 49°03′52″ N, 122°00′42″ W

VEDDER MOUNTAIN is home to a web of trails, as well as several community watersheds. The wooded outpost of the Skagit Range is known as Qoqó:lem ("drinking place") in Halq'eméylem, the language of the Stó:lō people. A spring jaunt on the mellow Vedder Mountain Ridge Trail is a great way to ease into the hiking season.

From the lower trailhead (560 m/1,840 ft), set off up the 4×4 road, which has big water bars. In 10 minutes, reach the signposted upper trailhead (670 m/2,200 ft; 49°04′16″ N, 122°00′36″ W). Start by crossing a dirt-bike trail, and go up the stairs and onto a double track; where it ends, bear right on a well-maintained path into the shady second growth. Follow the orange squares past a log bench and between clear-cuts.

After 1 hour on foot, a viewpoint off to the right faces Sumas Mountain (Kw'ekw'e'i:qw; Hike 61). The Sumas Prairie, once covered by Sumas Lake (Semá:th X̱ótsa), and Vedder Canal fill the valley below. Descend stairs and take the path straight ahead. Drop down to a pond and boardwalk, before arriving at a signed junction. Go left for the summit, 30 minutes away. Tackle steep and rocky bits with the aid of a fixed chain and knotted ropes.

Descending the Vedder Mountain Ridge Trail.

A viewpoint off to the right affords another look at Sumas Prairie farmland, before you arrive at treed Vedder Peak (2.5 hours up; 49°03′11″ N, 122°02′39″ W). Find plenty of seating room on open rock to the left. Enjoy lunch and savour the southeast outlook: Mount Amadis on International Ridge (Swíltcha Smá:lt), Isar Mountain, and Mount Baker (Kwelxá:lxw). Cultus Lake (Swíltcha) lies at the foot of Qoqó:lem but is hidden from view.

A rough route, indicated by pink flagging tape, continues southwest along the ridge toward a cutblock, but it's best to turn around here. Follow the same route back to the trailheads.

Qoqó:lem lies in S'ólh Téméxw, the territory of the Stó:lō people, including the Ts'elxwéyeqw Tribe. Founded in 2005, the Vedder Mountain Trails Association advocates for public access to the trail network and celebrated the establishment of Vedder Mountain Interpretive Forest in 2019.

GETTING THERE

Vehicle: On Trans-Canada Highway 1 in Abbotsford, take Exit 104. Following signs for Cultus Lake, head east on No. 3 Road. Turn right on Tolmie Road and quickly left on No. 3 Road. After entering Chilliwack, go left on Yarrow Central Road, which becomes Vedder Mountain Road. At the roundabout, go right on Cultus Lake Road, which continues south through the Soowahlie (Th'ewá:li) First Nation reserve as Columbia Valley Highway. Go right on (paved) Parmenter Road, 15 km (9.3 mi) from Highway 1. Bear right on Vedder Mountain Forest Service Road (the roads on either side are gated) and continue uphill on gravel (2WD). Bear left, passing gated Parmenter FSR. Arrive at a junction, with a signpost for the lower trailhead of the Vedder Mountain Ridge Trail, 4.2 km (2.6 mi) from Columbia Valley Highway. Park on the roadside. (**4WD** vehicles with high clearance can turn right and continue 800 m/0.5 mi on Tower Road to the upper trailhead.)

63
GLORIA LOOKOUT

Distance: 11 km (6.8 mi)
Time: 6.5 hours (out and back)
Elevation gain: 1,125 m (3,690 ft)
High point: 1,455 m (4,770 ft)
Season: June to October
Quality: ★★★
Difficulty: ◆
Maps: NTS 92-H/4 Chilliwack
Trailhead: 49°08′56″ N, 121°47′31″ W

WITH AN average grade of over 22 per cent, the Gloria Lookout Trail makes you work hard for views of the Fraser Valley and Cascade Mountains. Fortunately, the payoff for this relentless grind is suitably glorious.

Your hike begins in Chilliwack Community Forest on multi-use trails built and maintained by the Chilliwack Park Society. The forest lies in S'ólh Téméxw, the territory of the Stó:lō people—including the Pil'alt (Pelhó'lhxw) Tribe, represented by the Cheam (Xwchíyò:m), Kwaw-kwaw-Apilt (QweQwe'opelhp), and Skwah (Sqwá) First Nations. A few of the trails have names in the Halq'eméylem language.

From the trailhead kiosk (330 m/1,080 ft), set off on the gravel path. At the first junction, head left on Pí:txel (pronounced "PEET-hyul" and meaning "salamander"). Pass the Slug Trail. Go left on Cholqthet (pronounced "cholk-THET" and meaning "dropping in, like a bird falling out of the nest for the first time"). Make a left on the Broken Tree Loop, and take either side to the top of the community forest.

After 1.5 km (0.9 mi), come to a junction with benches (500 m/1,640 ft; 49°08′37″ N, 121°47′24″ W). Keep right to embark on the Gloria Lookout Trail, which is well maintained, exceedingly steep, and slippery when wet.

Mount MacFarlane (left) and Selísi from Skw'ikw'ets'tel Ridge.

A log bench and waterfall view mark the close-to-halfway point (830 m/2,720 ft). After 1.5 hours of hiking—2.5 km (1.6 mi) done, 3 km (1.9 mi) to go. Spurn the Magic Trail at the next junction. The incline eases as you encounter a beautiful patch of forest and approach the day's high point.

Finally, another bench and wooden signs welcome you to the crest of Skw'ikw'ets'tel Ridge. Left is the Gloria-Thurston Trail, offering access to Mount Thurston (Hike 64) in 4.5 km (2.8 mi)—and making possible a strenuous 20 km (12.4 mi) traverse over Elk Mountain. However, the right-hand path leads to our destination, now only 15 minutes (500 m/0.3 mi) away.

Before ridge walking and descending to the trail's end, savour the scene southward. Skw'ikw'ets'tel (pronounced "skee-kwet-sul" and meaning "cut fish"), the hanging valley of Elk Creek, lies before you. Slesse Mountain (Selísi) is the star of the show, and the tops of Liumchen Mountain (Loyú:mthel) and Mount Amadis (Swíltcha Smá:lt) are visible.

At Gloria Lookout (3.5 hours up; 1,346 m/4,420 ft; 49°07′46″ N, 121°46′54″ W), watch for bald eagles, ravens, and paragliders. Pick out Cultus Lake (Swíltcha), Sumas Mountain (Kw'ekw'e'i:qw; Hike 61), Harrison Lake (Peqwpa:qotel), Cheam Peak (Lhílheqey; Hike 65), and Lady Peak (Sqwemá:y). Mind the cliff edge. Retrace your steps to the trailhead.

GETTING THERE

Vehicle: On Trans-Canada Highway 1 in Chilliwack, take Exit 129 and head south on Annis Road. Quickly turn left on Hack Brown Road. In 1.4 km (0.9 mi), continue straight onto Nixon Road for 750 m (0.5 mi). Fork left for Allan Road, which turns to gravel (2WD). In 1.4 km (0.9 mi), turn right and continue up to the Chilliwack Community Forest parking lot (51642 Allan Road; toilet available).

64

MOUNT THURSTON

Distance: 16 km (9.9 mi)
Time: 7 hours (out and back)
Elevation gain: 1,000 m (3,280 ft)
High point: 1,630 m (5,350 ft)
Season: June to October

Quality: ★★★
Difficulty: ◆
Maps: NTS 92-H/4 Chilliwack; Trail Ventures BC Chilliwack East, Chilliwack West
Trailhead: 49°06′18″ N, 121°49′14″ W

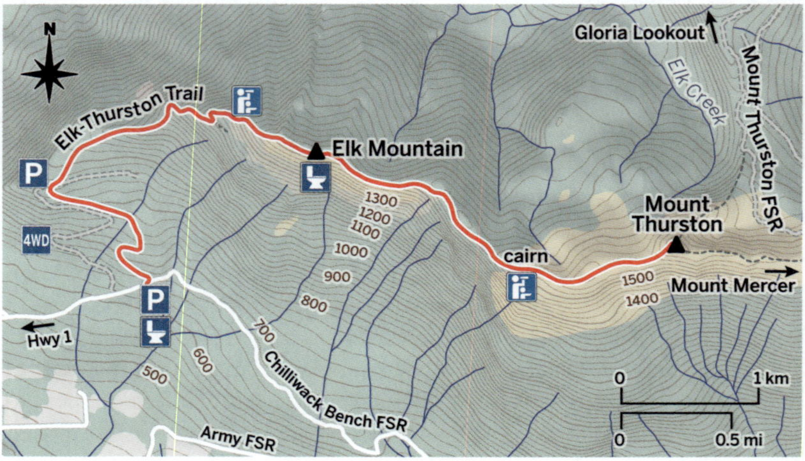

LOOKING FOR a hike that will test your mettle and suitably reward your efforts? The Chilliwack duo of Elk Mountain and Mount Thurston—in the territory of the Stó:lō people—is just the ticket, with its steep climb leading to gorgeous meadows and superlative views.

From Chilliwack Bench Forest Service Road (630 m/2,070 ft), the popular Elk-Thurston Trail dives into the forest, crosses a logging road with an outhouse and 4×4 parking at 1.5 km (0.9 mi), and grinds stiffly northward to Elk Mountain's west ridge. The path is badly braided due to shortcutting.

After 3.5 km (2.2 mi), a rocky lookout with a grand view of the Fraser Valley offers a taste of what's to come. Head east through subalpine meadows.

At 4 km (2.5 mi), reach the gentle summit of Elk Mountain (1,432 m/4,700 ft; 49°06′48″ N, 121°48′14″ W), almost halfway to your objective. If you're doing only the Chilliwack Grind, which equals the Grouse Grind (see Hike 7) in elevation gain (800 m/2,625 ft), turn around here. Mountaintop facilities include a windsock—it's a launch site for paragliders—and an outhouse.

However, with the hardest part behind you, the best lies ahead. Stroll along the ridge, savouring the high meadows and sweeping views of the valley

T'amiyehó:y, across the Ts'elxwéyeqw valley from the Elk-Thurston Trail.

of the Chilliwack River (Ts'elxwéyeqw [Ch-ihl-kway-uhk] in Halq'eméylem, the language of the Stó:lō), far below to your right. A cairn marks a false summit (1,542 m/5,060 ft) of Mount Thurston, 1.5 km (0.9 mi) past the top of Elk. For many hikers, this perch is a satisfying enough destination. Slesse Mountain (Selísi, "The Fang") pierces the sky to the southeast.

For the sake of completeness, press on for 2.5 km (1.6 mi) to the true summit of Mount Thurston (3.5 hours up; 49°06′25″ N, 121°46′05″ W), a couple of bumps east. Meet up with the Gloria-Thurston Trail, which connects to Gloria Lookout (Hike 63) on Skw'ikw'ets'tel Ridge and Chilliwack Community Forest. The treed mountaintop is a bit of a letdown, but it does offer a vista of Cheam Peak (Lhílheqey; Hike 65) and Lady Peak (Sqwemá:y).

Retrace your steps to the trailhead, 8 km (5 mi) away. Admire arctic lupine, red paintbrush, and spreading phlox in summer bloom. You follow in the tracks of the Pil'alt (Pelhó'lhxw) Tribe and Ts'elxwéyeqw Tribe, who have travelled this ridge for ages. Eye Mount McGuire (T'amiyehó:y) due south, Lookout Ridge below to the west, and the mighty Fraser River (Stó:lō) on its way to the Salish Sea. Hiking poles are advised for the descent.

GETTING THERE

Vehicle: On Trans-Canada Highway 1 in Chilliwack, take Exit 123. Head south on Prest Road. At the second roundabout, take the third exit (east) for Bailey Road. Fork right onto Elk View Road and continue for 10 km (6.2 mi). After Elk View becomes potholed Chilliwack Bench Forest Service Road (2WD), cross a clear-cut and look for the parking area on the left (toilet available). (High-clearance **4WD** vehicles can make a hard left in the clear-cut, drive 2 km (1.2 mi) up a spur, and park where the trail crosses the road.)

65

LHÍLHEQEY (CHEAM PEAK)

Distance: 9 km (5.6 mi)
Time: 4 hours (out and back)
Elevation gain: 690 m (2,260 ft)
High point: 2,104 m (6,900 ft)
Season: July to October

Quality: ★★★★★
Difficulty: ■
Maps: NTS 92-H/4 Chilliwack; Trail Ventures BC Chilliwack East
Trailhead: 49°10′06″ N, 121°41′39″ W

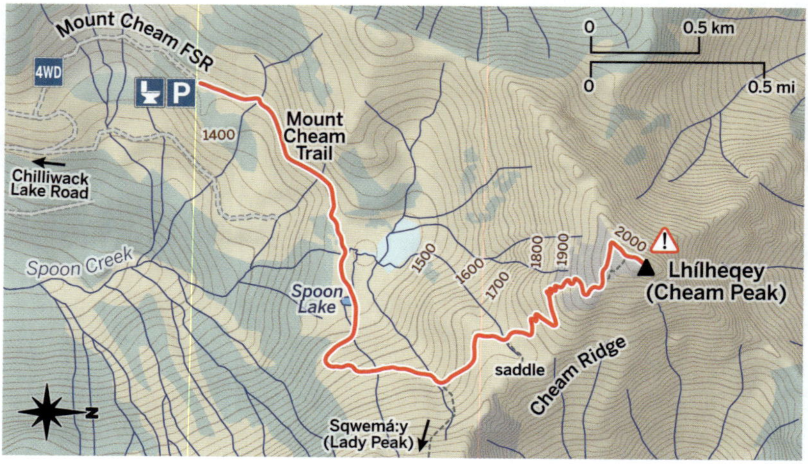

AT THE START of the Mount Cheam Trail, the west face of impressive Lady Peak draws your gaze upwards. From bottom to top, the scenery on this bustling trail is solid gold.

Although you are likely to see kids and dogs on the trail, this hike may not be suitable for all, due to the steepness and some exposure at the top. To the Stó:lō people, including the Pil'alt (Pelhó'lhxw) Tribe and Ts'elxwéyeqw Tribe, Cheam Peak is known by the Halq'eméylem name Lhílheqey (roughly pronounced "THEETH-uhl-kay")—a wife of Mount Baker (Kwelxá:lxw) and the mother of Mount Hood in Oregon. It's the formidable mountain that eastbound travellers on Trans-Canada Highway 1 in Chilliwack see towering over the Fraser Valley.

From the logging road barricade (1,415 m/4,640 ft), head north on the wide trail past the map board. In short order, American Border Peak, Canadian Border Peak, Tomyhoi Peak, and Mount Baker enter the view. The Mount Cheam Trail descends to the meadowy bowl below Cheam Peak and Lady Peak (Sqwemá:y [Lhílheqey's dog]; 2,178 m/7,150 ft), crossing two creeks on wooden bridges and going by near-circular Spoon Lake (Xwoqwsemó:leqw).

Sqwemá:y and the Skagit Range from the summit.

After 20 minutes, follow the main path as it switchbacks up Lady Peak, then angles north and climbs steadily toward the Lady-Cheam saddle. Blueberries and wildflowers—fireweed, green false hellebore, edible thistle, red paintbrush, and stream violet—line the trail. Preserve the lush meadows and respect this sacred place: stay on the path and don't shortcut.

Begin switchbacking northwest on Cheam Peak itself, 1 hour in. Join Cascade golden-mantled ground squirrels on the southwest ridge, and embark on the final windy walk to your objective. Hold on to your hat!

A well-worn track through the volcanic breccia leads to a wooden bench, then to the exhilarating summit (2 hours up; 49°11′11″ N, 121°40′56″ W). Clockwise from north, the breathtaking panorama includes the Fraser River (Stó:lō), Wahleach (Jones) Lake, Knight Peak and the rest of Cheam Ridge, Mount Shuksan, Mount Agassiz (Qweqwatchem; see Hike 60), Harrison Lake (Peqwpa:qotel), and Bear Mountain (Stemletsil). Watch your step around the precipice. Reverse your ascent route on the descent.

Camping, fires, mountain biking, and motorized vehicles are prohibited. Dogs must be leashed. Visitors are asked not to build memorial monuments.

GETTING THERE

Vehicle: On Trans-Canada Highway 1 in Chilliwack, take Exit 119. Head south on Vedder Road for 5.4 km (3.4 mi). At the roundabout before the Vedder Bridge, take the second exit and go east on Chilliwack Lake Road for 27 km (17 mi). After the Foley Creek bridge, turn left on Chilliwack Bench Forest Service Road (2WD). Recross Foley Creek and follow Bench left, spurning Foley Creek FSR. With high-clearance **4WD**, turn right on very rough and steep Chipmunk Creek FSR. Follow signs for the Mount Cheam Trail for 11 km (6.8 mi) to reach the parking area at the top of Mount Cheam FSR (toilet available). Beware of deep water bars, big puddles, and ATVs.

66

FORD MOUNTAIN

Distance: 12 km (7.5 mi)
Time: 5.5 hours (out and back)
Elevation gain: 1,010 m (3,310 ft)
High point: 1,421 m (4,660 ft)
Season: June to October

Quality: ★
Difficulty: ■
Maps: NTS 92-H/4 Chilliwack; Trail Ventures BC Chilliwack East
Trailhead: 49°05′44″ N, 121°35′55″ W

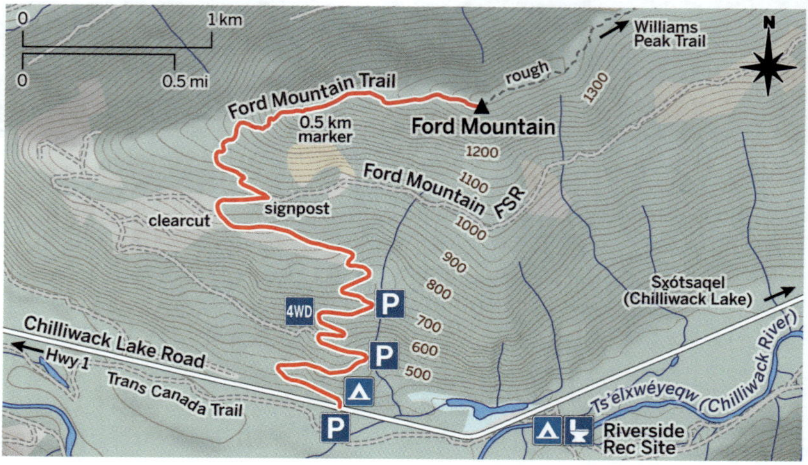

ONCE UPON A TIME, fire-watchers stationed atop Ford Mountain scanned the Chilliwack Valley for smoke. Today, all that remains of the fire lookout are its concrete footings. Nevertheless, the wooded knoll on the west end of Williams Ridge still beckons hikers interested in history and scenery, even with a lengthy logging-road approach.

Starting from Chilliwack Lake Road (410 m/1,345 ft), walk up Ford Mountain Forest Service Road, passing an unmaintained campsite at its base. Stick with the mainline for 3.6 km (2.2 mi) and steadily gain altitude. Near the bottom, water shoots out of a pipe on the roadside—perfect for rinsing off your boots on the way down. The gravel road develops deep ruts above the second bend and has an especially rough patch above the sixth bend. Follow the road along the top of a clear-cut, ignoring a leftward spur.

After 1.5 hours on foot, a burned and broken signpost for the Ford Mountain Trail indicates it's time to take a hard left (925 m/3,035 ft; 49°06′20″ N, 121°36′13″ W). Zigzag up to the top of this road in 20 minutes. With 1 hour to the top, continue onto a path denoted by occasional orange squares, negotiating switchbacks and deadfall. Pass the 0.5 km (0.3 mi) marker of the trail

The view of Selísi from Ford Mountain. *Photo by Cassie Markham*

proper, and gain the west shoulder. Begin a pleasant ridge walk with lichen-draped trees on your left and Skagit Range views to your right.

Spot the 1 km (0.6 mi) marker, step up an outcrop, and follow the ridge to the old fire lookout site (3 hours up, 49°06′35″ N, 121°35′17″ W). Lodgepole pines and subalpine firs impede the view, but take a gander at Slesse Mountain (Selísi, "The Fang," in the Halq'eméylem language of the Stó:lō people), Mount Pierce, and Mount MacFarlane rising on the far side of the Chilliwack River (Ts'elxwéyeqw).

Turn around here and retrace your steps down the mountain. A rough trail continues along the ridge to link up with the demanding Williams Peak Trail. Scramblers can use either trail to climb Williams Peak (2,123 m/6,965 ft), an ambitious objective requiring a much longer day.

Ford Mountain lies in S'ólh Téméxw, the territory of the Stó:lō people, including the Ts'elxwéyeqw Tribe. The Ts'elxwéyeqw encompass the Aitchelitz (Áthelets), Skowkale (Sq'ewqeyl), Shxwhá:y Village, Soowahlie (Th'ewá:li), Squiala (Sxwoyehálá), Tzeachten (Ch'íyáqtel), and Yakweakwioose (Yeqwyeqwí:ws) First Nations.

GETTING THERE

Vehicle: On Trans-Canada Highway 1 in Chilliwack, take Exit 119. Head south on Vedder Road for 5.4 km (3.4 mi). At the roundabout before the Vedder Bridge, take the second exit and go east on Chilliwack Lake Road for 29 km (18 mi). After passing the Ford Mountain Correctional Centre and Chilliwack Bench Forest Service Road, find the entrance to Ford Mountain FSR on the left. Park on the shoulder of Chilliwack Lake Road or in a pullout within the first two bends of the logging road (2WD). (High-clearance **4WD** vehicles can make it 1.8 km/1.1 mi or farther up the road.) Warning: Vehicle break-ins have been reported here.

67
PORCUPINE ROCK

Distance: 6 km (3.7 mi)
Time: 4.5 hours (out and back)
Elevation gain: 640 m (2,100 ft)
High point: 1,240 m (4,070 ft)
Season: June to October

Quality: ★★★
Difficulty: ◆
Maps: NTS 92-H/3 Skagit River; Trail Ventures BC Chilliwack East
Trailhead: 49°05′55″ N, 121°28′04″ W

LINDEMAN LAKE is a turquoise gem in Sx̱ótsaqel/Chilliwack Lake Provincial Park that's a mob scene on summer weekends. Known as Suxwi:ts ("pushing the water back and forth") in Halq'eméylem, the language of the Stó:lō people, the lake is an even more dazzling sight from above. To see for yourself, tackle the extremely steep and rough trail up Porcupine Ridge.

First, a caveat: This challenging hike is not suitable for dogs, young kids, beginners, or wet weather. To start, cross the boulder blockades (600 m/1,970 ft) and take the old road on the right, which parallels and then curves away from Chilliwack Lake Road. In several minutes, spot a single track on the left by a big boulder. Follow this path, which climbs sharply uphill at once and is marked with orange squares and flagging tape. Negotiate deadfall and tackle scrambly sections, employing your hands often.

A series of three fixed ropes helps with the slipperiest, stiffest inclines. The path forks and reunites. After 1.5 hours (2.2 km/1.4 mi) on foot, go right at the next fork on a short path to the first viewpoint (1,040 m/3,410 ft; 49°06′22″ N, 121°27′53″ W). Mind the drop-off at this promontory, where pixie cup lichens cover rock. Look up at Flora Peak (Hike 68), with The Gargoyles on its northwest

Suxwi:ts in Sx̱ótsaqel/Chilliwack Lake Provincial Park.

ridge, and down at gleaming Suxwi:ts in the valley of Post Creek (Kwôkwelem). If you're satisfied, you could turn around here.

For even more delightful vistas, continue onwards and upwards for another hour (800 m/0.5 mi). Discern the expanse of Sx̱ótsaqel ("sacred lake"), also known as Chilliwack Lake, through the trees as you head up the ridge. An airy path to the right leads to a precarious vantage of both lacustrine jewels. Just up the trail, find, with a clifftop overhang, the Porcupine Rock viewpoint (2.5 hours up; 49°06′30″ N, 121°28′01″ W), which makes a fine destination. Whisky-jacks might drop by. After lunch, retrace your footsteps and handholds, carefully, down the 21 per cent grade to the trailhead.

The described hike ends shy of Porcupine Ridge proper. From Porcupine Rock, the rough route continues up and along the lengthy ridge, eventually leading committed scramblers to Porcupine Peak (1,982 m/6,500 ft), also known as Goat Mountain (a name shared by many summits in B.C.).

Porcupine Rock sits on the margin of Sx̱ótsaqel/Chilliwack Lake Provincial Park, which lies in the territories of the Nlaka'pamux and Stó:lō peoples, including the Ts'elxwéyeqw Tribe. No drones, fires, mushroom or plant harvesting, off-road vehicles, smoking, or vaping.

GETTING THERE

Vehicle: On Trans-Canada Highway 1 in Chilliwack, take Exit 119. Head south on Vedder Road for 5.4 km (3.4 mi). At the roundabout before the Vedder Bridge, take the second exit and go east on Chilliwack Lake Road for 39 km (24 mi). After passing Paulsen Road, spot a logging-road entrance blocked by boulders on the left. Park on the roadside. This spot is 600 m (0.4 mi) west of B.C. Parks' Post Creek parking lot (toilet available). Warning: Vehicle break-ins have been reported here.

68
FLORA PEAK

Distance: 12 km (7.5 mi)
Time: 7 hours (out and back)
Elevation gain: 1,310 m (4,300 ft)
High point: 1,952 m (6,405 ft)
Season: July to October

Quality: ★★★★
Difficulty: ◆
Maps: NTS 92-H/3 Skagit River; Trail Ventures BC Chilliwack East
Trailhead: 49°05′56″ N, 121°27′30″ W

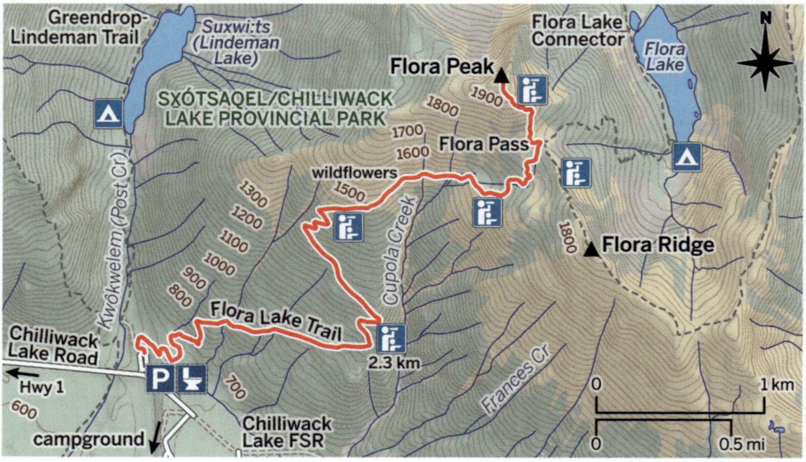

FLORA PEAK is a fabulous hiking destination. In addition to colourful wildflowers, panoramic views compensate for the considerable elevation gain. It's found in Sx̱ótsaqel/Chilliwack Lake Provincial Park and the territories of the Nlaka'pamux and Stó:lō peoples, including the Ts'elxwéyeqw Tribe.

The approach via the Flora Lake Trail starts at the same trailhead (640 m/2,100 ft) as the crowd-drawing Greendrop-Lindeman Trail. From the kiosk, set off on the gravel road. In 1 minute, turn right at the signed Flora Lake turnoff. Follow the old road and orange squares left. Go left again at the next fork. The trail curves right and begins climbing steadily. After a couple of switchbacks, make an ascending traverse through mossy outcrops. Earn a vista of Mount Webb (on the ridge known as Siya:meteq' in Halq'eméylem, the language of the Stó:lō people), and step over streams.

Switchback up to a viewpoint and unsanctioned campsite (1,120 m/3,675 ft) at the 2.3 km (1.4 mi) marker. Look out over Sx̱ótsaqel (pronounced "skot-sa-qel" and meaning "sacred lake"), a.k.a. Chilliwack Lake. Hit the third set of switchbacks. Traverse right, going by the 3.5 km (2.2 mi) marker. Another viewpoint and unsanctioned campsite await.

Flora Peak rises above Flora Pass.

Sidehill across steep, dry, rocky terrain at the headwaters of Cupola Creek. Coast penstemon, spreading phlox, and tiger lily star in the subalpine flower show. Negotiate a muddy section. A viewpoint spur offers a look back. Duck back into the trees for the penultimate push. Follow orange squares left at a bend, leaving the boot path to the right to revegetate.

After 3.5 hours (5.3 km/3.3 mi) on foot, look for a left-hand turnoff (1,735 m/5,690 ft; 49°06′36″ N, 121°25′32″ W) marked with pink flagging, shortly before the summit of Flora Pass. (Just over the crest, the Flora Lake Trail forks left en route to a backcountry campground at its namesake lake, eventually reuniting with the Greendrop-Lindeman Trail via the Flora Lake Connector.) With Flora Peak as your goal, follow pink tapes and orange squares steeply up through heather and trees for 600 m (0.4 mi).

In 40 minutes, reach the cairn and 1948 survey marker on the summit (4 hours up; 49°06′49″ N, 121°25′44″ W). Nearby are Mount Wittenberg to the northeast and Porcupine Peak (see Hike 67) to the northwest. Peer down at Flora Lake and Greendrop Lake (Pep'qwothet); Lindeman Lake (Suxwi:ts) is hidden from view. Unless you plan to overnight at Flora Lake (backcountry camping permit required), retrace your steps to the trailhead.

In 2019, the Wilderness Committee called for the watersheds of Paleface Creek and Depot Creek (Chechexem), which flow into Sx̱ótsaqel, to be set aside as protected areas.

GETTING THERE

Vehicle: On Trans-Canada Highway 1 in Chilliwack, take Exit 119. Head south on Vedder Road for 5.4 km (3.4 mi). At the roundabout before the Vedder Bridge, take the second exit and go east on Chilliwack Lake Road for 39.5 km (24.5 mi). Before the pavement ends, turn left into the Post Creek parking lot (toilet available), which fills up quickly on sunny days. Warning: Vehicle break-ins have been reported here.

69

ST'ÁM'YA (HOPE MOUNTAIN)

Distance: 8.5 km (5.3 mi)
Time: 6 hours (out and back)
Elevation gain: 690 m (2,260 ft)
High point: 1,844 m (6,050 ft)
Season: July to October

Quality: ★★★★
Difficulty: ■
Maps: NTS 92-H/6 Hope
Trailhead: 49°19′43″ N, 121°22′57″ W

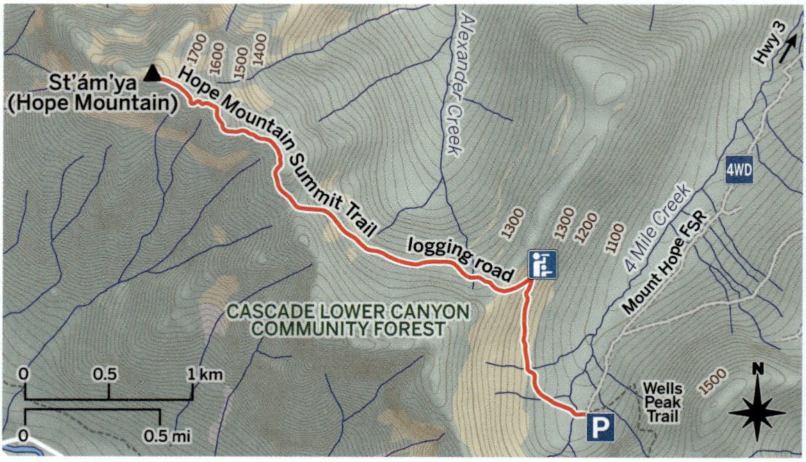

HOPE MOUNTAIN towers over its namesake municipality at the head of the Fraser Valley. The peak belongs to the Skagit Range and accords visitors fine views of its North Cascades relatives to the south. In Halq'eméylem, the language of the Stó:lō (People of the River), the mountain's name is St'ám'ya (meaning "what are you?").

From its cutblock trailhead (1,160 m/3,810 ft; right of the start of the trail to nearby Wells Peak, Hike 70), the flagged route to St'ám'ya descends west to cross 4 Mile Creek. The Hope Mountain Summit Trail then rises northward to the divide between 4 Mile and Alexander Creeks. Blueberries and saffron milk caps flourish along the path.

After pausing at the viewpoint on the divide, drop down the other side to pick up an old, easygoing logging road. Contour west across the head of a bowl scarred by clear-cuts, until the trail exits to the left, headed for Hope Mountain's southeast ridge. The path climbs steeply northwest—winding through heather, by ponds, and over rock—and crosses a ledge at one point.

Although three radio-repeater cones litter the mountaintop (3 hours up; 49°20′51″ N, 121°25′04″ W), the panorama more than compensates.

Descending St'ám'ya, with Wells Peak in the background.

Looking north from the summit cairn, you can see the Fraser River (Stó:lō in Halq'eméylem; Quoo.O Oy in Nłeʔkepmxcín, the Nlaka'pamux language) emerging from the Fraser Canyon, Ogilvie Peak (Qemqemó, "breasts," in Halq'eméylem) behind Hope (Ts'qó:ls) and Kawkawa Lake (Q'ówqèwem, "howling"), and the mountains around Coquihalla Pass.

An outcrop on the far side of a pond just below the summit offers a prime spot from which to admire the shapely valley of Silverhope Creek (Tl'akwelem) to the south. Wells Peak and the Silver Bluffs lord over Silver Lake (Páp-loshe-ka). Mount Baker (Kwelxá:lxw) stands tall across the Canada-U.S. border. Retrace your steps to the trailhead.

St'ám'ya lies in the territories of the Nlaka'pamux and Stó:lō peoples, including the Tiyt Tribe. It's surrounded by the Cascade Lower Canyon Community Forest, a partnership between the Yale (X̱wóx̱welá:lhp) First Nation, District of Hope, and Fraser Valley Regional District.

GETTING THERE

Vehicle: From Trans-Canada Highway 1 in Hope, head east on Crowsnest Highway 3 (Hope-Princeton Highway). Keep right and take Exit 177 in 6 km (3.7 mi) to stay on Highway 3 at its junction with Yellowhead Highway 5 (Coquihalla Highway). Shortly after, turn right on easy-to-miss Mount Hope Forest Service Road (opposite the closed entrance to Nicolum River Provincial Park). Stick with the narrow gravel mainline and yield to massive logging trucks. 2WD vehicles might make it as far as 5 km (3.1 mi) up, where a bridge crosses 4 Mile Creek. Thereafter, the rough road requires **4WD** and high clearance. At a signed fork, 8 km (5 mi) up, go right on a spur with large water bars for 500 m (0.3 mi). Park at the end.

70

WELLS PEAK

Distance: 6 km (3.7 mi)
Time: 4.5 hours (out and back)
Elevation gain: 700 m (2,300 ft)
High point: 1,863 m (6,110 ft)
Season: July to October

Quality: ★★★★
Difficulty: ■
Maps: NTS 92-H/6 Hope
Trailhead: 49°19′43″ N, 121°22′56″ W

WELLS PEAK delivers a satisfying panorama of the Skagit Range and beyond. It's also gained in quicker fashion—but feels more remote—than neighbouring Hope Mountain (St'ám'ya in Halq'eméylem, the language of the Stó:lō people; Hike 69).

At the end of the logging spur (1,160 m/3,810 ft), find the signed start of the Wells Peak Trail on the left (opposite the Hope Mountain Summit Trail). Set off into a logged area (part of the Cascade Lower Canyon Community Forest—a partnership between the Yale [X̱wóx̱welá:lhp] First Nation, District of Hope, and Fraser Valley Regional District) and cross a creek. Soon, leave the deciduous growth behind and zigzag stiffly up under the firs. Beginning a rightward traverse, pass beneath a rock wall and walk atop a downed log.

Continue uphill, encountering patches of pink mountain-heather. Break through timberline amid the buzzing of bees pollinating wildflowers. Ascend the steep meadow, passing big boulders and keeping an eye out for pink tapes and small cairns. The trail is braided and intermittent.

With Wells Peak's northeast face looming ahead, begin a leftward ascending traverse roughly following the boundary between meadow and boulder

Mount Grant and Tl'akwelem from the summit.

field. Eventually, cross loose rock and find a path that heads very steeply up through the heather and trees. (This part is slippery on the way down.)

Gain the southeast ridge at a meadow junction marked by a cairn (1,830 m/6,000 ft; 49°18′58″ N, 121°22′54″ W), 2.5 km (1.6 mi) from the trailhead. First, venture left for 250 m (270 yd) to take in the viewpoint at the end of the friendly ridge. Then head up-ridge for 150 m (165 yd), minding the cliff to the right, to the summit outcrop.

From the top, survey the valley of Silverhope Creek (Tl'akwelem). Close at hand, St'ám'ya stands behind Silver Bluffs. The sea of mountains includes Ogilvie Peak (Qemqemó), Macleod Peak (Yusoló:luk), Mount Baker (Kwelxá:lxw), Lady Peak (Sqwemá:y), Isolillock Peak and Silver Peak (Islléleqw), and Mount Lincoln (Popelehó:ys). Head back the way you came.

Wells Peak lies in the territories of the Nlaka'pamux and Stó:lō peoples, including the Tiyt Tribe. The Tiyt Tribe encompasses the Chawathil (Chowéthel), Seabird Island (Sq'éwqel), Shxw'ōwhámél, Skawahlook (Sq'ewá:lxw), Peters (Skw'átets), Popkum (Pópkw'em), Yale, and Union Bar (Iwówes) First Nations.

GETTING THERE

Vehicle: From Trans-Canada Highway 1 in Hope, head east on Crowsnest Highway 3 (Hope-Princeton Highway). Keep right and take Exit 177 in 6 km (3.7 mi) to stay on Highway 3 at its junction with Yellowhead Highway 5 (Coquihalla Highway). Shortly after, turn right on easy-to-miss Mount Hope Forest Service Road (opposite the closed entrance to Nicolum River Provincial Park). Stick with the narrow gravel mainline and yield to massive logging trucks. 2WD vehicles might make it as far as 5 km (3.1 mi) up, where a bridge crosses 4 Mile Creek. Thereafter, the rough road requires **4WD** and high clearance. At a signed fork, 8 km (5 mi) up, go right on a spur with large water bars for 500 m (0.3 mi). Park at the end.

71

TIKWALUS HERITAGE TRAIL

Distance: 12.5 km (7.8 mi)
Time: 7 hours (lollipop)
Elevation gain: 790 m (2,590 ft)
High point: 910 m (2,990 ft)
Season: May to October

Quality: ★★★
Difficulty: ■
Maps: NTS 92-H/11 Spuzzum, 92-H/14 Boston Bar
Trailhead: 49°43′23″ N, 121°25′18″ W

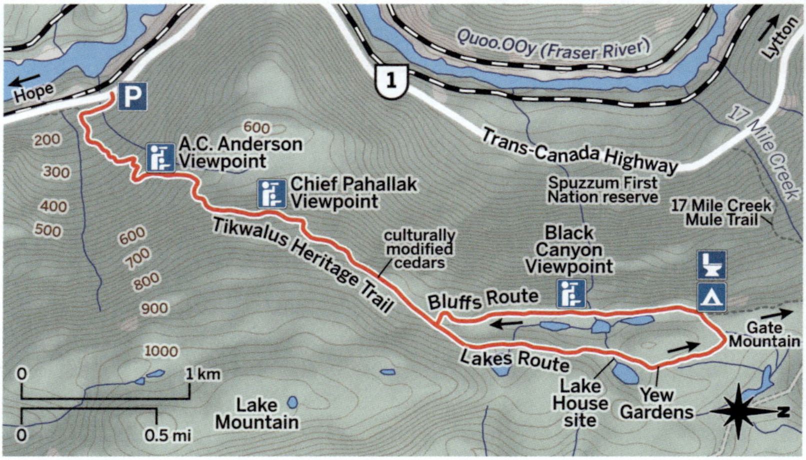

FORMERLY KNOWN as the First Brigade Trail, the Tikwalus Heritage Trail is replete with detailed interpretive panels so all visitors may learn about its place in Indigenous, fur trade, gold rush, and railway history.

Originally an ancient Nlaka'pamux route bypassing the cliffs of Hells Gate and the Black Canyon (Ch.etwik in Nłeʔkepmxcín, the Nlaka'pamux language) on the Fraser River (Quoo.OOy), the challenging trail over Lake Mountain was tapped for the fur trade by the Hudson's Bay Company (HBC) in 1848. In the first season, 70 horses died making the trip between Fort Kamloops and Fort Langley. Consequently, another route—now known as the HBC (1849) Heritage Trail (see Hike 75)—became the preferred way to cross the Cascade Mountains.

Arrive at the trailhead (120 m/390 ft) early and carry plenty of water to avoid heat exhaustion. Initially, the trail contours south before steeply switchbacking eastward up the forested mountainside. Within 2 hours, pass the A.C. Anderson Viewpoint and arrive at the Chief Pahallak Viewpoint, which has log benches. The trail drops a bit to visit some culturally modified trees—bark-stripped western red cedars (quatqulhp in Nłeʔkepmxcín).

The Tikwalus Heritage Trail follows an ancient Nlaka'pamux route.

Come to a key fork (850 m/2,790 ft; 49°44′25″ N, 121°24′08″ W), 4.2 km (2.6 mi) from the highway. Go right to do a counterclockwise loop, starting with the Lakes Route. After some more up, the trail breaks into the sunshine before passing through a patch of trees burned in a 2004 wildfire.

From the high point at the 5 km (3.1 mi) mark, descend to the shady Lake House site. During the early years of the Fraser Canyon gold rush, which began in 1858, miners could stop at the cabin for alcoholic refreshment. Yew Gardens, a dense grove of western yews (chkee-nakAlhp), is the next point of interest.

At 6.5 km (4 mi), reach the campsite at the far end of the Tikwalus loop (3.5 hours up; 830 m/2,720 ft; 49°45′16″ N, 121°24′10″ W). With a campfire ring, food cache, outhouse, butterflies, and views of Spuzzum Mountain and the Lillooet Ranges, it's a righteous lunch spot. (From the campsite, the rough Bluffs Trail leads north to a junction with the 17 Mile Creek Mule Trail and Gate Mountain Trail.)

Returning via the undulating Bluffs Route, hike south with lakes on your left and cliffs on the right. Back at the Lakes-Bluffs junction, go right and descend familiar terrain to the trailhead.

The Hope Mountain Centre for Outdoor Learning Society, Spuzzum (Spô'zêm) First Nation, and New Pathways to Gold Society deserve much credit for the trail's restoration and reopening in 2012.

Tikwalus (pronounced "TEEqualoosh") is the name of a nearby ancient Nlaka'pamux village site. No motorized vehicles on the trail. Be careful with fires.

GETTING THERE

Vehicle: From Hope, head north on Trans-Canada Highway 1. After passing Alexandra Bridge Provincial Park and the historic Alexandra Lodge, find the trailhead at a pullout on the east shoulder, 22 km (13.7 mi) north of Yale. Sadly, this parking lot is prone to break-ins.

72

ZUPJOK PEAK

Distance: 10 km (6.2 mi)
Time: 4.5 hours (out and back)
Elevation gain: 655 m (2,150 ft)
High point: 1,835 m (6,020 ft)
Season: July to October

Quality: ★★★★
Difficulty: ■
Maps: NTS 92-H/11 Spuzzum; John Baldwin Coquihalla Summit
Trailhead: 49°35′46″ N, 121°07′22″ W

WHILE YAK PEAK and Needle Peak lord over Coquihalla Pass, less conspicuous Zupjok Peak offers hikers in the area arguably the most bang for the buck.

From the washrooms (1,190 m/3,900 ft), walk west on the on-ramp shoulder past two big brake-check signs. Just after the second utility pole and before the on-ramp barrier ends, go right onto a double track. Gently descend to a wooden bridge over a branch of Boston Bar Creek, which flows into the Coquihalla River (Kw'ikw'iyá:la in Halq'eméylem, the language of the Stó:lō people). Encounter an avalanche control bunker. After crossing a tributary on logs, the old road, which leads to Ottomite Mountain, gradually gains elevation.

In 45 minutes (3 km/1.9 mi), spot a cairn at the road's second leftward bend, atop a cut slope (1,360 m/4,460 ft; 49°36′23″ N, 121°09′04″ W). Exit to the right for the trail to Zupjok Peak. Follow the muddy single track and flagging tape. Spurn a left fork that goes to Iago Peak (southwest of Zupjok). The grade steepens as you ascend a wooded ridge. Clamber up outcrops in increasingly open terrain.

Arrive at the summit outcrop (less than 2.5 hours up, 49°37′01″ N, 121°09′19″ W), 1.5 hours (2 km/1.2 mi) from the Ottomite road. The Eocene

Zopkios Ridge and Zupjok Peak in autumn.

granite is eroded into natural steps. Look back at Yak Peak and Needle Peak (c̓maqs in Nłeʔkepmxcín, the language of the Nlaka'pamux people) guarding Coquihalla Pass, and northwest to Steinbok Peak and Gemse Peak.

For bonus views, it's worth heading 15 minutes (600 m/0.4 mi) northwest to an outcrop just over the immediate shoulder. With enough daylight, energy, and supplies, experienced parties may wish to continue much farther, dropping to the col and ascending Llama Peak (1,914 m/6,280 ft) and Alpaca Peak (2,083 m/6,830 ft). Alpaca, Vicuna Peak, and Guanaco Peak are the eye-catching trio standing over the headwaters of the Coldwater River (Ntstlatko), a tributary of the Nicola River (Scw'ex), due north.

Return the way you came. Ottomite Mountain (1,470 m/4,820 ft; 49°36′09″ N, 121°09′12″ W) is another optional extension, just 30 minutes (1 km/0.6 mi) up the old road from the Zupjok turnoff. There's a rotten helipad and another perspective of Zupjok to be found on the flat summit, though trees block most of the views. In winter, both Zupjok and Ottomite are snowshoe-worthy destinations. With respect to avalanche risk, the Ottomite road sticks to simple terrain while the Zupjok trail traverses challenging terrain.

Zupjok Peak lies in the territories of the Nlaka'pamux and Stó:lō peoples, including the Scw'exmx. Dogs must be leashed.

GETTING THERE

Vehicle: Eastbound on Crowsnest Highway 3 (Hope-Princeton Highway), east of Hope, keep left (spurning Exit 177) to go north on Yellowhead Highway 5 (Coquihalla Highway) for 38 km (24 mi). Past the Great Bear Snowshed, take Exit 217 (unsigned northbound) on the right, before the summit of Coquihalla Pass. Turn left to go under the highway via a one-lane tunnel. Park at the Zopkios Rest Area (toilet available) on the other side. (If you miss Exit 217, turn around at Exit 221 and use the southbound Zopkios off-ramp.)

73

THE FLATIRON

Distance: 10 km (6.2 mi)
Time: 5.5 hours (out and back)
Elevation gain: 690 m (2,260 ft)
High point: 1,898 m (6,230 ft)
Season: July to October

Quality: ★★★★
Difficulty: ■
Maps: NTS 92-H/11 Spuzzum; John Baldwin Coquihalla Summit
Trailhead: 49°35′43″ N, 121°07′31″ W

THE STRIKING peaks of the Cascade Mountains that tower over Coquihalla Pass are underlain by a body of rock that geologists call the Needle Peak Pluton. The intrusive rock is the product of magma crystallizing within the Earth's crust during the Eocene epoch. Consequently, making an ascent of The Flatiron, in the territories of the Nlaka'pamux and Stó:lō peoples, means treading on 39-million-year-old granite.

Find the trailhead just west of the Needle Peak Trail parking area (on the south side of the highway), across Boston Bar Creek and along a pipeline right-of-way. Make sure to carry plenty of water; sources are scarce by late summer. The trail threads south into the woods, steepening as it weaves uphill amid Douglas-fir and devil's club.

In 45 minutes, the forest opens up, inviting a look back at the exfoliating south face of Yak Peak on Zopkios Ridge. Following orange squares, gain the crest of a lovely spur ridge, extending north from the west shoulder of Needle Peak (c̓maqs in Nłeʔkepmxcín, the language of the Nlaka'pamux), 15 minutes farther. The trail levels out before rising in a largely gentle fashion, encountering blueberries and Cascade golden-mantled ground squirrels and travelling over bare rock and through heather meadows.

A fall hike to The Flatiron.

Reach the signed "Needle Peak Saddle" (not a saddle) at the 3.3 km (2.1 mi) mark (1,800 m/5,910 ft; 49°34′12″ N, 121°08′14″ W). (Scramblers aiming to thread their way up the Needle bear left here.) Watching for flagging, drop right (southwest) to the actual Needle-Flatiron saddle (1,740 m/5,710 ft). The braided path skirts a cliff on your right, then climbs to a pretty tarn (Flatiron Lake) in the bowl on the east side of The Flatiron. Cross via an island and make a zigzagging ascent, following occasional cairns.

The broad summit plateau (3 hours up; 49°33′56″ N, 121°09′13″ W) comes 1.5 km (0.9 mi) past the Needle Peak junction. In addition to the two solar-powered radio-repeater cones, you might spot a sooty grouse. Illal Mountain (Hike 74), Jim Kelly Peak, and Coquihalla Mountain lie across the Coquihalla River (and Coquihalla Fault) to the southeast. Nearby Portia Peak is due south. Needle Peak, scrambled via its southwest ridge, dominates to the northeast, with Markhor Peak behind it. Descend the way you came.

No drones, fires, motorized vehicles, smoking, tree cutting, or vaping. Dogs must be leashed.

GETTING THERE

Vehicle: Eastbound on Crowsnest Highway 3 (Hope-Princeton Highway), east of Hope, keep left (spurning Exit 177) to go north on Yellowhead Highway 5 (Coquihalla Highway) for 38 km (24 mi). Past the Great Bear Snowshed, take Exit 217 (unsigned northbound) on the right, before the summit of Coquihalla Pass. From the northbound off-ramp, quickly turn right on a gravel road and immediately right again to find the Needle Peak Trail parking area (below the highway maintenance sheds). Alternatively, take the one-lane tunnel under the highway and park at the Zopkios Rest Area (toilet available) on the other side. (If you miss Exit 217, turn around at Exit 221 and use the southbound Zopkios off-ramp.)

74
ILLAL MOUNTAIN

Distance: 18 km (11.2 mi)
Time: 8.5 hours (out and back)
Elevation gain: 870 m (2,850 ft)
High point: 2,020 m (6,630 ft)
Season: July to October

Quality: ★★★★★
Difficulty: ◆
Maps: NTS 92-H/10 Tulameen, 92-H/11 Spuzzum; John Baldwin Coquihalla Summit
Trailhead: 49°31′51″ N, 120°57′45″ W

ILLAL MEADOWS is noted for high winds, scattered tarns, radiant wildflowers, and breathtaking sunsets. Less known is that the headwaters of Illal Creek are surrounded by volcanoes. A hike to this subalpine wonderland, in Nlaka'pamux and Stó:lō territories, is also a tour of the Coquihalla Volcanic Complex, part of the Miocene-age Pemberton Volcanic Belt.

Route-finding and navigation skills are essential on this hike, as the path is often ill-defined. From Tulameen River Forest Service Road (1,150 m/3,770 ft), set off west on the Illal Creek spur, inspecting a few washouts on the way. In 45 minutes (2.9 km/1.8 mi), reach the former upper parking area (49°32′04″ N, 120°59′48″ W) at the top of the road. Go forth on the well-established Illal Meadows Trail. Cross a stream and ascend the forest path.

After 1.5 hours on the trail, tread across talus slopes, with rocks clinking like dinner plates, encountering blueberries and huckleberries. The trail rises higher, through meadows and stream beds, before levelling out in wide-open terrain and becoming less distinct. Please keep to established paths.

Occasional flagging and cairns mark an intermittent path up the south (looker's left) side of Illal Meadows. Pass to the left of a pair of brook-fed

Dawn at Illal Meadows in the Cascade Mountains.

ponds en route to crystal-clear Jim Kelly Lake (49°31′51″ N, 121°02′40″ W), just northwest of Jim Kelly Peak, an andesite dome. Ignore a track breaking off left near the Coquihalla Mountain–Jim Kelly Peak col.

Continue west to the glorious crest of the windblown plateau and bear north (right) to close the distance with Illal Mountain. The hornblende andesite dome, with radiating columnar jointing and a talus apron, looms over striking Illal Lake (1,930 m/6,330 ft; 49°32′16″ N, 121°03′04″ W). From the lake's west end, follow a path around the back of the mountain.

Ascend its straightforward western slopes to the rocky summit (4.5 hours up; 49°32′23″ N, 121°02′51″ W). Coquihalla Mountain, a stratovolcano, and Jim Kelly Peak stand opposite Illal Meadows. The Flatiron (Hike 73), Needle Peak (č̓maqs in Nłeʔkepmxcín, the language of the Nlaka'pamux), and Yak Peak rise to the northwest in the Coquihalla Summit Recreation Area.

In any case, reverse course for the trip back to Tulameen FSR. Please observe Leave No Trace principles, such as hiking and camping on durable surfaces and packing out all food scraps and trash.

GETTING THERE

Vehicle: Eastbound on Crowsnest Highway 3 (Hope-Princeton Highway), east of Hope, keep left (spurning Exit 177) to go north on Yellowhead Highway 5 (Coquihalla Highway). In 50 km (31 mi), take Exit 228. From the off-ramp, turn right on Coquihalla Lakes Road (with the Britton Creek Rest Area ahead). Quickly take the left fork for Tulameen River Forest Service Road (2WD). Stay on the mainline for 19 km (12 mi), passing a turnoff for Lawless-Britton FSR (8 km/5 mi). The road is rough in parts, driven by logging trucks, and prone to washouts—check current conditions. Immediately after the road crosses a bridge over Illal Creek (in the middle of a horseshoe curve), park near the bottom of the spur on the right (don't block it) or in a pullout on the left.

75

PODUNK CREEK

Distance: 23 km (14.3 mi)
Time: 7 hours (out and back)
Elevation gain: 215 m (705 ft)
High point: 1,470 m (4,820 ft)
Season: June to October

Quality: ★★
Difficulty: ■
Maps: NTS 92-H/6 Hope, 92-H/7 Princeton; Hope Mountain Centre HBC Trail
Trailhead: 49°21′11″ N, 121°03′31″ W

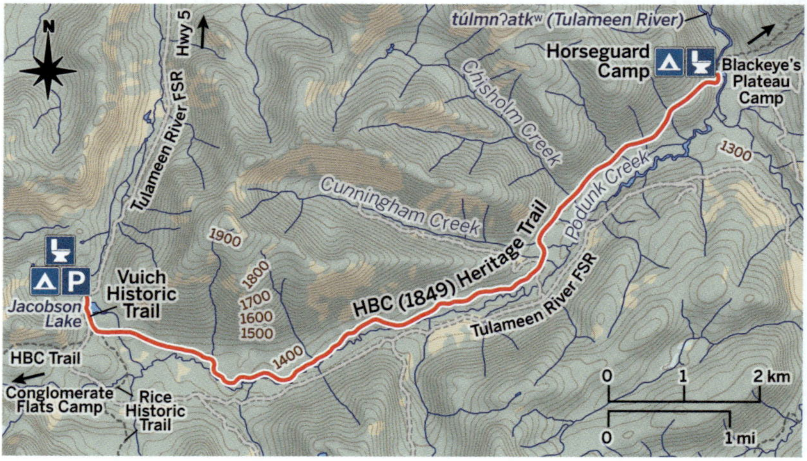

TRAVELLED BY First Nations hunters and traders, fur brigades, gold miners, and cattle ranchers, the Hudson's Bay Company (1849) Heritage Trail has a storied past. Crossing the Cascade Mountains, the HBC Trail extends 74 km (46 mi) from Hope to Tulameen, in the territories of the Nlaka'pamux, Stó:lō, and Syilx peoples, including the sməlqmíx.

Travelling eastward, the HBC Trail, a.k.a. Blackeye's Trail (for the sməlqmíx chief who showed the route to HBC trader Alexander Caulfield Anderson in 1846), culminates with a ford of the Tulameen River (túlmnʔatkʷ in nsyilxcən, the language of the sməlqmíx), west of its namesake community. Backpackers must also make a wet crossing of the Tulameen near the midpoint. It's optional on a pleasant day or overnight hike down Podunk Creek.

From the kiosk at Jacobson Lake (1,470 m/4,820 ft), go south on the Vuich Historic Trail for 400 m (0.2 mi). Turn left (east) on the HBC Trail (the Rice Historic Trail continues south). Follow the mellow single track for 11 km (6.8 mi), staying on river left of Podunk Creek all the way.

Merrily hiking gently downstream, negotiate deadfall and pass from the Engelmann spruce–subalpine fir to the montane spruce biogeoclimatic

Horseguard Camp on the HBC (1849) Heritage Trail.

zone. Pass Cunningham Creek and Chisholm Creek, both Podunk tributaries named after prospectors.

Finally, the remote trail climbs some and drops more to Horseguard Camp (3 hours down; 1,255 m/4,120 ft; 49°22′39″ N, 120°56′33″ W), which historically served as the third campsite of the HBC fur brigades. It's located on the left bank of the Tulameen River.

Set up your tent for riparian dreams or retrace your steps—upstream—back to Jacobson Lake.

Optionally, if the Tulameen is low enough to safely ford, carefully cross to the right bank. You can stay overnight at buggy Blackeye's Plateau Camp (1,860 m/6,100 ft), 6 km (3.7 mi) farther east. On the way, the HBC Trail navigates The Defiles, a stretch of steep-sided narrow valley meadows.

The Tulameen River was once known as the North Fork of the Similkameen River (nməlqitkʷ). The latter crosses the Canada-U.S. border and flows into the Okanogan River (qawsitkʷ), a tributary of the mighty Columbia River (nx̌ʷəntkʷitkʷ in nsyilxcən; Nch'i-Wána in Ichishkíin Sínwit, the language of the Yakama people).

Credit for the trail's restoration goes to the Hope Mountain Centre for Outdoor Learning Society, Back Country Horsemen Society of B.C., Okanagan Similkameen Parks Society, and New Pathways to Gold Society.

GETTING THERE

Vehicle: Eastbound on Crowsnest Highway 3 (Hope-Princeton Highway), east of Hope, keep left (spurning Exit 177) to go north on Yellowhead Highway 5 (Coquihalla Highway). In 50 km (31 mi), take Exit 228. From the off-ramp, turn right on Coquihalla Lakes Road (with the Britton Creek Rest Area ahead). Quickly take the left fork for Tulameen River Forest Service Road (2WD). Stay on the mainline for 45.8 km (28.5 mi), passing turnoffs for Lawless-Britton FSR (8 km/5 mi) and Lodestone FSR (26 km/16 mi). The road is rough in parts and prone to washouts—check current conditions. Park at the Jacobson Lake Recreation Site (toilet available).

76

SKAGIT BLUFFS

Distance: 12 km (7.5 mi)
Time: 4.5 hours (out and back)
Elevation gain: 350 m (1,150 ft)
High point: 930 m (3,050 ft)
Season: April to November

Quality: ★
Difficulty: ●
Maps: NTS 92-H/2, 92-H/3; Clark Geomatics 104 E.C. Manning
Trailhead: 49°13′44″ N, 121°03′22″ W

BUILT IN 1862, the Hope Pass Wagon Trail served as a key packhorse route between Hope (Ts'qó:ls in Halq'eméylem, the language of the Stó:lō people) and Princeton for over 60 years. Hike the Skagit Bluff Trail in E.C. Manning Provincial Park to experience 6 km (3.7 mi) of this historic thoroughfare.

Find the signed trailhead (775 m/2,540 ft) next to the yellow gate at the Cascade Recreation Area entrance. Enter the shady forest and gently rise above and away from the Hope-Princeton Highway, which your path parallels as it heads southeast through the Skagit Bluffs. Douglas-firs, vine maples, and Oregon grape line the trail. In 10 minutes, the traffic noise recedes.

Past the 1 km (0.6 mi) marker of the Hope Pass Wagon Trail, cross old rockslides with mossy boulders. The grade steepens. Hear and glimpse the Skagit River below to your right. The Skagit is known as sk̓aʔitkʷ in nsyilxcən, the language of the sməlqmíx people; upstream of the Klesilkwa River confluence, its Halq'eméylem name is Nuch-hái-cheen. Descend to the 2 km (1.2 mi) marker and step over small creeks. The undulating trail enters a dark grove of tall Douglas-firs and takes a wooden bridge over a bigger creek.

Follow the moss-lined path up to the Skagit Bluff Trail's main viewpoint (870 m/2,850 ft; 49°12′57″ N, 121°01′17″ W), featuring a log bench and fence,

Hiking the historic Skagit Bluff Trail.

3.7 km (2.3 mi) from the Cascade trailhead. Peer down at the Skagit River, where it flows under a highway bridge.

Opened in 1949, the Hope-Princeton Highway replaced the Allison Pass Trail of 1860. The highway was constructed, in part, by Nikkei forcibly relocated, dispossessed of property, and put to work during World War II. Between 1942 and 1946, Tashme, the country's largest Japanese Canadian internment camp, housed up to 2,644 people in Sunshine Valley, just outside Manning's west gate.

Another bench lies just up the Skagit Bluff Trail, but trees partially obscure the view. Cross another bridge over a creek. Pass the 5 km (3.1 mi) marker, and walk the planks over Campsite Creek. Reach a junction (2 hours one way; 800 m/2,625 ft; 49°12′22″ N, 120°59′53″ W), 6 km (3.7 mi) from the Cascade Recreation Area. If you had the forethought to leave a second car at Cayuse Flats, go right and head down to the trailhead, just steps away, and (carefully) cross the highway. Otherwise, turn around here.

From the Cayuse Flats junction, the Hope Pass Trail continues 24 km (15 mi) northeast along the Skaist River.

The Skagit Bluff Trail lies in the territories of the Nlaka'pamux, Stó:lō, and Syilx peoples, including the sməlqmíx, who refer to Manning as saʕtikn.

GETTING THERE

Vehicle: From Trans-Canada Highway 1 in Hope, head east on Crowsnest Highway 3 (Hope-Princeton Highway). Keep right and take Exit 177 in 6 km (3.7 mi) to stay on Highway 3 at its junction with Yellowhead Highway 5 (Coquihalla Highway). Turn left into the Cascade Recreation Area, 12.5 km (7.8 mi) east of the marmot carving at E.C. Manning Provincial Park's west gate. Park in the first lot on the left. (Toilet available at the second lot.)

77

THREE BROTHERS MOUNTAIN

Distance: 21 km (13 mi)
Time: 6.5 hours (out and back)
Elevation gain: 480 m (1,575 ft)
High point: 2,272 m (7,450 ft)
Season: July to October

Quality: ★★★★★
Difficulty: ■
Maps: NTS 92-H/2 Manning Park; Clark Geomatics 104 E.C. Manning
Trailhead: 49°05′56″ N, 120°45′54″ W

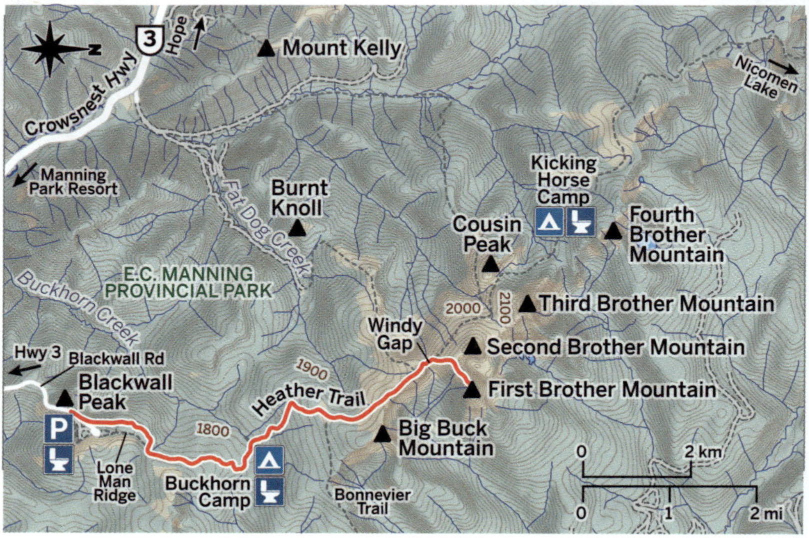

READY FOR one of the best wildflower hikes in B.C.? It's no secret why hikers flock to the Heather Trail every July and August. At peak bloom, the subalpine meadows burst into a sea of red (Elmer's paintbrush), orange (slender agoseris), yellow (heart-leaved arnica), blue (arctic lupine), purple (Davidson's penstemon), and pink (spreading phlox).

From the trailhead (1,940 m/6,365 ft) on Blackwall Peak, head north on the Heather Trail. Hiking in the territories of the Nlaka'pamux and Syilx peoples, including the sməlqmíx, contour along the western slopes of Lone Man Ridge and merge with a trail from the upper parking lot. Lose a bunch of elevation—which you can look forward to regaining on the return—en route to the backcountry campsite (reservation required, no fires) and low point at Buckhorn Creek (1,790 m/5870 ft), 5 km (3.1 mi) in. Switchbacks lead up and out of the valley.

Stay left at the Bonnevier Trail junction at the 7 km (4.3 mi) mark. Stroll northwest through the floral rainbow, staying on the path to avoid trampling the fragile meadows. Traversing the west flank of Big Buck Mountain, there's

Ridge walking on First Brother Mountain.

ample opportunity to gaze at Frosty Mountain (Hike 79), Hozomeen Mountain, and the rest of the North Cascades to the south.

At Windy Gap, part ways with the Heather Trail, 10 km (6.2 mi) from Blackwall Peak. Go right to ascend the rocky path to the saddle east of Second Brother Mountain (2,250 m/7,380 ft). Once on the crest, face northeast and relish the elating ridge walk to First Brother Mountain (3 hours up; 49°09′58″ N, 120°46′06″ W), the highest summit of Three Brothers Mountain.

This mountaintop pierces the alpine tundra biogeoclimatic zone; look for moss campion and krummholz, stunted trees deformed by freezing winds. For peak baggers, the Second and Third Brothers are within scramble range. Fourth Brother Mountain stands estranged, even farther away than Cousin Peak. The Similkameen River (nməlqitkʷ in nsyilxcən, the language of the sməlqmíx) watershed surrounds you.

Hiking back on the Heather Trail, you'll see more than one species of its namesake evergreen shrub. Pink mountain-heather, western bell heather, and yellow mountain-heather grow in the subalpine meadows.

For backpackers, the Heather Trail continues northwest to the Kicking Horse (no fires) and Nicomen Lake campsites (backcountry permit required at both). From Nicomen Lake, it's either 21 km (13 mi) back on the Heather Trail or a 17 km (10.6 mi) crossover to the Cayuse Flats parking lot via the Grainger Creek Trail and Hope Pass Trail.

Dogs must be leashed in E.C. Manning Provincial Park (saʕtikn).

GETTING THERE

Vehicle: From Trans-Canada Highway 1 in Hope, head east on Crowsnest Highway 3 (Hope-Princeton Highway) for 66 km (41 mi). At the Manning Park Resort, turn left and immediately left again on Blackwall Road (closed in winter for cross-country skiing). Drive 15 km (9.3 mi)—on gravel (2WD) beyond the Cascade Lookout—to the lower Blackwall Peak parking area (toilet available).

78

WINDY JOE MOUNTAIN

Distance: 15 km (9.3 mi)
Time: 5 hours (out and back)
Elevation gain: 665 m (2,180 ft)
High point: 1,825 m (5,990 ft)
Season: July to October

Quality: ★★
Difficulty: ■
Maps: NTS 92-H/2 Manning Park; Clark Geomatics 104 E.C. Manning
Trailhead: 49°03′49″ N, 120°47′52″ W

FOR THOSE of us harbouring long-distance hiking dreams, a visit to Windy Joe Mountain is a must. On a day hike, you can experience the home stretch of the epic Pacific Crest Trail (PCT), the U.S. national scenic trail that runs 4,260 km (2,650 mi) from Mexico to Canada. If you're lucky enough to encounter a thru-hiker, they will have spent five months or so backpacking the PCT.

Even without the PCT, there are lots of other reasons to do this hike in the territories of the Nlaka'pamux and Syilx peoples, including the sməlqmíx. Firstly, it's in E.C. Manning Provincial Park and, therefore, lies among the northernmost peaks of the Cascade Range (officially the Cascade Mountains in Canada). Secondly, it's topped by an intact fire lookout, complete with an old-school fire finder and views in every direction. Thirdly, the old road to the top welcomes use in all seasons (with snowshoes in winter).

Start at the Manning Park sign (1,190 m/3,900 ft) on the south side of Gibson Pass Road. Immediately, fork left for the Similkameen Trail, which stays on the right side of the Similkameen River (nməlqitkʷ in nsyilxcən,

This way to the Pacific Crest Trail.

the language of the sməlqmíx). A minor incline leads to a junction in 2.1 km (1.3 mi); go right on the Windy Joe Trail. At 5.5 km (3.4 mi), the trail forks and you head left, parting ways with the PCT.

The 8 km (5 mi) marker is nailed to the Windy Joe Fire Tower (2.5 hours up; 49°02′37″ N, 120°45′17″ W), a two-storey hut dating back to 1950. On the second floor, signs help visitors identify The Parks, jagged Castle Peak, Frosty Mountain (Hike 79), and other prominences. Windy Joe's true summit (1,843 m/6,050 ft) lies off-trail to the south. Retrace your steps to the trailhead.

For decades, many fire lookouts were staffed and played a lead role in wildfire detection. B.C. is home to 320 fire lookout sites, with around 25 considered active.

Back at the 5.5 km (3.4 mi) junction, heading left would soon lead to another decision point. Left is for the PCT, with a backcountry campsite nearby, to Monument 78 on the 49th parallel. Right is an alternative way to ascend Frosty Mountain's east peak.

Established in 1941, Manning (saʕtikn) is adjacent to Skagit Valley Provincial Park. Environmentalists on both sides of the border have long sought protection of the Donut Hole (nixʷtúlaʔxʷ) surrounded by the two parks. In 2019, the B.C. government halted logging in the area. Facing opposition to gold exploration from several First Nations and Tribes, Imperial Metals Corporation surrendered its mineral tenures in a 2022 deal with the province and Skagit Environmental Endowment Commission.

GETTING THERE

Vehicle: From Trans-Canada Highway 1 in Hope, head east on Crowsnest Highway 3 (Hope-Princeton Highway) for 66 km (41 mi). At the Manning Park Resort, turn right on Gibson Pass Road. In 1.2 km (0.7 mi), cross a bridge over the Similkameen River and find the Windy Joe/Pacific Crest Trail parking area on the left side of the road.

79

FROSTY MOUNTAIN

Distance: 21 km (13 mi)
Time: 7.5 hours (out and back)
Elevation gain: 1,170 m (3,840 ft)
High point: 2,409 m (7,900 ft)
Season: July to October

Quality: ★★★★★
Difficulty: ■
Maps: NTS 92-H/2 Manning Park; Clark Geomatics 104 E.C. Manning
Trailhead: 49°03′44″ N, 120°49′39″ W

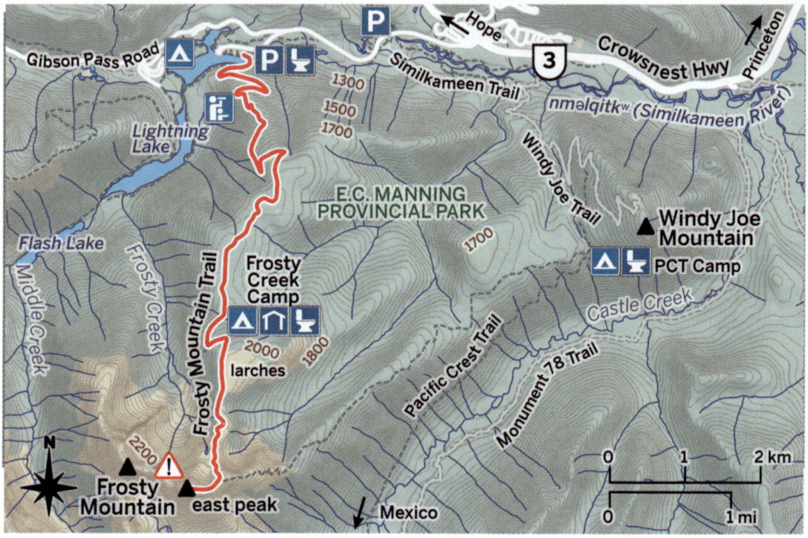

FROSTY MOUNTAIN has the distinction of being the highest summit in E.C. Manning Provincial Park. However, the destination for hikers is the lower east peak. That's because the west peak is a sketchy climb on loose rock. In the fall, hikers flock to Frosty's larch meadows.

Start at the kiosk by the Lightning Lake beach (1,240 m/4,070 ft)—in the territories of the Nlaka'pamux, Stó:lō, and Syilx peoples, including the sməlqmíx. Head east on the paved path and across the 1960s-era dam at the end of the lake. The Frosty Mountain Trail quickly strikes off to the left.

Zigzag upward in the Engelmann spruce–subalpine fir biogeoclimatic zone. Soon there are picturesque downvalley views of two of the Lightning Lakes (Skwa-kwa-eets in Halq'eméylem, the language of the Stó:lō; Hike 80)—Lightning and Flash.

In 6.5 km (4 mi), reach Frosty Creek Camp (1,850 m/6,070 ft), featuring a rustic emergency shelter and space for a few tents (backcountry camping permit required). Beyond 7 km (4.3 mi) lies a subalpine larch forest (49°01′34″ N, 120°49′50″ W). When the deciduous conifer's needles change from pale blue

The golden glow of subalpine larches amid autumn snow. *Photo by Andy Gibb*

green to golden yellow in autumn, it's a magical sight. Past the larch grove, the east and west peaks of Frosty Mountain reveal themselves.

After benefiting from a mostly pleasant grade, switchback sharply up the harsh (and possibly icy) talus—home to moss campion and American pikas—to the rocky crest, merging with the longer approach via the Windy Joe Trail (see Hike 78). Turn right (west) for a magnificent ridge walk to the summit post of the east peak (4 hours up; 49°00′39″ N, 120°50′15″ W).

From this perch close to the Canada-U.S. border, survey Frosty's main peak (2,423 m/7,950 ft) to the west, Quiniscoe Mountain and Grimface Mountain in Cathedral Provincial Park (kʷaniɬkʷaʔitkʷ in nsyilxcən, the language of the sməlqmíx) to the east, and Castle Peak in the Pasayten Wilderness (saʕtitkʷ) to the south. Return the way you came.

If planned for—definitely not spur of the moment—Frosty can be done as an ambitious loop (27 km/17 mi). Descend the ridge trail to the east. Keep left at junctions with the Pacific Crest Trail (backcountry campsite nearby), Windy Joe Trail, and Similkameen Trail. At the Windy Joe/Pacific Crest Trail parking area, take the Little Muddy Trail left to the Lightning Lake day-use area to close the loop.

Dogs must be leashed. Make sure to bring enough water on this trip.

East of Manning (saʕtikn), the Lower Similkameen Indian Band designated the Ashnola River (nʔaysnúlaʔxʷ) watershed, including Cathedral Provincial Park, as a sməlqmíx Protected and Conserved Area in 2022.

GETTING THERE

Vehicle: From Trans-Canada Highway 1 in Hope, head east on Crowsnest Highway 3 (Hope-Princeton Highway) for 66 km (41 mi). At the Manning Park Resort, turn right on Gibson Pass Road. In 3 km (1.9 mi), turn left and park at the Lightning Lake day-use area (toilet available).

80

SKWA-KWA-EETS (LIGHTNING LAKES)

Distance: 19.5 km (12.1 mi)
Time: 6.5 hours (out and back)
Elevation gain: 100 m (330 ft)
High point: 1,260 m (4,130 ft)
Season: May to October

Quality: ★★★
Difficulty: ■
Maps: NTS 92-H/2 Manning Park; Clark Geomatics 104 E.C. Manning
Trailhead: 49°03′32″ N, 120°50′26″ W

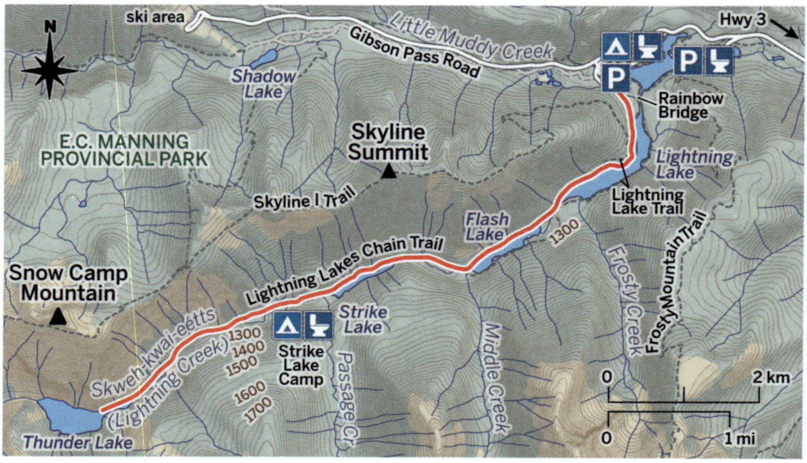

LIGHTNING LAKE in E.C. Manning Provincial Park has plenty on offer—camping, hiking, fishing, paddling, and swimming—so it's not lacking for summer visitors. Leave the masses behind with a hike to the quieter members of the Lightning Lakes chain: Flash, Strike, and Thunder. Skwa-kwa-eets is the name for the Lightning Lakes area in Halq'eméylem, the language of the Stó:lō people.

From the kiosk at the Spruce Bay parking lot (1,250 m/4,100 ft), head right (south) and go through a gate. Keep right at four junctions on the old fire road, joining the Lightning Lake Trail in the process. In 15 minutes, pass the eastern terminus of the Skyline I Trail (see Hikes 81 and 82). At Lightning Lake's beaver-dammed outlet, the Lightning Lake Trail turns left to cross a bridge over Lightning Creek (Skweh-kwai-eétts). However, continue straight onto the Lightning Lakes Chain Trail, which is of particular interest to beginner backpackers, lake baggers, and portaging canoeists.

Keep right at both ends of Flash Lake. Avalanche terrain makes it dangerous to travel past Flash Lake in winter and spring.

The Lightning Lakes Chain Trail ends at Thunder Lake.

After 1.5 hours (6.5 km/4 mi), arrive at rustic Strike Lake Camp (49°02′05″ N, 120°53′57″ W) in the trees. There are tent sites (backcountry camping permit required), log benches, firepits (campfires are discouraged), food caches, and an outhouse. The trail is overgrown beyond this point, but it's worth continuing downvalley for 3.2 km (2 mi) to remote Thunder Lake. Navigate open rocky terrain, with the help of cairns, below Snow Camp Mountain.

Near the desolate head of Thunder Lake, a wooden sign advises it's "dangerous to proceed past this point." Heeding the warning, leave the trail, descend the rocky slope, and make your way to the muddy lakeshore (3 hours one way; 1,160 m/3,810 ft; 49°01′20″ N, 120°56′02″ W). Heading upstream to return to the parking lot, stay left at all junctions, except the one for the Skyline I Trail.

Formerly known as the Quartet Lakes, the Lightning Lakes sit in a valley deepened and widened by erosion during the Wisconsin Glaciation. Lightning Creek empties into Ross Lake (tkcnwixʷtn in nsyilxcən, the language of the sməlqmíx people), a hydroelectric reservoir on the Skagit River (sk̓aʔitkʷ). Due to a 1968 dam, Lightning Lake actually drains into two watersheds. To the east, it feeds Little Muddy Creek, a tributary of the Similkameen River (nməlqitkʷ) and part of the Columbia River (nx̌ʷəntkʷitkʷ) system.

The Lightning Lakes lie in the territories of the Nlaka'pamux, Stó:lō, and Syilx peoples, including the sməlqmíx. Dogs must be leashed.

GETTING THERE

Vehicle: From Trans-Canada Highway 1 in Hope, head east on Crowsnest Highway 3 (Hope-Princeton Highway) for 66 km (41 mi). At the Manning Park Resort, turn right on Gibson Pass Road. Pass the Lightning Lake day-use area turnoff in 3 km (1.9 mi). Turn left into the Lightning Lake campground entrance, 5 km (3.1 mi) from the highway. Keep right to arrive at the Spruce Bay parking lot. (Toilet available in the campground.)

81

SKYLINE SUMMIT

Distance: 14 km (8.7 mi)
Time: 5.5 hours (out and back)
Elevation gain: 750 m (2,460 ft)
High point: 1,996 m (6,550 ft)
Season: July to October

Quality: ★★★
Difficulty: ■
Maps: NTS 92-H/2 Manning Park; Clark Geomatics 104 E.C. Manning
Trailhead: 49°03′32″ N, 120°50′26″ W

SAVOUR A ridge walk and earn views of Lightning Lakes (Skwa-kwa-eets in Halq'eméylem, the language of the Stó:lō people; Hike 80) and the Hozameen Range. These are just a couple of reasons to hike the original eastern branch of the Skyline Trail to the highest point on the scenic traverse between E.C. Manning and Skagit Valley Provincial Parks.

From the kiosk at the Spruce Bay parking lot (1,250 m/4,100 ft), head right (south) and pass through a gate. Keep right at four junctions on the wide path, joining the Lightning Lake Trail in the process. In 15 minutes (1.1 km/0.7 mi), turn right at a signpost marking the Skyline I Trail's eastern terminus (49°03′02″ N, 120°50′25″ W).

The well-maintained Skyline I Trail begins gently, with a long ascending traverse across steep forest slopes. Cross little bridges over two creeks en route to the first switchback. The path turns westward to gain and follow the ridge crest. After 1.5 hours of hiking, reach the first meadow and partial viewpoint. Spot Frosty Mountain (2,423 m/7,950 ft; Hike 79) to the south.

Enter a burned forest, evidence of a 1994 wildfire. Say bye to the shady woods but hello to almost continuous views and colourful butterflies. With

Subalpine meadows on the Skyline I Trail.

the twin towers of Hozomeen Mountain (Hoz-o-méen) in Washington looming ahead, ridge walk into a minor dip and rise to a good viewpoint. Peer down Lightning Creek (Skweh-kwai-eétts) at Strike Lake and Thunder Lake and across the valley (and Canada-U.S. border) to Castle Peak.

Enjoy the unburned ridgetop ahead. Pass the Skyline I Trail's 10 km (6.2 mi) marker (in reference to the northern trailhead at Strawberry Flats) and drop into another dip. Ascend, skirting a broad subalpine meadow, to your destination, a cairned summit (3 hours up; 49°02′59″ N, 120°52′55″ W), 6 km (3.7 mi) from the Lightning Lake Trail. Spy Shawatum Mountain (Sleha:wetem) and Silvertip Mountain to the west.

Turn around here—or wander forth for more wildflowers and views. At Sky Junction, 3 km (1.9 mi) away, the Skyline I Trail turns north and descends to Strawberry Flats. For backpackers, the Skyline II Trail continues west to Lone Goat Mountain (Hike 82), Mowich Camp (backcountry camping permit required), and Silver Skagit Road. By leaving a second vehicle at the Strawberry Flats parking area, day trippers can do the Skyline I Trail as a 16 km (9.9 mi) crossover. The South Gibson Trail links Strawberry Flats and Spruce Bay and makes possible an ambitious loop of 20 km (12.4 mi).

The Skyline Trail lies in the territories of the Nlaka'pamux, Stó:lō, and Syilx peoples, including the sməlqmíx, who refer to Manning as saʕtikn in the nsyilxcən language.

GETTING THERE

Vehicle: From Trans-Canada Highway 1 in Hope, head east on Crowsnest Highway 3 (Hope-Princeton Highway) for 66 km (41 mi). At the Manning Park Resort, turn right on Gibson Pass Road. Pass the Lightning Lake day-use area turnoff in 3 km (1.9 mi). Turn left into the Lightning Lake campground entrance, 5 km (3.1 mi) from the highway. Keep right to arrive at the Spruce Bay parking lot. (Toilet available in the campground.)

82
LONE GOAT MOUNTAIN

Distance: 22 km (13.7 mi)
Time: 8 hours (out and back)
Elevation gain: 640 m (2,100 ft)
High point: 2,004 m (6,575 ft)
Season: July to October

Quality: ★★★★
Difficulty: ■
Maps: NTS 92-H/2 Manning Park; Clark Geomatics 104 E.C. Manning
Trailhead: 49°04′00″ N, 120°53′05″ W

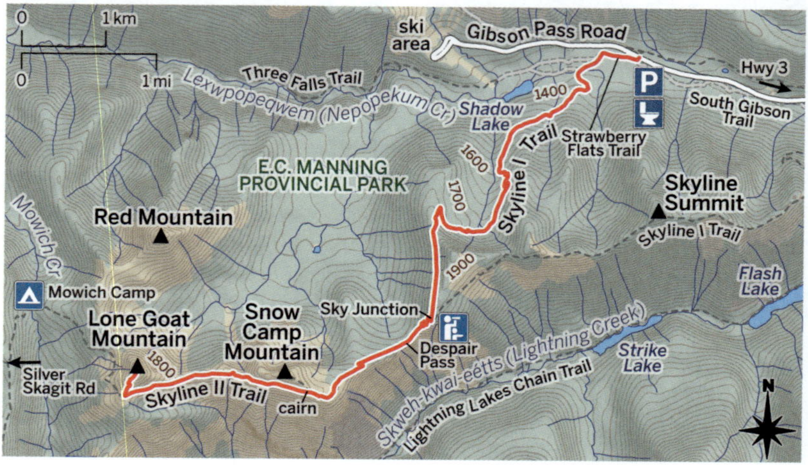

WITH ITS greenstone towers, Hozomeen Mountain (2,459 m/8,070 ft) in Washington's North Cascades is an unmistakable landmark for hikers across the border in E.C. Manning Provincial Park. Venturing onto the three-pronged Skyline Trail, which links Manning with Skagit Valley Provincial Park, means getting an eyeful of the double peak that Jack Kerouac describes as the "most mournful mountain I ever seen" in his 1958 novel *The Dharma Bums*.

Indigenous people blazed the Skyline Trail, which would later be travelled by fur traders and gold prospectors. Known as the Roach River Trail for a time, the Skyline was incorporated into the fading Centennial Trail of the 1960s. Today, Lone Goat Mountain makes a fine destination for day hikers.

Find the Strawberry Flats trailhead (1,360 m/4,460 ft) on the south side of the road at Gibson Pass. Go right on a double track, and turn left at a junction marking the start of the northern branch of the Skyline Trail. The Skyline 1 Trail steadily gains elevation. Watch out for black bears.

At the 6 km (3.7 mi) mark (49°02′19″ N, 120°55′10″ W), after 2 hours on foot, hit Sky Junction. Skyline 1 goes left to a high point (Skyline Summit, Hike 81) and its eastern terminus at Lightning Lake. Before you make a hard

Snow Camp Mountain (left), Thunder Lake, and Lone Mountain from the summit.

right on the Skyline II Trail, though, check out the soaring viewpoint ahead for your first look at the valley of Lightning Creek (Skweh-kwai-eétts in the Halq'eméylem language of the Stó:lō people) and Hozomeen Mountain.

Drop west into Despair Pass (1,710 m/5,610 ft), then rise up to the wildflowers of Snow Camp Mountain. A cairn calls attention to a side path to the summit (1,980 m/6,500 ft; 49°02′00″ N, 120°56′33″ W)—and a shorter hike option (round trip: 6 hours)—2.2 km (1.4 mi) from Sky Junction.

With Lone Goat Mountain as your goal, stick with Skyline II as it crosses dry meadows and descends to a col. An ascending traverse leads to an unmarked junction in a meadow on the south side of Lone Goat. Turn right, leaving the main trail, and march skywards to gain the summit (4 hours up; 49°02′03″ N, 120°58′02″ W), 2.8 km (1.7 mi) from the Snow Camp turnoff.

Hozomeen Mountain dominates the scene; its name is attributed to a word in Nłeʔkepmxcín, the language of the Nlaka'pamux people, meaning "sharp, like a sharp knife." Steel yourself for the return via Despair Pass.

Backpackers can push on to Mowich Camp for the night (12.5 km/7.8 mi from Strawberry Flats; backcountry camping permit required), perhaps en route to completing the Skyline II Trail crossover to Silver Skagit Road (13 km/8.1 mi farther), south of Hope (Ts'qó:ls).

The Skyline Trail lies in the territories of the Nlaka'pamux, Stó:lō, and Syilx peoples, including the sməlqmíx, who refer to Manning as saʕtikn in the nsyilxcən language. Be sure to bring sun protection and plenty of water.

GETTING THERE

Vehicle: From Trans-Canada Highway 1 in Hope, head east on Crowsnest Highway 3 (Hope-Princeton Highway) for 66 km (41 mi). At the Manning Park Resort, turn right on Gibson Pass Road. Keep right at the Lightning Lake turnoff in 3 km (1.9 mi). Reach the Strawberry Flats parking lot (toilet available), where the road is gated in summer, 9 km (5.6 mi) from the highway.

83
MOUNT GARDNER

Distance: 14 km (8.7 mi)
Time: 5.5 hours (lollipop)
Elevation gain: 720 m (2,360 ft)
High point: 727 m (2,385 ft)
Season: Most of the year

Quality: ★★★
Difficulty: ■
Maps: NTS 92-G/6 North Vancouver
Trailhead: 49°22′50″ N, 123°20′03″ W

AN ISLAND day hike can feel as invigorating as a week away. The ferry from Horseshoe Bay (Ch'ax̱áy) to Bowen Island (Nex̱wlélex̱wem), in Squamish Nation (Sḵwx̱wú7mesh Úxwumixw) territory, takes 20 minutes. Foot passengers can scale the island's highest peak and be back in Vancouver for dinner.

From the Snug Cove ferry dock, walk 100 m (110 yd) west on Bowen Island Trunk Road. Turn right on Cardena Road and head past the visitor centre. Enter Crippen Regional Park on the left (elevation: 10 m/30 ft). Fork right for the Alder Grove Trail. Optionally, visit the tranquil Bowen Island Memorial Garden on the right and take in the view of Deep Bay (Kwíl'aḵm in Sḵwx̱wú7mesh Sníchim, the Squamish language), a.k.a. Mannion Bay.

Up the Alder Grove Trail, the fish ladder at Bridal Veil Falls is another diversion. Go right on Miller Road and over Killarney Creek, then cross the street to take the Killarney Creek Trail. Pass junctions with the Collins Trail and Meadow Trail. Keep left at the Cedar Trail fork. Turn left on Magee Road.

After 30 minutes (2.2 km/1.4 mi), cross Mount Gardner Road and go forth on the new Mount Gardner Connector Trail. Take a right fork (where a steep bike path goes left). Reach a junction featuring one of many new signposts installed by the Bowen Island Trail Society. Turn left on the Lower

A helipad on the north summit overlooks Átl'ḵa7tsem.

Skid Trail, starting a clockwise loop. Briefly jog left on the Denis Lynn Trail, an old road, then go right on the Mid Skid Trail. Follow orange diamonds uphill in the cool forest—ignoring a rightward exit to Hikers Trail Road.

Go left on the Upper Skid Trail (spurning the Canyon Trail) at a T-junction. At the next decision point, turn right to ascend the steep and scrambly South Summit Grind. Take in a partial view of Lighthouse Park's Point Atkinson (Sḵ'íw̓itsut, "go around"), before cairns mark the inconspicuous south summit (49°22′35″ N, 123°23′25″ W), the day's high point. Thereafter, keep right at the South Ridge Express and North Summit Bypass junctions.

Break into the open on the north summit (3 hours up; 719 m/2,360 ft; 49°22′46″ N, 123°23′19″ W), 7 km (4.3 mi) from the Cardena Road trailhead. It's a swell lunch spot in spite of the telecom towers. Wooden helipads offer views in two directions: east to the Twin Sisters (Ch'ich'iyúy), English Bay, and Spanish Bank (P'ekwchá); west to Port Mellon (Ḵ'iḵ'élx̱n).

From the west-facing pad, follow markers down an abrupt gully, aided by a fixed cord, on the North Summit Trail (rather than taking Easy Street to the right). Follow signs to Hikers Trail Road, keeping right and earning a view of Keats Island (Lheḵ'tínes) on the way. Go right on the gravel road and stick with it until a junction near the bottom. Turn right on Lower Skid Trail, then left on the Mount Gardner Connector Trail. Retrace your steps to Snug Cove.

Dogs must be leashed in Crippen Regional Park.

GETTING THERE

Transit: Take TransLink Bus 250 (Horseshoe Bay), 257 (Horseshoe Bay Express), or 262 (Lions Bay–Brunswick) to the Horseshoe Bay ferry terminal.
Vehicle: From Vancouver, take Trans-Canada Highway 1 west to the B.C. Ferries terminal at Horseshoe Bay (Exit 3) in West Vancouver. Park in the long-term parking lot. (If you bring a vehicle to the island, park at the Snug Cove picnic area [toilet available], off Dorman Road.)

84

MCNAIR LAKE

Distance: 20 km (12.4 mi)
Time: 7.5 hours (out and back)
Elevation gain: 190 m (620 ft)
High point: 1,130 m (3,710 ft)
Season: May to November

Quality: ★★★
Difficulty: ◆
Maps: NTS 92-G/12 Sechelt Inlet
Trailhead: 49°36′11″ N, 123°40′18″ W

SEARCHING FOR SOLITUDE? In Tetrahedron Provincial Park, you have a better chance of finding it down by Chapman Lake than up on Mount Steele (Hike 85). This hike ventures into a wild, remote valley in the territory of the shíshálh Nation. Route-finding skills are essential, as the path is indistinct here and there. Be bear aware!

From the upper parking lot (940 m/3,080 ft), hike east on a logging road. Pass the turnoff for the Batchelor Lake Cabin and reach Victor's Landing. The clear-cut-scarred scenery of the Tetrahedron Plateau improves as you near Edwards Lake. The trail swings left to rise above its north shore.

In 1.5 hours (4.5 km/2.8 mi), arrive at Edwards Lake Cabin (49°35′40″ N, 123°37′25″ W), built and maintained by the Tetrahedron Outdoor Club. If you stay overnight, be sure to pay the posted hut fee. Cross Steele Creek, 500 m (0.3 mi) past the cabin.

Turn right for the challenging 5.2 km (3.2 mi) traverse to McNair Lake Cabin. (Left goes to Mount Steele Cabin.) The southward path loses plenty of elevation en route to a long-suffering bridge over Chapman Creek (ts'úḵw'um stulu in she shashishalhem, the language of the shíshálh).

Panther Peak (left), mala, Chapman Lake, and McNair Lake (middle right) from Mount Steele.

After passing several ponds, the muddy path reaches the south shore of Chapman Lake (976 m/3,200 ft), whose outflow is controlled by a dam.

Next, the wet and intermittent path takes aim at Panther Peak before curving south and ascending to far-flung McNair Lake Cabin (3.5 hours up; 1,040 m/3,410 ft; 49°34′40″ N, 123°35′20″ W), which is often buried by snow in winter. McNair Lake itself lies beyond the cabin, over the Howe Sound (Átl'ḵa7tsem in Sḵwx̱wú7mesh Sníchim, the language of the Squamish Nation [Sḵwx̱wú7mesh Úxwumixw]) divide. Northwest of the cabin is mala (Hind-Smith Lake); its shíshálh toponym was the ancestral name of respected shíshálh Elder Albert Louie (1935–2012). Head back the way you came.

Dogs, drones, fires, mountain biking, motorized vehicles, smoking, swimming, tenting, and vaping are prohibited in Tetrahedron Provincial Park. Each cabin has room for 12 guests and is first-come, first-served.

GETTING THERE

Vehicle: B.C. Ferries offers daily sailings between West Vancouver and the Sunshine Coast via the Horseshoe Bay–Langdale route. In Sechelt Village, where northbound Highway 101 (Sunshine Coast Highway) turns left, go right (north) on Wharf Avenue. Turn right on Porpoise Bay Road, which becomes Sechelt Inlet Road. After crossing Gray Creek, 8 km (5 mi) from Sechelt Village, turn right on Gray Creek Road (Sechelt Dakota Forest Service Road). In 1 km (0.6 mi), take the left fork for Sechelt Gray FSR (Branch 9; rough 2WD). At 6 km (3.7 mi), keep right to recross Gray Creek. Ignore Branch 17 on the right. The lower parking lot (820 m/2,690 ft; toilet available) is 11 km (6.8 mi) from the pavement. With high-clearance **4WD**, keep right and continue 1 km (0.6 mi) on Branch 500 to the upper parking lot.

85
MOUNT STEELE

Distance: 17 km (10.6 mi)
Time: 7 hours (out and back)
Elevation gain: 720 m (2,360 ft)
High point: 1,659 m (5,440 ft)
Season: July to October
Quality: ★★★★
Difficulty: ◆
Maps: NTS 92-G/12 Sechelt Inlet
Trailhead: 49°36′11″ N, 123°40′18″ W

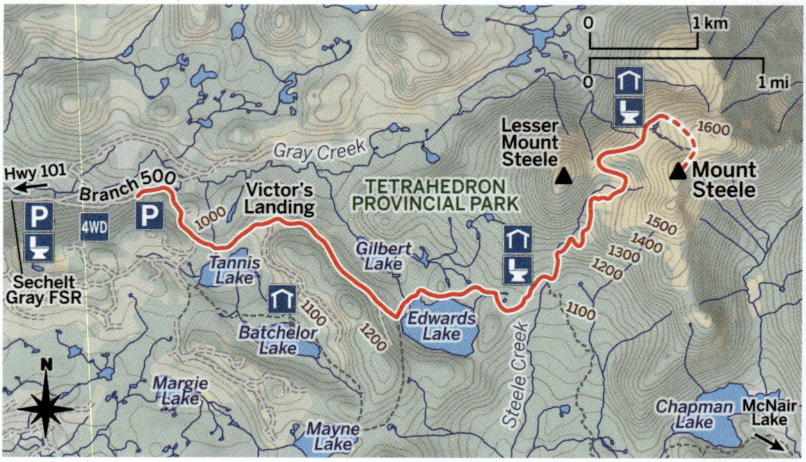

MOUNT STEELE is the main draw for hikers, snowshoers, and ski tourers in Tetrahedron Provincial Park. From the summit, in the territory of the shíshálh Nation, the sensational panorama stars Tetrahedron Peak and Panther Peak, also in the park, alongside the Earle Range, Salmon Inlet (skwúpa in she shashishalhem, the language of the shíshálh), Tantalus Range, and Salish Sea.

From the upper parking lot (940 m/3,080 ft), hike east on a degrading logging road. Pass the right-hand turnoff for the Batchelor Lake Cabin and reach Victor's Landing. Clear-cuts give the trail a disheartening kickoff, but the scenery of the Tetrahedron Plateau changes for the better as you near Edwards Lake. The trail swings left to rise above its north shore.

In 1.5 hours (4.5 km/2.8 mi), arrive at Edwards Lake Cabin (1,130 m/3,710 ft; 49°35′40″ N, 123°37′25″ W), erected by the Tetrahedron Outdoor Club (formerly the Tetrahedron Ski Club) in 1987. If you stay overnight, be sure to pay the posted hut fee to support maintenance.

Cross Steele Creek, 500 m (0.3 mi) past the cabin. Turn left to ascend Mount Steele over the next 3.5 km (2.2 mi). (Right goes to McNair Lake Cabin [see Hike 84].) The steep path switchbacks northeast, then curves 180 degrees

Mount Steele Cabin and spipiyus swiya at sunset.

in a scenic subalpine bowl before turning back eastward in the saddle between Lesser Mount Steele and your objective.

A glorious ramble up the northeast ridge is all that separates the Mount Steele Cabin (1,500 m/4,920 ft) and the summit (3.5 hours up; 49°36′18″ N, 123°36′18″ W). Scan the horizon and pick out (clockwise from north): Phantom Mountain, Nch'ḵaỷ (Mount Garibaldi), Mount Arrowsmith (kał-ka-č'ałḥ in nuučaan̓uł to the Hupačasath First Nation) on Vancouver Island, Mount Shepherd on Texada Island (spílḵsen in she shashishalhem), and Mount Hallowell in the Caren Range (spipiyus swiya). Return the way you came.

The park protects the headwaters of Chapman Creek (ts'úḵw'um stulu) and Gray Creek, which support salmon runs and supply drinking water to Sechelt (ch'atlich) and much of the Sunshine Coast Regional District. Dogs, drones, fires, mountain biking, motorized vehicles, smoking, swimming, tenting, and vaping are prohibited in Tetrahedron Provincial Park. Each cabin has room for 12 guests and is first-come, first-served.

GETTING THERE

Vehicle: B.C. Ferries offers daily sailings between West Vancouver and the Sunshine Coast via the Horseshoe Bay–Langdale route. In Sechelt Village, where northbound Highway 101 (Sunshine Coast Highway) turns left, go right (north) on Wharf Avenue. Turn right on Porpoise Bay Road, which becomes Sechelt Inlet Road. After crossing Gray Creek, 8 km (5 mi) from Sechelt Village, turn right on Gray Creek Road (Sechelt Dakota Forest Service Road). In 1 km (0.6 mi), take the left fork for Sechelt Gray FSR (Branch 9; rough 2WD). At 6 km (3.7 mi), keep right to recross Gray Creek. Ignore Branch 17 on the right. The lower parking lot (820 m/2,690 ft; toilet available) is 11 km (6.8 mi) from the pavement. With high-clearance **4WD**, keep right and continue 1 km (0.6 mi) on Branch 500 to the upper parking lot.

86

SHÉLKÉM (MOUNT DANIEL)

Distance: 4.5 km (2.8 mi)
Time: 2.5 hours (out and back)
Elevation gain: 360 m (1,180 ft)
High point: 449 m (1,470 ft)
Season: Most of the year

Quality: ★★★★
Difficulty: ■
Maps: NTS 92-F/9 Texada Island
Trailhead: 49°38′48″ N, 124°00′22″ W

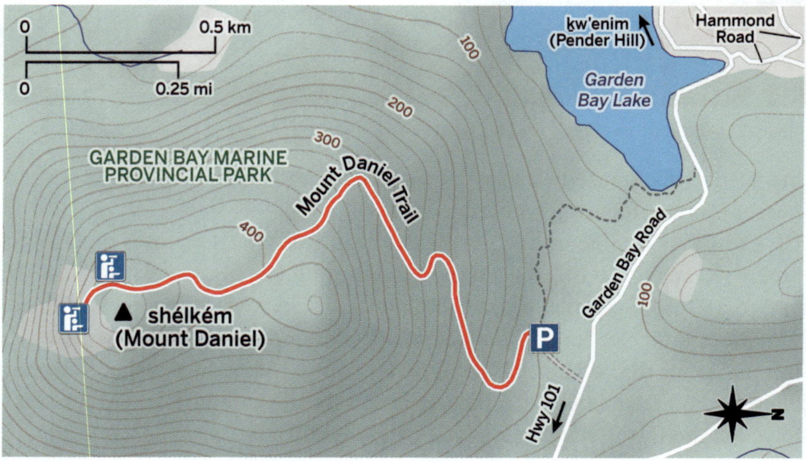

OVERLOOKING K̲ALPILIN (Pender Harbour), Mount Daniel rises in the heart of shíshálh swiya, the territory of the shíshálh Nation, on the Sunshine Coast. Known as shélkém in the she shashishalhem language, this roche moutonnée, shaped by glacial erosion, has long served as an important cultural, spiritual, and defence site for the shíshálh.

Today, shélkém is protected by Garden Bay Marine Provincial Park and included in the shíshálh's k̲alpilin-stséx̲wena kw'enit sim alap (Pender Harbour–Sakinaw Cultural Emphasis Area). From the access road (90 m/295 ft), the four-season Mount Daniel Trail zigzags south.

Steadily gain elevation in the mixed forest and ferny understory. Watch out for slugs and snails underfoot. Scan your surroundings for black bears, Columbian black-tailed deer, and cougars. Admire the peeling cinnamon bark of arbutus trees, but please don't add your name to the careless graffiti scarring their trunks.

A clearing on the right calls for a break, 45 minutes up. The trail jogs left and drops briefly before rising to blufftop viewpoints near the summit of Mount Daniel (1 hour up; 49°38′12″ N, 124°00′25″ W), formerly known as

Hotel Lake and shélkém from k̲w'enim.

Mount Arthur. Feast on the delicious Salish Sea views from this shíshálh lookout point on the Sechelt Peninsula.

Peer southwest at Lily Lake, Bargain Bay, Gerrans Bay, and the Francis Peninsula. Cecil Hill (wah-wey-we'-lath), a training ground for young shíshálh men, rises across Gunboat Bay. Texada Island (spílk̲sen) lies across the Malaspina Strait (sínkwu) to the west. Return the way you came.

If a doubleheader interests you, Pender Hill (k̲w'enim, "looking") is located nearby and overlooks the entrance of k̲alpilin. It's another short-and-sweet hike, taking 1 hour (1.6 km/1 mi) return. From the Mount Daniel trailhead, drive (or bike) west on Garden Bay Road, continue straight onto Irvines Landing Road, and turn right on Lee Road to find Pender Hill Park (4331 Coastview Drive).

Both shélkém and k̲w'enim make ideal outings for campers staying at Porpoise Bay Provincial Park in Sechelt (ch'atlich). Bike campers can ride the Suncoaster Trail to bypass a chunk of Highway 101.

Dogs must be leashed. No drones, littering, smoking, or vaping. Please stay on trails and don't shortcut.

GETTING THERE

Vehicle: B.C. Ferries offers daily sailings between West Vancouver and the Sunshine Coast via the Horseshoe Bay–Langdale route. From Sechelt Village, head north on Highway 101 (Sunshine Coast Highway) for 37 km (23 mi). By the gas station in Kleindale, turn left on Garden Bay Road. In 3.3 km (2.1 mi), after passing Oyster Bay Road, turn left on a dirt road. Park by the entrance or just up the road, where a Mount Daniel sign points to the left fork.

87

FAIRVIEW BAY

Distance: 13.5 km (8.4 mi)
Time: 4.5 hours (out and back)
Elevation gain: 130 m (430 ft)
High point: 130 m (430 ft)
Season: All year

Quality: ★★★
Difficulty: ●
Maps: NTS 92-F/16 Haslam Lake; Tourism Powell River Recreation
Trailhead: 49°47′03″ N, 124°10′30″ W

JOLTED INTO action by the disappearing old-growth forests of the Upper Sunshine Coast, Eagle Walz and a merry band of outdoor enthusiasts began building the Sunshine Coast Trail (SCT; see also Hike 90) in 1992. The SCT largely traverses the treaty territory of the Tla'amin (ɬaʔamɩn) Nation, from Sarah Point to sḵelhp (Saltery Bay). A north-to-south journey of 10-plus days, the footpath covers 178 km (111 mi), with 15 huts along the way.

To section-hike the final leg of the SCT, set out from the southern trailhead at sḵelhp on the scenic Fairview Bay Trail, in shíshálh Nation territory. Follow the SCT distance markers and signs east for 6.8 km (4.2 mi). Initially, keep right to cross a bridge over Saltery Creek. Above Rose Beach, go left to bypass Honeysuckle Harbour Point and ascend the Escalator switchbacks to the day's high point. Descend to the Pirates Cove picnic site.

The SCT heads up to join a power-line road en route to the big B.C. Hydro pylons at Ahlstrom Point, which support high-voltage wires spanning lekw'emin (Jervis Inlet).

The trail gets closer to sea level at Ahlstrom Bench and Plantation Cove. Arrive at lovely Fairview Bay Hut (2 hours one way; 49°47′23″ N, 124°07′19″ W),

Fairview Bay Hut on the Sunshine Coast Trail. *Photo by Emma Levez Larocque*

the southernmost overnight shelter on the SCT. Built in 2009 and renovated in 2014, the enclosed shelter sleeps 10 people. The rocky beach outside is littered with oyster shells, purple sea stars, and rusty chains.

Return the way you came. Otherwise, spend more time on the SCT by following the red squares north for 2.7 km (1.7 mi) to the Rainy Day Lake Trail junction. Hang a left to visit the Rainy Day Lake Hut on Hailstone Bluff. The swimming is excellent here. With a night in the sleeping loft, you might consider ascending Mount Troubridge (1,304 m/4,280 ft), the highest summit on the SCT. It's 9.2 km (5.7 mi) north of the Rainy Day Lake junction.

From Rainy Day Lake, the Saltery Bay Trail provides an alternative way to loop back to the trailhead, with little difference in distance. In 2009, the B.C. government recognized sk̲elhp, an ancient toponym in the she shashishalhem language for Saltery Bay, as the official name of the body of water.

Dogs must be leashed and are not allowed in SCT huts, which are first-come, first-served. If you stay in one, please make a donation to the qathet Parks and Wilderness Society, which built and maintains the SCT.

GETTING THERE

Transit: Powell River Regional Transit Bus 12 (Stillwater) offers limited service to the Saltery Bay ferry terminal. (Sunshine Coast Connector offers once-a-day coach service between the Langdale and Earls Cove ferry terminals.) From the Saltery Bay terminal, walk 200 m (220 yd) east on Saltery Bay Forest Service Road.

Vehicle: B.C. Ferries offers daily sailings on the Horseshoe Bay–Langdale and Earls Cove–Saltery Bay routes, which are connected by Highway 101 (Sunshine Coast Highway) through Sechelt (ch'atlich). Leaving the Saltery Bay ferry terminal (toilet available), immediately turn right (east) on Saltery Bay FSR (2WD). Drive 200 m (220 yd) to the Sunshine Coast Trail parking lot.

88

EMMA LAKE

Distance: 11.5 km (7.1 mi)
Time: 6.5 hours (out and back)
Elevation gain: 1,150 m (3,770 ft)
High point: 1,360 m (4,460 ft)
Season: July to October

Quality: ★★★★★
Difficulty: ◆
Maps: NTS 92-K/1 Powell Lake; Tourism Powell River Recreation
Trailhead: 50°06′59″ N, 124°12′14″ W

EMMA LAKE is an alpine gem in qathet (formerly the Powell River Regional District) and the treaty territory of the Tla'amin (ɬaʔamɩn) Nation. It's also the midpoint of the South Powell Divide, a high route (for experienced backpackers only) with days of tricky terrain. The trail to Emma Lake is brutally stiff. Fortunately, the destination makes up for the journey.

As the A800 Branch kiosk (210 m/690 ft) advises, expect to take 3 to 6 hours to climb the Emma Lake Trail. The first half is a steadily rising double track, shared with ATVs (all-terrain vehicles), under tree cover. Pass a waterfall fed by Kay Lake, followed by a smaller cascade.

In 1.7 km (1.1 mi), come to the base of Emma Falls. Wade or boulder-hop Emma Creek. After the rocky track switchbacks, get a downvalley vista from boulders off to the right. The road ends (640 m/2,100 ft; 50°07′47″ N, 124°11′12″ W), 1.1 km (0.7 mi) past Emma Falls, at a viewpoint.

What lies ahead is 3 km (1.9 mi) of relentlessly steep single track with a 24 per cent grade (compared with 15 per cent for the road). Follow pink tapes and blue diamonds a regenerating clear-cut to another valley view. Pass the remains of a wooden helipad and head into mature conifers.

Crossroads Peak (left) and Thunderdome Peak across Emma Lake.

Skip the side trail to Scrub Lake (right), unless energy is in good supply; your destination is 600 m (0.4 mi) away. Exit a tunnel formed by boulders with a fixed-rope assist. Finally, rejoice at the sight of Emma Lake Cabin ahead.

Arrive at the cabin junction (4 hours up; 50°07′56″ N, 124°09′49″ W). Go forth to the gorgeous tarn, presided over by Crossroads Peak (Hike 89), Thunderdome (Edington) Peak, and the mountain called Pickles and Puzzles. Venture left for the composting outhouse and Edge of the World bluff viewpoint. Or, head right for the outlet bridge and cascade. Emma Lake feeds into the Eldred River, which drains into Powell Lake (θaʔyɛɬ in ʔayʔaǰuθəm, the language of the Tla'amin). Retrace your steps to A800 Branch.

Emma Lake Cabin is maintained by the Knuckleheads Winter Recreation Association. If you use the hut, please register at the trailhead and make a donation.

GETTING THERE

Vehicle: B.C. Ferries offers daily sailings on the Horseshoe Bay–Langdale and Earls Cove–Saltery Bay routes, which are connected by Highway 101 (Sunshine Coast Highway) through Sechelt (ch'atlich). From the Saltery Bay ferry terminal, drive west on Highway 101 for 12 km (7.5 mi). At Lang Bay, turn right on Dixon Road, which curves right and turns to gravel (2WD). At a stop sign, go left on Goat Main Hookup Road, following one-way directions. Continue straight onto Goat Lake Main and stay on it. (Distance markers are in miles.) After the 8 mi (13 km) call point, go left at a major junction with Tin Hat Connector (which you'll use to take Stillwater Main on the way out). Stay left where Goat Lake 1 branches off. Goat Main gets narrower and rougher, with potholes and washboarding. Spot an Emma Lake Trail sign at a fork, 50 km (31 mi) from the highway. With high clearance, continue right on A800 Branch for 600 m (0.4 mi). Otherwise, park in a pullout on the mainline and walk 10 minutes to the trailhead.

89
CROSSROADS PEAK

Distance: 16.5 km (10.3 mi)
Time: 9 hours (out and back)
Elevation gain: 1,415 m (4,640 ft)
High point: 1,625 m (5,330 ft)
Season: July to October

Quality: ★★★★★
Difficulty: ◆
Maps: NTS 92-K/1 Powell Lake; Tourism Powell River Recreation
Trailhead: 50°06′59″ N, 124°12′14″ W

DAY AND overnight hikers can sample the delights of the South Powell Divide with a visit to Crossroads Peak, in Tla'amin (ɬaʔamɩn) treaty territory. The South Powell Divide is an alpine route on the height of land between Powell Lake (θaʔyɛɬ in the ʔayʔaǰuθəm language of the Tla'amin Nation) and Jervis Inlet (lekw'emin). Due to challenging terrain and tricky route-finding, a full traverse of the divide is best left to the most seasoned backpackers.

Start up the Emma Lake Trail (Hike 88) from the A800 Branch kiosk (210 m/690 ft). The first half is a steadily rising double track, shared with ATVs. In 1.7 km (1.1 mi), come to Emma Falls. Wade or boulder-hop Emma Creek. The road ends, 1.1 km (0.7 mi) past Emma Falls, at a viewpoint.

What lies ahead is 3 km (1.9 mi) of steep single track. Follow pink tapes and blue diamonds through a regenerating clear-cut. Enter the subalpine and skip the side trail to Scrub Lake (right). Exit a tunnel formed by massive boulders with a fixed-rope assist. Finally, spot Emma Lake Cabin ahead.

Arrive at the cabin junction (1,360 m/4,460 ft; 50°07′56″ N, 124°09′49″ W), after 4 hours on foot. Signs point the way north (toward Little Crater Lake) and south (toward Skwim Mountain) on the South Powell Divide. Identify Crossroads Peak, 1.5 hours away, to the east-northeast.

Snowy Peak (top left), Pickles and Puzzles, and Emma Lake from Crossroads Peak.

Set off northeast, following beaten paths, cairns, and intermittent flagging. Enjoy a viewpoint of Snowy Peak, Pickles and Puzzles, and Emma Lake. Gain the crest of Canada Ridge. Stick with the ridge where the B Branch Trail, the old approach to Emma Lake, drops left to Maria Lake.

Reach the summit cairn of Crossroads Peak (5.5 hours up; 50°08′13″ N, 124°08′17″ W), 2.4 km (1.5 mi) from the cabin, on the divide proper. Davidson's penstemon blooms violet on the mountaintop. The splendid panorama includes Mount Alfred, k̲'els (Anchor Mountain, formerly Mount Victoria), Diadem Mountain, Thunderdome (Edington) Peak, Beartooth Mountain, Mount Baldy, and Slide Mountain. Arctic Lake fills the cirque southeast.

Retrace your steps to Emma Lake Cabin and A800 Branch. Beyond Crossroads, the cairns are sparse, the route-finding is gnarly, and it's easy to wander into cliffy terrain. The north section of the South Powell Divide continues over two peaks before bypassing The Fist and dropping to remote Cairn Lake (1,300 m/4,265 ft), 3 hours (4 km/2.5 mi) from Crossroads.

GETTING THERE

Vehicle: B.C. Ferries offers daily sailings on the Horseshoe Bay–Langdale and Earls Cove–Saltery Bay routes, which are connected by Highway 101 (Sunshine Coast Highway) through Sechelt (ch'atlich). From the Saltery Bay ferry terminal, drive west on Highway 101 for 12 km (7.5 mi). At Lang Bay, turn right on Dixon Road, which curves right and turns to gravel (2WD). At a stop sign, go left on Goat Main Hookup Road, following one-way directions. Continue straight onto Goat Lake Main and stay on it. (Distance markers are in miles.) Go left at a major junction with Tin Hat Connector. Stay left where Goat Lake 1 branches off. Goat Main gets narrower and rougher, with potholes and washboarding. Spot an Emma Lake Trail sign at a fork, 50 km (31 mi) from the highway. With high clearance, continue right on A800 Branch for 600 m (0.4 mi).

90 CONFEDERATION LAKE

Distance: 20 km (12.4 mi)
Time: 7 hours (out and back)
Elevation gain: 540 m (1,770 ft)
High point: 660 m (2,165 ft)
Season: March to November
Quality: ★★★
Difficulty: ■
Maps: NTS 92-F/16 Haslam Lake; Tourism Powell River Recreation
Trailhead: 49°55′08″ N, 124°28′53″ W

ANCIENT GROVES of western red cedars and Douglas-firs are the raison d'être of the 178 km (111 mi) Sunshine Coast Trail (SCT; see also Hike 87). You'll get a sense why on the hike to secluded Confederation Lake in the treaty territory of the Tla'amin (ɬaʔamɩn) Nation.

From the Inland Lake campground (120 m/390 ft), join the Inland Lake Trail, a link in the SCT. Head counterclockwise on the pleasant loop, built with wheelchair accessibility in mind in the 1980s but since fallen into disrepair.

After 2.8 km (1.7 mi), bear right and away from the lake on the challenging Confederation Lake Trail (49°56′29″ N, 124°29′06″ W). Follow SCT signs for another 7.3 km (4.5 mi), gaining height on the lush western slopes of Mount Mahony. Stairs and switchbacks help negotiate the stubbornly steep climb.

At 7 km (4.3 mi), the Loon Bluffs viewpoint, off to the left, affords an elevated look at Inland Lake, a.k.a. Loon Lake. The grade relents as you crest Pearson Pass. Keep right to round the east shore of Confederation Lake in its forested bowl.

In 2016, the Powell River Parks and Wilderness Society (now the qathet Parks and Wilderness Society, or qPAWS) constructed the new Confederation

The Sunshine Coast Trail in Inland Lake Provincial Park.

Lake Hut (3.5 hours up; 640 m/2,100 ft; 49°58′33″ N, 124°27′20″ W), next to the original, deteriorating log cabin near the 74 km (46 mi) mark of the SCT. There's also a tent pad, picnic table, and composting toilet.

A sign just past the hut may entice you a little bit farther: Vomit Vista beckons 800 m (0.5 mi) north, with a view of Tin Hat Mountain and Goat Lake. Retrace your steps to the Inland Lake campground.

Looking for something easier? Leave Confederation Lake for another day and circumnavigate Inland Lake. The loop (13 km/8.1 mi) takes 3 hours. In ʔayʔaǰuθəm, the language of the Tla'amin, θaʔyɛɬ ("Thah yetl") is a place name for nearby Powell Lake and Haslam Lake; Powell River is known as tiskʷat ("Teeskwat").

Dogs must be leashed and are not allowed on beaches or in SCT huts, which are first-come, first-served. If you stay in one of the huts, please make a donation to qPAWS. Hut etiquette: One-night stays only, thru-hikers get priority, and groups of eight or more should stay in tents.

GETTING THERE

Vehicle: B.C. Ferries offers daily sailings on the Horseshoe Bay–Langdale and Earls Cove–Saltery Bay routes, which are connected by Highway 101 (Sunshine Coast Highway) through Sechelt (ch'atlich). From the Saltery Bay ferry terminal, drive west on Highway 101 (Sunshine Coast Highway) for 27 km (17 mi), continuing onto Thunder Bay Street in Powell River. Turn right on Joyce Avenue. At a T-junction, go left on Manson Avenue. Quickly turn right on Cassiar Street and left on Yukon Avenue. In 1 km (0.6 mi), go right on Haslam Street. Continue straight onto Inland Lake Forest Service Road. Stick with the mainline, turning right at the Haywire Bay Road (Branch 3) junction. Enter Inland Lake Provincial Park, fork left for the campground, and keep right two times to find the parking lot (toilet available).

91
MOUNT ERSKINE

Distance: 5 km (3.1 mi)
Time: 3 hours (lollipop)
Elevation gain: 380 m (1,250 ft)
High point: 448 m (1,470 ft)
Season: All year

Quality: ★★★★★
Difficulty: ■
Maps: NTS 92-B/13 Duncan
Trailhead: 48°51′23″ N, 123°33′33″ W

SURE, MOUNT ERSKINE isn't the loftiest peak on Saltspring Island—known as ĆUÁN in SENĆOŦEN, the language of the W̱SÁNEĆ people. Those bragging rights belong to Bruce Peak. No matter—Erskine is undoubtedly the most magical of Saltspring's prominences.

From Collins Road (70 m/230 ft), enter the Lower Mount Erskine Nature Reserve, located in the territories of the Quw'utsun, Semiahmoo (se'mya'me), Tsawwassen (scəw̓aθən), and W̱SÁNEĆ peoples. The small Islands Trust Conservancy property is home to arbutus and hairy manzanita. Keep left at the first fork. At the Mount Erskine Provincial Park boundary, the Jack Fisher Trail becomes the Mount Erskine Trail (Trail #1).

A half-hour in, follow Trail #1 right at a four-way junction to start a counterclockwise loop. Go right at the next fork for Trail #3 to discover charming little fairy doors and two enchanting viewpoints popular with dragonflies.

To the northwest, Halalt Island (Xulelthw in Hul'q'umi'num', the language of the Quw'utsun Nation), a.k.a. Willy Island, and Penelakut Island (Puneluxutth' in Hul'q'umi'num'; PENÁ,LEXEȾ in SENĆOŦEN) line Stuart Channel. Penelakut was the site of the Catholic-run Kuper Island

Xulelthw, Stuart Channel, and Puneluxutth' from Trail #3.

residential school, where Coast Salish children were subjected to cruel experiments, sexual abuse, and other atrocities. Opened in 1889, the school finally closed circa 1975. The Hwlitsum First Nation, which is seeking federal recognition, is connected to a winter village site, Lamalchi, on Penelakut.

Trail #4 enters from the left before the upper viewpoint, after which Trail #3 swings sharply left at a log with an orange marker. A fairy door lies on the other side. (A sketchy path continues south, passing a cave before petering out on a ledge. An exposed scramble and more ledges ensue.)

Trail #3 merges with Trail #1 en route to the inviting summit (1.5 hours up; 48°50′49″ N, 123°32′58″ W) with its expansive views. A concrete water bowl is dedicated to Rosie the dog (1990–2001).

Continue southeast to pick up mellow Trail #2. Turn left at the junction with Trail #5. (Optionally, take Trail #5 into the Manzanita Ridge Nature Reserve, owned by the Salt Spring Island Conservancy and protected by a covenant. Then return to the loop.) Descend in shady forest to the four-way junction, where you go straight to follow Trail #1 back to the trailhead.

Mount Erskine Provincial Park was established in 2006 after the Salt Spring Island Conservancy led a campaign to protect the mountain.

GETTING THERE

Vehicle: B.C. Ferries offers daily sailings to Saltspring Island via three routes: Tsawwassen–Long Harbour, Swartz Bay–Fulford Harbour, and Crofton–Vesuvius Bay. From the Long Harbour ferry terminal, head west on Long Harbour Road. At T-junctions, turn left on Upper Ganges Road and right on Lower Ganges Road. In 2 km (1.2 mi), go left on Booth Canal Road and merge onto Rainbow Road. (From Fulford Harbour, head north on Fulford-Ganges Road for 14 km/8.7 mi. Turn left on Lower Ganges Road and left on Rainbow Road.) Where Rainbow dead-ends, bear left on Collins Road. In 700 m (0.4 mi), park in a small pullout on the right, opposite the trailhead.

92

HWMET'UTSUM (MOUNT MAXWELL)

Distance: 6.5 km (4 mi)
Time: 3 hours (lollipop)
Elevation gain: 280 m (920 ft)
High point: 593 m (1,945 ft)
Season: All year

Quality: ★★★
Difficulty: ■
Maps: NTS 92-B/13 Duncan, 92-B/14 Mayne Island
Trailhead: 48°48′19″ N, 123°29′42″ W

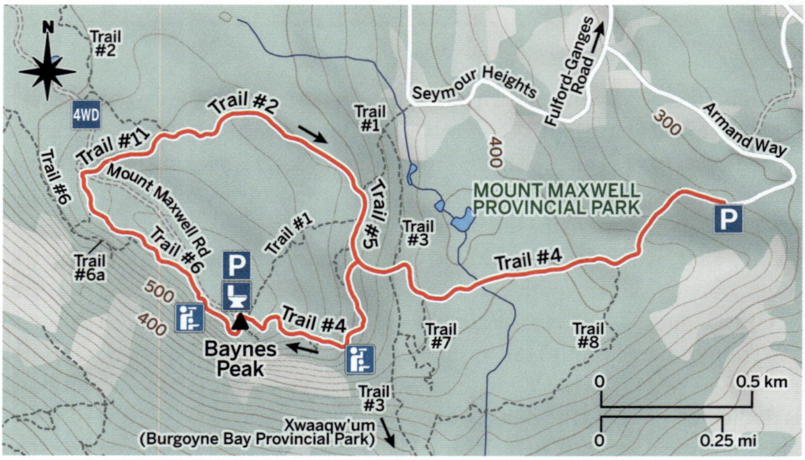

A SACRED MOUNTAIN that looms large in the past, present, and future of the Quw'utsun Nation, Hwmet'utsum on Saltspring Island overlooks a storied landscape. More recently known as Mount Maxwell, Hwmet'utsum (meaning "bent over place" in the Hul'q'umi'num' language) and its surrounds are central to Quw'utsun cultural practices, oral traditions, and resource harvesting.

Take a hike in the territories of the Quw'utsun, Semiahmoo (se'mya'me), Tsawwassen (scəw̓aθən), and W̱SÁNEĆ peoples, and enjoy the magnificent view from the top. Set off west on the Armand Way Trail (Trail #4). After entering Mount Maxwell Provincial Park, stay right at junctions with the Sunshine Trail (#8) and Little View Trail (#7). Cross the Girlfriend Trail (#3).

Keep left at a junction with the Link Trail (#5) to stick with Trail #4 and begin a clockwise loop. Soon enough, you encounter wow views of Fulford Harbour (Hwnen'uts in Hul'q'umi'num'; W̱ENÁ¸NEĆ in SENĆOŦEN, the language of the W̱SÁNEĆ), the southernmost Gulf Islands (ṮEṮÁĆES, "relatives of the deep," in SENĆOŦEN), and Mount Baker (ĆEḴ PEK SṈÁNET). Trail #4 swings right to meet the Mountain Trail (#1) near a parking lot.

A view of ṮEṮÁĆES and the Salish Sea from the Armand Way Trail.

Find the conglomerate summit of Baynes Peak (1 hour up; 48°48′05″ N, 123°31′02″ W) above fenced-off cliff. Near Bold Bluff Point (Shhwehwa'uselu in Hul'q'umi'num'), to the southwest, is a fabled home of the Thunderbird (S'hwa'hwa'us). Look out at Burgoyne Bay (Xwaaqw'um, "female merganser duck place," in Hul'q'umi'num'; XOEȻȻEM in SENĆOŦEN) and Maple Bay (Hwtl'upnets in Hul'q'umi'num') in Sansum Narrows.

Follow the fence west to pick up the Rim Trail (#6). Go right to cross Mount Maxwell Road on the Brian Trail (#11). Take the Gary Trail (#2) right to the Link Trail (#5), ignoring Trail #1 on the left and then the right. Upon reaching Trail #4, turn left to return to Armand Way.

The SENĆOŦEN name for Saltspring Island is ĆUÁN.

The Stqeeye' Learning Society works to preserve the Quw'utsun village site, restore wetlands, and connect Indigenous youth to the land at Xwaaqw'um.

GETTING THERE

Transit: From the Fulford Harbour ferry terminal or the Ganges visitor centre, take Salt Spring Island Transit Bus 2 (Fulford Harbour) to Burgoyne Bay Road. Walk west on Burgoyne Bay Road for 1.5 km (0.9 mi) to the parking lot in Burgoyne Bay Provincial Park. Hike up the Girlfriend Trail (#3).

Vehicle: B.C. Ferries offers daily sailings to Saltspring Island via three routes: Tsawwassen–Long Harbour, Swartz Bay–Fulford Harbour, and Crofton–Vesuvius Bay. From the Long Harbour ferry terminal, head west on Long Harbour Road. At T-junctions, turn left on Upper Ganges Road and right on Lower Ganges Road. Keep right to continue on Fulford-Ganges Road for 6 km (3.7 mi). Turn right on Dukes Road. (From Fulford Harbour, head north on Fulford-Ganges Road for 8 km/5 mi. Turn left on Dukes Road.) Go left on Seymour Heights and left on Armand Way. Park at the cul-de-sac.

93
MOUNT WORK

Distance: 6 km (3.7 mi)
Time: 3 hours (out and back)
Elevation gain: 310 m (1,020 ft)
High point: 449 m (1,470 ft)
Season: Most of the year

Quality: ★★
Difficulty: ●
Maps: NTS 92-B/11 Sidney
Trailhead: 48°33′00″ N, 123°29′24″ W

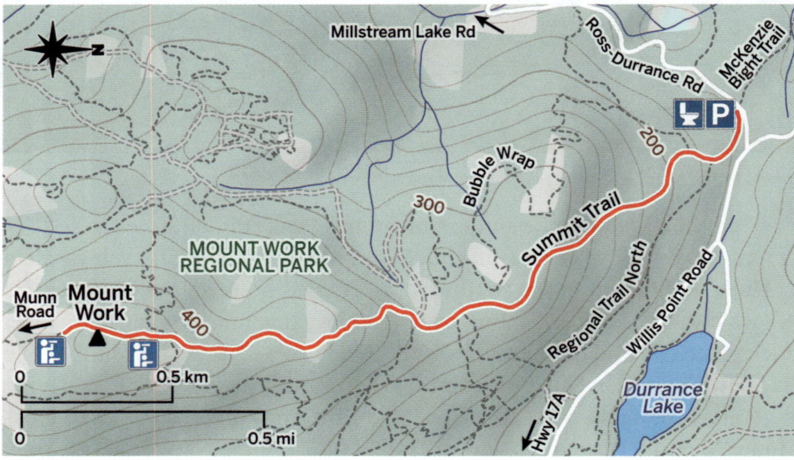

MOUNT WORK is gneiss—its exposed bedrock, that is—and popular with trail runners. The highest peak on the Saanich Peninsula is a monadnock (bedrock hill) that survived the erosion of the Fraser Glaciation, 15,000 years ago. It's in the Gowlland Range, part of the Insular Mountains, which run from Vancouver Island to Haida Gwaii.

From the map board at the large gravel parking lot (140 m/460 ft), tread the wide path into Mount Work Regional Park—in the territories of the Malahat (MÁLEXEȽ) and W̱SÁNEĆ peoples. In 180 m (200 yd), fork right for the Summit Trail. Bracket fungi, Oregon grape, and sword fern grow in the understory. As you ascend southward, the mixed forest thins out and arbutus trees, with their peeling cinnamon bark, increase in number.

Look for yellow plates to stay on the rocky and rooty trail, and ignore numerous side paths. In 1 hour, reach a broad viewpoint overlooking Jocelyn Hill (W̱QEN¸EL¸EȽ in SENĆOŦEN, the language of the W̱SÁNEĆ; Hike 94), Pease Lake, and Saanich Inlet, a.k.a. W̱SÁNEĆ Inlet, a glacially carved fjord, to the northwest. Kinnikinnick and hairy manzanita line the path.

A metal sign marks the view-challenged summit (48°31′51″ N, 123°28′49″ W), after 2.9 km (1.8 mi) on foot. Don't stop here—continue several minutes

A southward view of W̱SÁNEĆ from Mount Work.

south for mossy ground, open rock, and expansive views (1.5 hours up). Watch the ravens and bald eagles, and survey Skirt Mountain (SPAET), Mount Finlayson (S¸ELEꝀTEŁ; Hike 95), the anchorage of Royal Roads, the Salish Sea, and the snowy Olympic Mountains in Washington. Return the way you came.

Mount Work Regional Park sits on land subject to the 1852 Douglas Treaty with the Saanich Tribe—now represented by the Pauquachin (BOḰEĆEN), Tsartlip (W̱JOŁEŁP), Tsawout (SȾÁUTW̱), and Tseycum (W̱SIKEM) First Nations—covering North Saanich. The mountain is named for John Wark (ca. 1792–1861), a chief factor of the Hudson's Bay Company and legislative councillor for the British Crown colony of the Island of Vancouver and its Dependencies.

Legs need more work? After descending Mount Work, cross Ross-Durrance Road to enter Gowlland Tod Provincial Park (dogs must be leashed). Follow the trail down to McKenzie Bight (W̱MÍEŦEṈ, "place of deer") and back.

No camping, fires, flower picking, motorized vehicles, smoking, or vaping. Mount Work Regional Park is open from sunrise to sunset.

GETTING THERE

Vehicle: B.C. Ferries offers frequent sailings between Delta and North Saanich via the busy Tsawwassen–Swartz Bay route. From the Swartz Bay ferry terminal, head south on Highway 17 (Patricia Bay Highway) for 11 km (6.8 mi) to Central Saanich. Turn right on Mount Newton Cross Road, then left on Wallace Drive. Go left on Highway 17A (West Saanich Road) for 5 km (3.1 mi). In Saanich, turn right on Wallace Drive. Quickly make a left on Willis Point Road. Go left on Ross-Durrance Road. Enter Highlands and find Mount Work Regional Park's main entrance on the left (toilet available).

94

W̱QEN¸EL¸EŁ (JOCELYN HILL)

Distance: 9 km (5.6 mi)
Time: 4 hours (circuit)
Elevation gain: 220 m (720 ft)
High point: 434 m (1,420 ft)
Season: Most of the year

Quality: ★★★★
Difficulty: ●
Maps: NTS 92-B/12 Shawnigan Lake
Trailhead: 48°30′32″ N, 123°31′57″ W

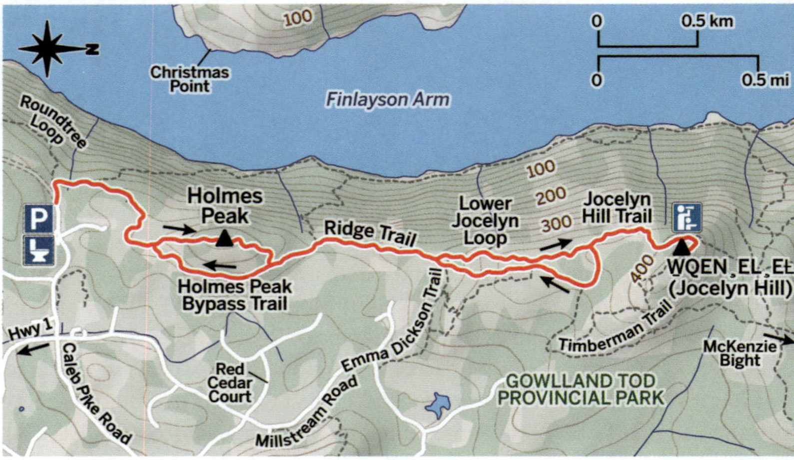

RISING IN the Gowlland Range, Jocelyn Hill overlooks the deep and steep-sided Finlayson Arm. Orcas, grey and pilot whales, and harbour seals frequent this unique fjord, which sees its anoxic (oxygen-deficient) bottom waters refreshed only once a year. In SENĆOŦEN, the language of the W̱SÁNEĆ people, the area of Jocelyn Hill and Repulse Rock, which protrudes from the inlet below, is known as W̱QEN¸EL¸EŁ.

Jocelyn Hill is the centrepiece of Gowlland Tod Provincial Park, created in 1995. From the Caleb Pike trailhead (230 m/755 ft), head north on the undulating Ridge Trail. Quickly take a right fork. Thereafter, keep left all the way to today's objective. Follow orange markers under two sets of transmission lines, with Scotch broom–infested corridors, and up the wooded ridge.

Spurning a bypass trail, surmount Holmes Peak (327 m/1,070 ft; 48°30′59″ N, 123°31′47″ W) in 1.3 km (0.8 mi). Pause and take a gander at the Warwick Range across Finlayson Arm, accompanied by the noise pollution of Malahat Drive. Continue north along the lovely, lovely ridge.

Watch your step on the bluffs. Stay on designated trails to preserve the sensitive habitat of the rare, rain-shadowed coastal Douglas-fir biogeoclimatic

Finlayson Arm, part of W̱SÁNEĆ Inlet, from Holmes Peak.

zone. Logged in the 1940s and '50s, the uplands are speckled with very gneiss outcrops adorned with arbutus (ḰEḰEYIȽĆ, a sacred tree to the W̱SÁNEĆ), hairy manzanita (an arbutus relative), shore pine, and Garry oak.

En route to the Lower Jocelyn Loop fork, you're treated to further rewarding views of Finlayson Arm. Stay left for the Jocelyn Hill Trail. The best vantages come before the summit, when you break out of the trees. The trail U-turns before arriving at the Jocelyn Hill viewpoint (2 hours up; 48°32′16″ N, 123°31′47″ W), off to the left, at the 4.4 km (2.7 mi) mark.

From the grassy, arbutus-fringed outcrop, gaze north up Squally Reach to the mouth of Saanich Inlet (W̱SÁNEĆ Inlet) and beyond to Saltspring Island (ĆUÁN). Retrace your steps to the Caleb Pike entrance. Vary portions of your return by taking the eastern branch of the Lower Jocelyn Loop and the Holmes Peak Bypass Trail. (Just don't descend the Timberman Trail or Emma Dickson Trail, which lead east and away from the ridge.)

Jocelyn Hill's name was formalized by a British admiralty chart in 1911. Gowlland Tod Provincial Park lies in the territories of the Malahat (MÁLEXEȽ) and W̱SÁNEĆ peoples and is covered by the 1852 Douglas Treaty for North Saanich. In SENĆOŦEN, W̱SÁNEĆ ("Emerging People") is not only the name of the Indigenous people of this land, but also that of the Saanich Peninsula.

GETTING THERE

Vehicle: B.C. Ferries offers frequent sailings between Delta and North Saanich via the busy Tsawwassen–Swartz Bay route. From the Swartz Bay ferry terminal, head south on Highway 17 (Patricia Bay Highway) for 25 km (15.5 mi) to Saanich. Take Exit 7. Keep right to join Trans-Canada Highway 1. In Langford, take Exit 14. Proceed north on Millstream Road to Highlands. In 6.5 km (4 mi), turn left on Caleb Pike Road and continue to Gowlland Tod Provincial Park's south entrance (toilet available).

95

S̨ELEꝀTEȽ (MOUNT FINLAYSON)

Distance: 7 km (4.3 mi)
Time: 3 hours (loop)
Elevation gain: 415 m (1,360 ft)
High point: 419 m (1,375 ft)
Season: Most of the year

Quality: ★★★
Difficulty: ◆
Maps: NTS 92-B/5 Sooke
Trailhead: 48°28′44″ N, 123°32′45″ W

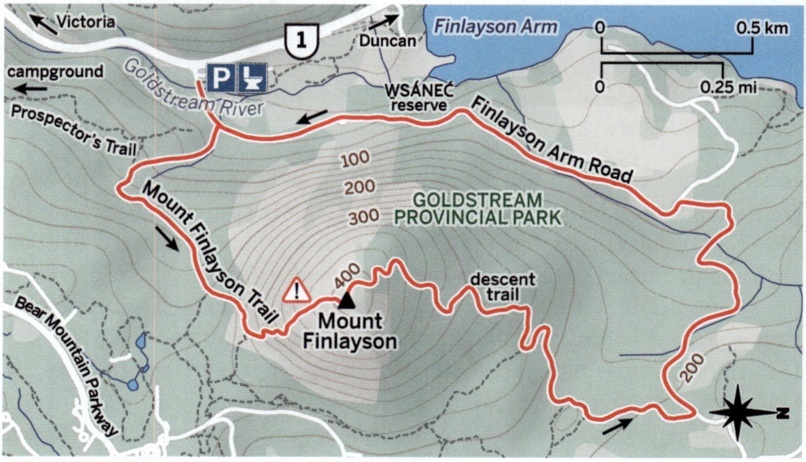

IN GEOMORPHOLOGICAL TERMS, Mount Finlayson is a roche moutonnée eroded by a passing glacier. In SENĆOŦEN, the language of the W̱SÁNEĆ people, the Mount Finlayson and Goldstream River area is known as S̨ELEꝀTEȽ. For hikers, this rounded peak in the Gowlland Range is the big draw in Goldstream Provincial Park, even though it was only added to the park in 1994.

This scrambly outing is not recommended for young kids or rainy days. From the day-use area, walk east on Finlayson Arm Road over the Goldstream River. Find the start of the steep Mount Finlayson Trail (and the end of the Prospector's Trail, from the campground) on the right.

Keeping left, ascend Finlayson's lower slopes. In the territories of the lək̓ʷəŋən, Malahat (MÁLEXEȽ), and W̱SÁNEĆ peoples, including the Esquimalt (Xwsepsum) and Songhees First Nations, head southeast and then northeast. After dropping to cross a creek, the path rockets up through the arbutus trees following orange bars. In a half-hour, reach the bluffs.

Get ready for some scrambly fun. Heeding arrows, head up the rock and traverse to the right. (Dangerous when wet!) Follow a crack up to a ramp that

Looking south to SPAET from the summit.

rises to the right, but cut back left before it tops out. Take note of the urban sprawl devouring Skirt Mountain (SPAET) to the south—where in 2006 a real estate developer destroyed a limestone cave, sacred to the Songhees and Tsartlip (W̱JOȽEȽP) First Nations, for a road.

Ascend more ramps to the right, and switchback up ledges and rocky slopes to the open summit (1 hour up; 48°28′58″ N, 123°32′18″ W), with its commemorative plaques, 1.7 km (1.1 mi) from the trailhead. A SENĆOŦEN name associated with the west face of Mount Finlayson is W̱QENNELEȽ. Along with PKOLS (Mount Douglas), Mount Finlayson is a boundary marker of the W̱SÁNEĆ ÁLEṈENEȻ (homeland). Scan for turkey vultures. Spy Mount Wells, another roche moutonnée, to the south.

Arrows point the way to the mellow second half of today's counterclockwise loop. Keep left on the descent trail as it zigzags 2.2 km (1.4 mi) north to Finlayson Arm Road. Hang a left and follow the quiet byroad for 3.1 km (1.9 mi) to the day-use area.

Established in 1958, Goldstream Provincial Park is home to Canada's other Niagara Falls and was the site of a gold rush in the mid-1800s.

GETTING THERE

Transit: From Langford Exchange, take Victoria Regional Transit Bus 58 (Goldstream Meadows) to Humpback Road at Rock Hill Place. Walk north on Golden Gate Road to enter the Goldstream Provincial Park campground. Keep right to find the Prospector's Trail in 700 m (0.4 mi) by campsite 18B. Hike 1.5 km (0.9 mi) northwest to join the Mount Finlayson Trail.

Vehicle: B.C. Ferries offers frequent sailings between Delta and North Saanich via the busy Tsawwassen–Swartz Bay route. From the Swartz Bay ferry terminal, head south on Highway 17 (Patricia Bay Highway) for 25 km (15.5 mi) to Saanich. Take Exit 7. Keep right to join Trans-Canada Highway 1 and continue north to Langford. In 13 km (8.1 mi), turn right on Finlayson Arm Road and park at the day-use area (toilet available).

96
MOUNT BRADEN

Distance: 16 km (9.9 mi)
Time: 6 hours (double lollipop)
Elevation gain: 340 m (1,115 ft)
High point: 473 m (1,550 ft)
Season: Most of the year

Quality: ★★★
Difficulty: ■
Maps: NTS 92-B/5 Sooke
Trailhead: 48°25′01″ N, 123°35′07″ W

RAMBLE ACROSS grassy balds, caress the peeling bark of arbutus trees, and peer over forested hills at the Salish Sea. If that sounds enticing, take a hike to Sugarloaf and Mount Braden in Sooke Hills Wilderness Regional Park and the territories of the Sc'ianew and T'Sou-ke First Nations.

From the Sooke Road parking lot (150 m/490 ft), start up the multi-use Veitch Creek Trail, quickly leaving the din of highway traffic behind. After crossing the Veitch Creek bridge, make a hard left on the Sugarloaf Summit Trail. Follow the well-signed path to the big boulder at the Townsend Trail junction, earning views of nearby Mount Helmcken from two balds en route.

Head left and over the summit of Sugarloaf (358 m/1,175 ft). Find a 270-degree panorama atop a sweet bluff (48°24′54″ N, 123°36′13″ W), 1.5 hours (4 km/2.5 mi) from the trailhead. Don't trundle rocks on sport climbers possibly below. Thunderbird Mountain stands out to the northwest.

Backtrack to the boulder junction. Take the Townsend Trail, keep left atop Townsend Hill, and drop down to the Veitch Creek Trail. Turn left on the easygoing road. Keep right at the Shephard Creek Trail junction. Go under a power line, bear left at a junction (with a watershed gate to the right), and find the signposted start of the Mount Braden Summit Loop Trail on the right.

Looking southwest to the Sooke Basin from the Sugarloaf viewpoint.

Head up the steep and rough path, negotiate deadfall, and scramble up outcrops on a Scotch broom-infested ridge. Yellow reflective plates nailed to rock help you stay on track. Pass a cairn and an erratic. A bump on the left offers a preview of the wide-angle perspective awaiting on the mountaintop.

Finally, 2.5 hours (6 km/3.7 mi) after leaving Sugarloaf, gain the exposed bedrock of the south ridge of Mount Braden (4 hours up; 48°26′43″ N, 123°35′53″ W). To the southwest, spot Mount Maguire (Hike 98) and Mount Manuel Quimper (Hike 97). Among the Olympic Mountains (sxʷƛ̓ayəm̓áɬ in nəxʷsƛ̓ay̓əmúcən, the Klallam language), Mount Angeles stands south by east across the Juan de Fuca Strait.

After a well-deserved lunch, follow the path past the treed summit. At a bald, the path goes hard left and down. Rise to bonus views from Castle Peak (455 m/1,490 ft), then begin the descent to Veitch Creek. Cross two bridges, with a left turn in between. Tread south on the Veitch Creek Trail. Return to the trailhead, 1.5 hours (6 km/3.7 mi) after departing Mount Braden.

GETTING THERE

Transit: From Langford Exchange, take Victoria Regional Transit Bus 61 or 65 (Sooke) to the 3770 block of Sooke Road. Carefully walk 600 m (0.4 mi) back to the parking lot on the narrow (and not so pleasant) shoulder.

Vehicle: B.C. Ferries offers frequent sailings between Delta and North Saanich via the busy Tsawwassen–Swartz Bay route. From the Swartz Bay ferry terminal, head south on Highway 17 (Patricia Bay Highway) for 25 km (15.5 mi) to Saanich. Take Exit 7 and keep right to go west on McKenzie Avenue for 1.8 km (1.1 mi). Use the right lane to join northbound Trans-Canada Highway 1 for 11 km (6.8 mi). In Langford, go left on West Shore Parkway for 4.2 km (2.6 mi). Turn right on Highway 14 (Sooke Road) and drive 3.3 km (2.1 mi) west to Metchosin. Turn right into the parking lot (toilet available).

97

MOUNT MANUEL QUIMPER

Distance: 12 km (7.5 mi)
Time: 4.5 hours (loop)
Elevation gain: 470 m (1,540 ft)
High point: 548 m (1,800 ft)
Season: Most of the year

Quality: ★★
Difficulty: ■
Maps: NTS 92-B/5 Sooke
Trailhead: 48°23′54″ N, 123°39′53″ W

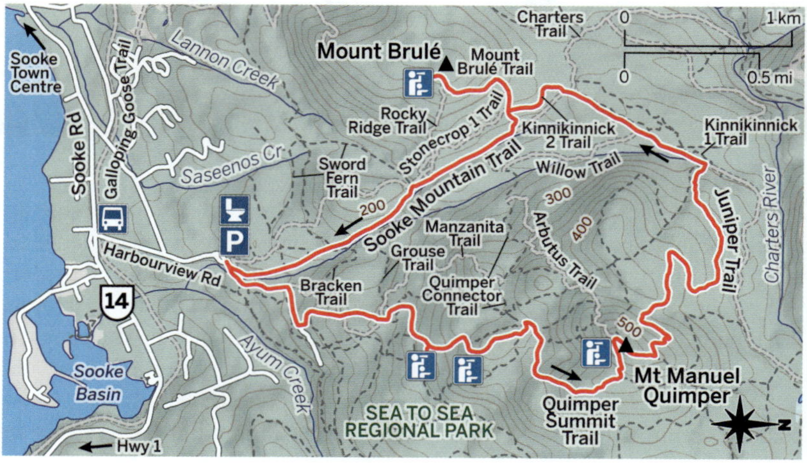

AN OLD FIRE LOOKOUT beckons atop Mount Manuel Quimper in the Sooke Hills. The mountain's namesake is Spanish naval officer Manuel Quimper Benítez del Pino, who charted the Juan de Fuca Strait in 1790 while in command of the *Princesa Real*, a captured British sloop.

Your mini-expedition begins at the Harbourview Road entrance of Sea to Sea Regional Park, located in the territories of the Sc'ianew and T'Sou-ke First Nations. Pass the trailhead kiosk (80 m/260 ft), and fork right to start up the Quimper Summit Trail, which is shared with horse riders and mountain bikers.

Steadily ascend for 4.2 km (2.6 mi), spurning the Bracken, Grouse, Quimper Connector, and Arbutus trails. Spy the Goodridge Islands from two midway viewpoints. You might startle a sooty grouse or vice versa en route to the summit of Mount Manuel Quimper (2 hours up; 48°25′11″ N, 123°39′32″ W).

Inside the fire tower, built in 1951, you'll find benches and windows but not much else. Survey the surrounds to spot Victoria (Matoolia in lək̓ʷəŋən, the language of the Esquimalt [Xwsepsum] and Songhees First Nations), Mount Maguire (Hike 98), Sooke Harbour (sú?əkʷ in nəxʷsƛ̓ay̓əmúcən, the Klallam language), and the Olympic Mountains (sxʷƛ̓ayəm̓áɬ).

The fire tower, built in 1951, on the summit.

Continue north on the Quimper Summit Trail to the next junction. Going left, descend the Juniper Trail (2.7 km/1.7 mi) and enjoy the winding single track. Take bypasses to avoid technical trail features meant to challenge mountain bikers. (Stay alert!) At the bottom, turn left on the Sooke Mountain Trail and follow this thoroughfare south to the map at the Charters Trail junction. Just ahead, take the Kinnikinnick 2 Trail on the right.

An hour past the fire lookout—and 1.5 km (0.9 mi) from the base of Juniper—arrive at the Mount Brulé Trail junction. It's worth a 30-minute side quest (700 m/0.4 mi one way) to unlock an additional elevated prospect. Therefore, head right (immediately forking right to skip the Stonecrop 1 Trail) and climb the rocky roadbed to the near-summit viewpoint on Mount Brulé (380 m/1,250 ft; 48°24′33″ N, 123°40′49″ W).

Drop back down the Mount Brulé Trail. Finish off Kinnikinnick 2 and turn right on the Sooke Mountain Trail to return to the parking lot.

GETTING THERE

Transit: From Langford Exchange, take Victoria Regional Transit Bus 61 or 65 (Sooke) to Sooke Road at Harbourview Road. Walk 700 m (0.4 mi) north on Harbourview, crossing the Galloping Goose Regional Trail, to the park gate.

Vehicle: B.C. Ferries offers frequent sailings between Delta and North Saanich via the busy Tsawwassen–Swartz Bay route. From the Swartz Bay ferry terminal, head south on Highway 17 (Patricia Bay Highway) for 25 km (15.5 mi) to Saanich. Take Exit 7 and keep right to go west on McKenzie Avenue for 1.8 km (1.1 mi). Use the right lane to join northbound Trans-Canada Highway 1 for 11 km (6.8 mi). In Langford, go left on West Shore Parkway for 4.2 km (2.6 mi). Turn right on Highway 14 (Sooke Road) and drive 13 km (8.1 mi) west to Sooke. Turn right on Harbourview Road and continue to the parking lot at the end (toilet available).

98

MOUNT MAGUIRE AND BABBINGTON HILL

Distance: 16 km (9.9 mi)
Time: 6 hours (circuit)
Elevation gain: 250 m (820 ft)
High point: 268 m (880 ft)
Season: All year

Quality: ★★★
Difficulty: ■
Maps: NTS 92-B/5 Sooke
Trailhead: 48°21′34″ N, 123°39′40″ W

MOUNT MAGUIRE is the highest point in East Sooke Regional Park. Babbington Hill, on the other hand, delivers a bigger view. Hit both of these humble summits and enjoy quiet woods on the crest of Vancouver Island's East Sooke Peninsula, in the territories of the Sc'ianew and T'Sou-ke First Nations.

From the parking lot (20 m/65 ft), head up the shady Anderson Cove Trail, watching for slugs underfoot. Keep right at signed junctions with the Babbington Hill, Interior, and Swamp Bypass trails. Cross a road (Copper Mine Trail) and spot your path continuing to the right.

Shortly thereafter, take the right turnoff for Mount Maguire. The path forks. Left goes to a bench viewpoint facing the Olympic Mountains (sxʷƛ̕ayəm̓áɬ in nəxʷsƛ̕ay̓əmúcən, the Klallam language) in Washington. Right leads to the treed summit (1.5 hours up; 48°21′13″ N, 123°41′07″ W), 4.3 km (2.7 mi) from the trailhead.

A view of xʷčiyánəxʷ and x̣ʷáyəŋ from Babbington Hill.

Next is the 5.8 km (3.6 mi) traverse to Babbington Hill. Return to the Anderson Cove Trail and backtrack to the Interior Trail junction, going right. Tackle lots of ups and downs. Turn left to briefly merge with the Parkheights Trail, then leave to the right, sticking with the Interior Trail. At a map post, go left. Then immediately keep right to spurn the Endurance Ridge Trail for the time being and begin a small counterclockwise loop.

At the Babbington Hill turnoff, go left. Take a right spur to the summit outcrop (2.5 hours from Mount Maguire; 228 m/750 ft; 48°19′55″ N, 123°39′30″ W), with its wooden sign. Follow the path to a grand viewpoint on a rock bluff. Look east-southeast to identify Becher Bay (xʷčiyánəxʷ in nəxʷsƛ̓ay̓əmúcən; W̱ĆIYÁNEW̱ in the SENĆOŦEN, the original language of the W̱SÁNEĆ people), the Bedford Islands, and the lighthouse at Race Rocks (x̣ʷáyəŋ in nəxʷsƛ̓ay̓əmúcən; X̱EL¸LEṈ in SENĆOŦEN; both meaning "swift water").

The trailhead is 1.5 hours (5.7 km/3.5 mi) away. Leave the summit and continue on the little loop. Descend to the Endurance Ridge Trail and go left to return to the Interior Trail; follow the latter back to the Parkheights Trail. At the T-junction, turn right. Quickly make a left on the Babbington Hill Trail. A final right on the Anderson Cove Trail delivers you back to the parking lot.

GETTING THERE

Transit: From Sooke Town Centre, take Victoria Regional Transit Bus 64 (East Sooke) to the 5900 block of East Sooke Road (weekdays only, infrequent service). Alternatively, arrange for Orange Taxi to shuttle you between Sooke and the park.

Vehicle: B.C. Ferries offers frequent sailings between Delta and North Saanich via the Tsawwassen–Swartz Bay route. From the Swartz Bay terminal, head south on Highway 17 (Patricia Bay Highway) for 25 km (15.5 mi) to Saanich. Take Exit 7 and keep right to go west on McKenzie Avenue for 1.8 km (1.1 mi). Use the right lane to join northbound Trans-Canada Highway 1 for 11 km (6.8 mi). In Langford, go left on West Shore Parkway for 4.2 km (2.6 mi). Turn right on Highway 14 (Sooke Road) and drive 8.9 km (5.5 mi) west to Sooke. Turn right for Gillespie Road, go under the overpass, and continue on Gillespie for 6 km (3.7 mi). Make a right on East Sooke Road. In 1.9 km (1.2 mi), turn left into the Anderson Cove parking lot (toilet available).

99

PINE AND CEDAR LAKES TRAIL

Distance: 12 km (7.5 mi)
Time: 5 hours (circuit)
Elevation gain: 460 m (1,510 ft)
High point: 560 m (1,840 ft)
Season: Most of the year

Quality: ★★
Difficulty: ■
Maps: USGS Bellingham South; Square One Chuckanut Recreation Area
Trailhead: 48°41′26″ N, 122°27′10″ W

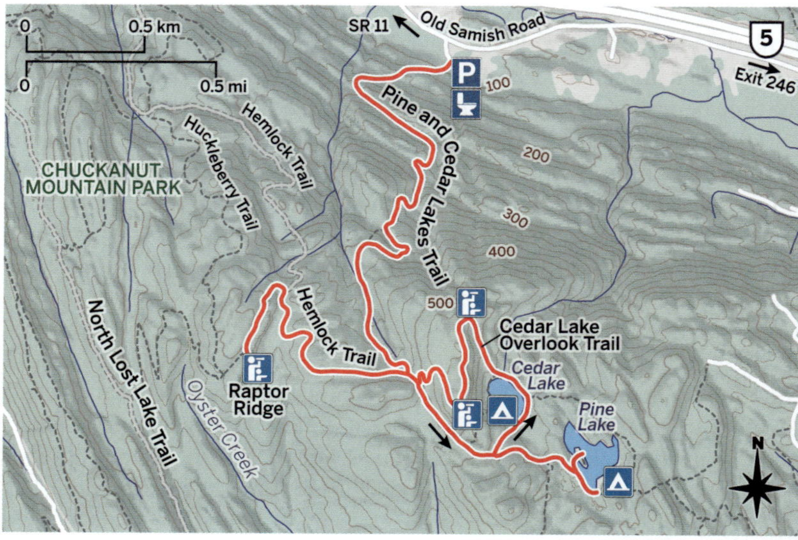

FOR SOME Metro Vancouver residents, Bellingham is synonymous with cross-border shopping and hazy memories of a pizza buffet. However, locals know there's decent hiking immediately south of the 96,000-strong "City of Subdued Excitement"—in the sandstone foothills of Chuckanut Mountain. One pleasant shoulder-season hike is the Pine and Cedar Lakes Trail, which begins within earshot of Interstate 5 but finds peace and quiet in the woods. Located in Whatcom County, the trail passes through Larrabee State Park, Chuckanut Mountain Park, and the Whatcom Wildlife Area.

From the parking area (100 m/330 ft), the multi-use trail winds south for 2.6 km (1.6 mi) to a junction with the Hemlock Trail (490 m/1,610 ft). For now, go left (east) to stay on the Pine and Cedar Lakes Trail. Ignore a few paths on the left (for Cedar Lake) and follow boardwalks to one or both of the backcountry campsites at Pine Lake (1.5 hours up; 480 m/1,575 ft; 48°40′32″ N, 122°26′43″ W), 3.5 km (2.2 mi) in.

Double back to the last Cedar Lake turnoff, and keep right to round the northeast side of the lake. Turn right on the Cedar Lake Overlook Trail to score a few viewpoints. The best vista showcases majestic Mount Baker (Kwelshan in Xwlemi Chosen, the language of the Lummi [Lhaq'temish] Nation) and Twin Sisters Mountain (Kwetl'kwítl' Smánit, "red mountain," in Lhéchelesem to the Nooksack [Noxws'á?aq] Tribe). Past the high point, follow switchbacks down to the Pine and Cedar Lakes Trail and head back to the Hemlock Trail junction.

Walking the planks at Pine Lake.

Before you drop down to the trailhead, a side trip to Raptor Ridge is in order. About 1 km (0.6 mi) west on the Hemlock Trail, turn left on the Raptor Ridge Trail and soon left again for the signed viewpoint. This lovely, rocky spot overlooks the forested valley of Oyster Creek. Now you can retrace your steps to the parking area.

Pine Lake and Cedar Lake are both stocked with rainbow and cutthroat trout. Dogs must be leashed. No fires or motorized vehicles.

GETTING THERE

Vehicle: On Interstate 5, south of Bellingham—and 49 km (30 mi) south of the Canada-U.S. border—take Exit 246 (North Lake Samish Drive). From either off-ramp, turn right. On the south side of the freeway overpass, turn west on Old Samish Road. Drive 4.2 km (2.6 mi) to the Pine and Cedar Lakes trailhead on your left (toilet available). Discover Pass required (purchase in advance).

100

OYSTER DOME

Distance: 13 km (8.1 mi)
Time: 6 hours (lollipop)
Elevation gain: 570 m (1,870 ft)
High point: 616 m (2,020 ft)
Season: Most of the year

Quality: ★★★
Difficulty: ■
Maps: USGS Bellingham South, Bow; Square One Chuckanut Recreation Area
Trailhead: 48°36′31″ N, 122°26′00″ W

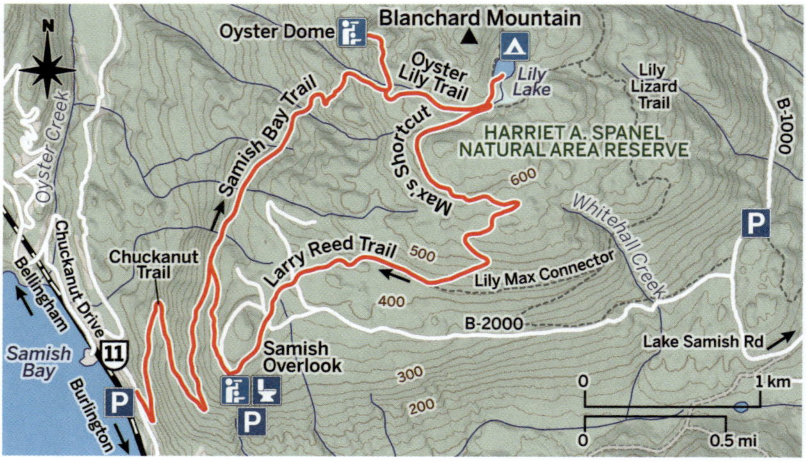

DON'T HAVE three months to spare? Get a quick taste of the long-distance Pacific Northwest Trail (PNT)—and an excellent south-of-the-border perspective of the Salish Sea—on Blanchard Mountain, one of the hills that make up Chuckanut Mountain in Skagit County. Our enjoyable loop tours the Harriet A. Spanel Natural Area Reserve in Blanchard State Forest, managed by the Washington State Department of Natural Resources.

From EMS Checkpoint Z (50 m/160 ft), hit the busy Chuckanut Trail, switchbacking up the steep hillside east of Chuckanut Drive and earning a view of Samish Bay. In 2.6 km (1.6 mi), leave the PNT for the time being; turn left on the Samish Bay Trail (2.3 km/1.4 mi), which starts out mellow before making a sweat-inducing ascent to the Oyster Dome turnoff.

Head left and up to a rocky clifftop (2.5 hours up; 48°37′37″ N, 122°24′54″ W) with a dynamite view of the San Juan Islands. Look across Samish Bay to Mount Erie (Hike 101) on Fidalgo Island, Guemes Island (Qweng7qwengila7—"lots of dogs," a reference to the Coast Salish woolly dog, now extinct—in Xws7ámeshqen, the language of the Samish [Xws7ámesh] Nation), Cypress Island (Séyenglhnelh, "Blood Across Neck Island"), and Lummi Peak on

Samish Bay from the clifftop viewpoint.

Lummi Island (Smemiekw in Xwlemi Chosen, the language the Lummi [Lhaq'temish] Nation). Keep back from the edge.

After lunch, return to the last junction and turn left (east) on the Oyster Lily Trail (600 m/0.4 mi). Go left for a brief side trip to Lily Lake, where a campground (no toilet) awaits. Backtrack to the junction and continue east—briefly. With a quick right turn, rejoin the PNT and head south on quiet Max's Shortcut (2.4 km/1.5 mi). Spurn the Acorn Trail, which goes right to the BL-1616 logging road. Bear right on the Larry Reed Trail (1.4 km/0.9 mi), which crosses a clear-cut.

Farmland on the Samish River floodplain fills the scene to the south of the drive-up Samish Overlook (48°36′35″ N, 122°25′34″ W), which has toilets. Find the Chuckanut Trail to the right. It's just 3.2 km (2 mi) down to the trailhead.

Unlike the Mexico-to-Canada Pacific Crest Trail, the PNT hasn't been the subject of a *New York Times* number one bestseller and a Hollywood film adaptation. However, the 1,900 km (1,200 mi) footpath traversing Montana, Idaho, and Washington, from the Continental Divide to the Pacific Ocean, beckons backpackers looking for an off-the-beaten path adventure.

After years of campaigning, Conservation Northwest and fellow advocates celebrated the protection of Blanchard Mountain's core from logging in 2019.

GETTING THERE

Vehicle: On Interstate 5 in Bellingham, 41 km (25 mi) south of the Canada-U.S. border, take Exit 250. Head west on State Route 11 (Old Fairhaven Parkway). Sticking with SR 11, turn left on 12th Street and bear left on Chuckanut Drive. Follow SR 11 south to find the trailhead on the east roadside, just before milepost 10. Park on the west shoulder. Discover Pass required (buy in advance).

101

MOUNT ERIE

Distance: 7.5 km (4.7 mi)
Time: 4 hours (reverse lollipop)
Elevation gain: 265 m (870 ft)
High point: 388 m (1,275 ft)
Season: All year

Quality: ★★
Difficulty: ●
Maps: USGS Anacortes South, Deception Pass; Green Trails 41S Deception Pass
Trailhead: 48°28′03″ N, 122°37′46″ W

SURE, SIGHTSEERS drive all the way up to the modest summit of Mount Erie, but the grand views are even more satisfying after a couple of hours of hiking. The scenery includes volcanoes of the North Cascades, Puget Sound (x̌ʷəlč, "saltwater," in txʷəlšucid, the language of the Puyallup [spuyaləpabš] Tribe), and the Olympic Mountains—not to mention hawks and rock climbers.

Mount Erie lies in the Anacortes Community Forest Lands, owned by the City of Anacortes on Fidalgo Island, in Treaty of Point Elliott territory. In the 1980s, a public outcry halted clear-cutting in the forest. Since the creation of a conservation easement program in 1998, donors have protected much of the area from logging and mining.

It's easy to get off track in the labyrinth of numbered trails, so pay close attention to markers. From the trailhead kiosk (120 m/390 ft), strike off on Trail 215 (Sugarloaf Trail). Stay right at junctions with Trails 320 and 225.

Go left on Trail 227, right on Trail 226, and left on Trail 238 to reach the delectable viewpoint and grassy ledges atop Sugarloaf (270 m/890 ft), the day's appetizer, in 30 minutes. Spot your entree, Mount Erie, and Skagit Bay to the south, as well as jagged Whitehorse Mountain (Subalihalli in

Sugarloaf in the Anacortes Community Forest Lands.

dxʷləšucid, the dialect of the Sauk-Suiattle [Sah-ku-méhu] Tribe) and Three Fingers (Gues-talb) to the east.

Briefly backtrack and turn left (west) on Trail 228 and left on Trail 215 to hit Mount Erie Road. Follow the road left momentarily, taking a left on Trail 26. Go right on Trail 216 (Mount Erie Summit Trail). Ascend the switchbacking, steepening path for 1.4 km (0.9 mi) to Mount Erie's car-park summit (2 hours up; 48°27′13″ N, 122°37′36″ W).

Take your pick of eye-filling viewpoints. Spot Mount Baker (təqʷúbəʔ) and Glacier Peak (Tda-ko-buh-ba) to the east—and even Mount Rainier (təqʷuʔmaʔ in txʷəlšucid), much farther, to the south. All three are "very high threat" stratovolcanoes, in terms of risk to people and property, according to a 2018 U.S. Geological Survey report.

After lunch, double back on Trail 216, but go right (east) on Trail 207 (not left on Trail 26) to vary your return. Keep right at the Trail 230 junction and turn left on Trail 21. Follow the double track for 1.4 km (0.9 mi), then make a left on Trail 320 and a right on Trail 215 to re-emerge at the trailhead.

The Friends of the Anacortes Community Forest Lands and Skagit Land Trust deserve credit for preserving these woods and their all-season, multi-use trails. Dogs must be leashed and dog poop carried out.

GETTING THERE

Vehicle: On Interstate 5 in Burlington, 75 km (47 mi) south of the Canada-U.S. border, take Exit 230. Head west on State Route 20 to Anacortes. Use the left lane at the SR 20 Spur junction to stay on the mainline. In 2.9 km (1.8 mi), turn right on Campbell Lake Road. Stay right at the Sharpe Road intersection to continue onto Heart Lake Road. Take the right fork, avoiding Rosario Road. Go right at the Mount Erie viewpoint sign onto Ray Auld Drive. Don't turn right on Mount Erie Road; use the parking lot straight ahead. Warning: Vehicle break-ins have been reported here.

102

SX'Á7LEX' (MOUNT CONSTITUTION)

Distance: 13.5 km (8.4 mi)
Time: 6 hours (loop)
Elevation gain: 460 m (1,510 ft)
High point: 734 m (2,405 ft)
Season: Most of the year

Quality: ★★★
Difficulty: ■
Maps: USGS Mount Constitution
Trailhead: 48°39′17″ N, 122°49′08″ W

STARING AT each other across Mountain Lake, Mount Constitution and Mount Pickett are decidedly different in character. Sure, both peaks are found in Moran State Park on Orcas Island. However, the bustling Mount Constitution, the tallest mountain in the San Juan Islands, has a road to its top, which boasts panoramic views. Meanwhile, quieter Mount Pickett has a treed summit and is largely protected by a natural area preserve.

Our grand tour takes in both mountains on the island known as Sx'wálex' ("scattered reef netting") in Xws7ámeshqen, the language of the Samish (Xws7ámesh) Nation. The Xws7ámeshqen name for Mount Constitution is Sx'á7lex'. Begin by the Mountain Lake picnic shelter (280 m/920 ft) and set off on the Little Summit Trail. In 1.9 km (1.2 mi), go right at a junction to bypass Little Summit and continue north for 3.2 km (2 mi).

As the trail gains elevation on the east side of False Summit, bluffs afford a vantage of Mount Pickett across gleaming Mountain Lake. Snow-capped Mount Baker (ĆEḴ PEK SṈÁNET in SENĆOŦEN to the W̱SÁNEĆ people; swáʔləx̣ in nəxʷsƛ̓ay̓əmúcən, the Klallam language) looms in the background.

Mount Pickett and Mountain Lake from the Little Summit Trail.

Stay right at the Cold Springs Trail junction, pass Summit Lake, and earn more Salish Sea views en route to the high point of our clockwise loop.

Sx'á7lex' is crowned by a medieval-style stone tower (2 hours up; 48°40′39″ N, 122°49′52″ W). Designed by Seattle architect Ellsworth Storey, it was built in 1936 by the Great Depression–era Civilian Conservation Corps. Up top, five photo plaques identify landmarks in sight, including Twin Sisters Mountain (Kwetl'kwítl' Smánit in Lhéchelesem to the Nooksack [Noxws'á?aq] Tribe) and Lummi Island (Smemiekw in Xwlemi Chosen to the Lummi [Lhaq'temish] Nation).

Cross the parking lot and descend the Mount Constitution Trail for 2.4 km (1.5 mi) to Twin Lakes, our loop's midpoint. Keep right at Big Twin Lake (336 m/1,103 ft) and Little Twin Lake—but spurn a rightward path to Mountain Lake—to pick up Mount Pickett Road.

In 2.4 km (1.5 mi), the pleasant forest walk leads southeast over Mount Pickett's low-key summit (536 m/1,757 ft; 48°40′00″ N, 122°48′00″ W). Stay right at all junctions until going left on the Mountain Lake Loop Trail. Thereafter, keep right to pass below the Mountain Lake dam and follow the lake loop back to the parking area.

Dogs must be leashed. No hunting or shooting. Most of the described loop is shared with mountain bikers from September to May.

GETTING THERE

Vehicle: Washington State Ferries offers daily service between Anacortes and Orcas Island. From the Orcas Island ferry dock, go left on Orcas Road and drive north for 13 km (8.1 mi) to Eastsound. Turn right on Main Street, which becomes Crescent Beach Drive. Hang a right on Olga Road. After passing Cascade Lake, go left on Mount Constitution Road. Take the right-hand turnoff to arrive at the Mountain Lake parking area (toilet available). Discover Pass required (purchase in advance).

103
HELIOTROPE RIDGE TRAIL

Distance: 8 km (5 mi)
Time: 4 hours (out and back)
Elevation gain: 490 m (1,610 ft)
High point: 1,600 m (5,250 ft)
Season: July to September

Quality: ★★★★★
Difficulty: ■
Maps: USGS Groat Mountain, Mount Baker; Green Trails 13SX Mount Baker Wilderness
Trailhead: 48°48′08″ N, 121°53′44″ W

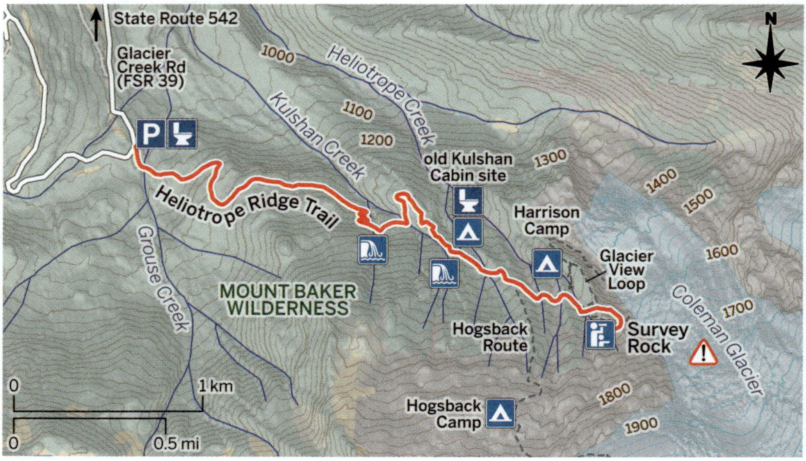

HIKE THE Heliotrope Ridge Trail to be dazzled by the imposing seracs and crevasses of the Coleman Glacier and the radiant blooms of alpine wildflowers. You'll join mountaineers tackling the Coleman-Deming route, the most popular way up Mount Baker. The active stratovolcano is known as Kweq' Smánit ("white mountain") in Lhéchelesem to the Nooksack (Noxws'áʔaq) Tribe and təqʷúbəʔ ("permanently snow-covered mountain") in dxʷləšucid to the Skagit (sqáǰət) people.

From the trailhead (1,110 m/3,640 ft), take a bridge over Grouse Creek and enter the Mount Baker Wilderness. Cross two branches of Kulshan Creek, earning waterfall sightings. Stream levels can rise dramatically during the day—approach fords with caution. In 1 hour, pass a toilet and campsites.

At a junction (1,520 m/4,990 ft; 48°47′43″ N, 121°52′04″ W) between the forks of Heliotrope Creek, the trail splits into the Glacier View Loop (left) for hikers and Hogsback Route (right) for climbers. Choose the left option. Thereafter, spurn leftward paths to Harrison Camp. Tackle the trickiest ford. Crest a wooded moraine and follow it upward, keeping away from the overhanging edge and feeling awestruck by the Coleman Glacier icefall.

The Coleman Glacier icefall from the Glacier View Loop.

Spot Survey Rock up the ridge, pass to its left, and surmount its far side to reach the viewpoint (2 hours up; 48°47′37″ N, 121°51′42″ W). Heliotrope Ridge rises south of your columnar-jointed perch; Chromatic Moraine lies to the north. Peer northwest at the valley of Glacier Creek (Nuxwchx̲áchu, "always has a lake," in Lhéchelesem), a tributary of the North Fork Nooksack River (Chuw7álich). Look for ice climbers digging their ice tools and crampons into the icefall. Retrace your steps to the trailhead.

If the Heliotrope Creek crossing proves too difficult or unsafe, the Hogsback Route offers an alternative destination for hikers. From Hogsback Camp, most mountaineers ascend the Coleman Glacier and Roman Headwall to reach Grant Peak (3,286 m/10,781 ft), the summit of Mount Baker. Leave the glacier travel to properly equipped and experienced mountaineers.

The Heliotrope Ridge Trail lies in Mount Baker–Snoqualmie National Forest. Wilderness regulations stipulate a maximum party size of 12. Visitors are asked to use blue bags (available at the trailhead) to collect, pack out, and dispose of solid human and dog waste (in trash bins, not vault toilets). If you encounter a Washington Trails Association work party doing maintenance, please thank the volunteers.

GETTING THERE

Vehicle: From the Sumas border crossing, head south on State Route 9 (Cherry Street). Turn left on SR 547 (Front Street). Follow SR 547 for 17 km (10.6 mi) to a roundabout. Take the second exit. Continue east on SR 542 (Mount Baker Highway). In 17 km (10.6 mi), visit the Glacier Public Service Center (10091 Mount Baker Highway) on the right and buy a National Forest Recreation Pass. Continue 1 km (0.6 mi) on SR 542. Turn right on Glacier Creek Road (Forest Service Road 39), which turns to gravel (2WD). (Check road conditions before you go—FSR 39 is prone to washouts.) Park at the Heliotrope Ridge trailhead (toilet available) on the left in 13 km (8.1 mi).

104
YELLOW ASTER BUTTE

Distance: 13 km (8.1 mi)
Time: 6.5 hours (out and back)
Elevation gain: 770 m (2,530 ft)
High point: 1,902 m (6,240 ft)
Season: July to October

Quality: ★★★★★
Difficulty: ◆
Maps: USGS Mount Larrabee; Green Trails 13SX Mount Baker Wilderness
Trailhead: 48°56′36″ N, 121°39′46″ W

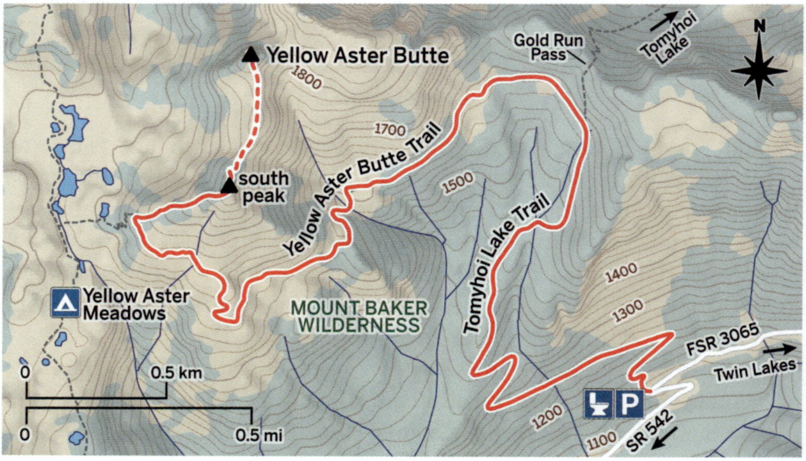

YELLOW ASTER BUTTE has it all: a rich profusion of wildflowers, berries, and alpine views—and a summit scramble to boot. But a butte it is not.

Starting on the Tomyhoi Lake Trail (1,130 m/3,710 ft), switchback up an avalanche path with thimbleberries. Enter the forest and the Mount Baker Wilderness (maximum party size: 12), gradually ascending west and then north.

Trading woods for meadows, reach a fork (48°57′07″ N, 121°39′56″ W) after 1 hour of hiking. Go left on the Yellow Aster Butte Trail to contour around the head of a scenic bowl. (The Tomyhoi Lake Trail continues right, climbing over Gold Run Pass and dropping to Coyote Flats and Tomyhoi Lake.)

Gaze upon American bistort, edible thistle, fireweed, green false hellebore, red paintbrush, subalpine daisy, western pasqueflower, lots of bees and blueberries (save some for the bears), perhaps a sooty grouse, and of course the glory of the North Cascades. Traverse west and cross a couple of creeks (snow lingers into late summer). Prepare to be amazed by the magical tarns of Yellow Aster Meadows, where camping is allowed on snow, rock, or bare ground. Leave No Trace practices are a must!

At 5.7 km (3.5 mi) from the trailhead, go right at an unsigned junction (48°56′57″ N, 121°41′16″ W) and head steeply up the meadowy ridge to

Ridge walking on Yellow Aster Butte.

the south peak (1,870 m/6,140 ft). Savour the splendid panorama: Tomyhoi Peak (Pút-lush-go-hap in Lhéchelesem, the language of the Nooksack [Noxws'á?aq] Tribe), Canadian and American Border Peaks, Mount Larrabee, Goat Mountain (Yi7íman), Mount Shuksan (Shéqsan), and Mount Baker (Kweq' Smánit in Lhéchelesem; Kwelxá:lxw in Halq'eméylem, the language of the Stó:lō people).

The horn rising 500 m (0.3 mi) north is Yellow Aster Butte's true summit (3 hours up; 48°57′16″ N, 121°40′56″ W). The easy scramble (best left to experienced hikers) entails a highly enjoyable ridge walk. Watch your step on the steep bits at both ends. From the rocky perch, peer down at Tomyhoi Lake. Retrace your steps to Forest Service Road 3065.

Visitors are asked to use blue bags (available at the trailhead) to collect, pack out, and dispose of solid human and dog waste (in trash bins, not vault toilets).

Camping is prohibited within 1.6 km (1 mi) of the Yellow Aster Butte Trail, except at the tarns. No bikes, drones, fires, snowmobiles, or trail shortcutting.

GETTING THERE

Vehicle: From the Sumas border crossing, head south on State Route 9 (Cherry Street). Turn left on SR 547 (Front Street). Follow SR 547 for 17 km (10.6 mi) to a roundabout. Take the second exit. Continue east on SR 542 (Mount Baker Highway). In 17 km (10.6 mi), visit the Glacier Public Service Center (10091 Mount Baker Highway) on the right and buy a National Forest Recreation Pass. Continue 20 km (12.4 mi) on SR 542. Turn left on Twin Lakes Road (Forest Service Road 3065). Drive 7 km (4.3 mi) on rough gravel (2WD) to the Tomyhoi Lake–Yellow Aster Butte trailhead and find roadside parking (toilet available).

105

CHAIN LAKES TRAIL

Distance: 11.5 km (7.1 mi)
Time: 5.5 hours (loop)
Elevation gain: 375 m (1,230 ft)
High point: 1,640 m (5,380 ft)
Season: July to October

Quality: ★★★★★
Difficulty: ■
Maps: USGS Shuksan Arm; Green Trails 13SX Mount Baker Wilderness
Trailhead: 48°50′48″ N, 121°41′31″ W

DELIVERING POSTCARD mountainscapes at every turn, the Chain Lakes Trail enters the Mount Baker Wilderness, within Mount Baker–Snoqualmie National Forest. Wilderness regulations limit the size of hiking parties to 12. Shortcutting trails is prohibited.

The hike to the Galena Chain Lakes begins at perhaps the most scenic parking lot in these parts. From Artist Point's vault toilets (1,555 m/5,100 ft), descend the upper section of the Wild Goose Trail (4 km/2.5 mi)—crossing the highway and passing the trail to Lake Ann—with jaggy Mount Shuksan (Shéqsan in Lhéchelesem, the language of the Nooksack [Noxws'áʔaq] Tribe) before you. Fancy cairns show the way.

At Terminal Lake, admire the reflection of Table Mountain (1,750 m/5,742 ft), the lava plateau you'll be circumnavigating. Head north to the nearby Austin Pass picnic area to chase Wild Goose's lower section. This leads to the Bagley Lakes trailhead and the start of the Chain Lakes Trail, in the glaciovolcanic wonderland of Heather Meadows.

Follow the throng of beaming hikers over the old Bagley Dam and head west above the shore of Lower Bagley Lake. At Upper Bagley Lake, a picturesque stone arch bridge spans the outlet.

Kweq' Smánit and Iceberg Lake from Hermann Saddle.

Stay on the north side to ascend a rockslide and switchbacks to Hermann Saddle (3 hours up; 48°51′32″ N, 121°42′36″ W), between Mazama Dome and Table Mountain, 3.8 km (2.4 mi) from the Bagley Lakes trailhead. Don't resist the urge to stop for lunch here—at the midpoint of our counterclockwise loop and just past the high point. Mount Baker (Kweq' Smánit) and the columnar andesite walls of Table Mountain dominate the eye-popping scene.

Then descend south and east, following the trail between Iceberg Lake (1,461 m/4,793 ft) and Hayes Lake, the two largest of the four Galena Chain Lakes. Keep left at two campsite junctions, visiting the west shore of Iceberg Lake (watch out for ice calving) and passing above Mazama Lake.

Turn left at the Ptarmigan Ridge Trail junction. (To extend your hike, go right and sample a bit of Ptarmigan Ridge.) The Chain Lakes Trail's busy home stretch slices across the plunging south slopes of Table Mountain to Artist Point. With rock ledges, waterfalls, a dramatic view of Shéqsan, and, if you're lucky, a dozen mountain goats grazing in the meadow far below, it's a spectacular and leisurely way to finish.

GETTING THERE

Vehicle: From the Sumas border crossing, head south on State Route 9 (Cherry Street). Turn left on SR 547 (Front Street). Follow SR 547 for 17 km (10.6 mi) to a roundabout. Take the second exit. Continue east on SR 542 (Mount Baker Highway). In 17 km (10.6 mi), visit the Glacier Public Service Center (10091 Mount Baker Highway) on the right and buy a National Forest Recreation Pass. Continue 39 km (24 mi) on SR 542, passing the Mount Baker ski area, to the huge Artist Point parking lot (toilet available) at the road's end. In winter and spring, Artist Point is buried in snow and closed to vehicles. The parking lot typically opens by early July and closes with the first major snowfall of autumn.

FACING: Sunrise on the Owl-Tenquille Traverse (see Hike 44).

ACKNOWLEDGEMENTS

THIS HIKING GUIDEBOOK is a labour of love. Without the help and generosity of many friends, trail partners, and drivers, I wouldn't have made it to 105 again.

Special thanks to Jaime Adams, Jasmine Alexander, Jacqueline Ashby, Mariam Besada, Esther Brysch, Julius Brysch, Stefan Brysch, Verena Brysch, Colleen Craig, Jason Cusator, Patrick Hui, Laszlo Hulicsko, Maria Kelly, Ella Li, Peter Locher, Louise Morrin, Carol-Anne Nicol, Rasham Rai, Saeed Refaei, Brianne Riehl, Craig Romano, Joan Septembre, Svetlana Tkacova, and Erin Watkins. Particular thanks to Simon Dyer, Matt Horne, Adil Kassam, Jeremy Moorhouse, and Nikki Way for accompanying me to the Sti'yen divide.

I'm grateful to Si:yémiya Albert (Sonny) McHalsie for writing a compelling foreword for the second edition and enlightening me about trails in S'ólh Téméxw. Kayla Brolly and Douglas Pope (North Shore Rescue Team Society) and Tori Ball (Canadian Parks and Wilderness Society–British Columbia) delighted me with their insightful contributions on safety and the environment, respectively. I'm indebted to T'uy't'tanat Cease Wyss, whose wonderful foreword opened the first edition.

It's always a pleasure to work with Rob Sanders, Jen Gauthier, Jennifer Croll, Meghan Vestad, Lara LeMoal, Fiona Siu, Megan Jones, Sydney Marchand, and the whole team at Greystone Books. My editor, Lucy Kenward, deserves special recognition for her unfailing support, sharp editing, and bottomless trail knowledge. The topographic maps are the result of another solid collaboration with Steve Chapman (Canadian Map Makers). Thanks to Cassie Markham, Andy Gibb, and Emma Levez Larocque for contributing photographs. Thanks also to Meg Yamamoto for the meticulous copy editing.

I'm thankful for conversations with Marilyn Baptiste, Karen Dunstan, Cecilia Point (who wrote the foreword for *Destination Hikes In and Around Southwestern British Columbia*), Nenh glunyadz Curtis Rattray (Tū'desē'cho Wholistic Indigenous Leadership Development Society), q̓wintkʷ Lauren Terbasket (Lower Similkameen Indian Band), Tiwenomot Mavis Underwood, and Chief Roger William (Xeni Gwet'in First Nations). Each generously shared insights—about unbreakable connections between people, lands, and waters—that stayed on my mind as I prepared the second edition.

This book could not have arrived at trail's end without the support of Ollie and Nicole. Lydia Kwa, Alexandra Oosterom, and Jamie Sullivan helped me find a path through the boulders. Thanks also to Ian Rocksborough-Smith, Aaron Pete (*Bigger Than Me Podcast*), Charles Demers, Cara Ng, Betsy Agar, Pieta Woolley, and David Newland; Mark Gifford, Sherry Yano, Hedy Rubin, Jen McCaffrey, Kimiko Johanson, Naxginkw Tara Marsden, the Indigenous Community Leaders Circle, and all my colleagues at the Real Estate Foundation of B.C.; and my fellow commissioners on the Skagit Environmental Endowment Commission.

I'd like to acknowledge the Wanderung Outdoor Recreation Society, along with Nature Vancouver (Vancouver Natural History Society), the North Shore Hikers Society, and NatureKids B.C. for enriching my outdoor adventures. I've appreciated help from Sandra Riches (AdventureSmart/B.C. Search and Rescue Association), Dave Scanlon and Kathleen Cheng (B.C. Mountaineering Club), Kristine Pérez de León (Hope Mountain Centre for Outdoor Learning Society), Eagle Walz (qathet Parks and Wilderness Society), and Louise Pedersen (Outdoor Recreation Council of B.C.).

Many other organizations deserve recognition for their conservation, education, inclusion, safety, or trail work, including the Alpine Club of Canada, Avalanche Canada, B.C. Marine Trails Network Association, B.C. Mobility Opportunities Society, B.C. Parks Foundation, Bowen Island Trail Society, Chilliwack Outdoor Club, Chilliwack Park Society, Colour the Trails, Conservation Northwest, Coquitlam Search and Rescue Society (long-time volunteer Michael Coyle contributed the safety essay for the first edition), Federation of Mountain Clubs of B.C., Friends of Cypress Provincial Park Society, Friends of Garibaldi Park Society, Friends of the Anacortes Community Forest Lands, Howe Sound Biosphere Region Initiative Society, Indigenous Life Sport Academy, Indigenous Women Outdoors Society (founder Welwál̓tnaat Myia Antone wrote the foreword for *Best Hikes and Nature Walks With Kids In and Around Southwestern British Columbia*), Knuckleheads Winter Recreation Association, Pacific Northwest Trail Association, Pemberton Valley Trails Association, Pemberton Wildlife Association, Ridge Meadows Outdoor Club, Salt Spring Island Conservancy, Skagit-Whatcom-Island Trail Maintenance

Organization, Stqeeye' Learning Society, Take a Hike Foundation, Tetrahedron Outdoor Club, Trails Society of B.C., Tsleil-Waututh (səlilwətaɬ) Nation Sacred Trust Initiative, Varsity Outdoor Club, Washington Trails Association, and Wilderness Committee.

As hikers, we owe much to the land and water stewardship—past, present, and future—of many First Nations and Tribes among the Coast Salish, St'át'imc, Nlaka'pamux, Syilx, Tŝilhqot'in, and Secwépemc peoples. Accordingly, we can give back to the Indigenous Peoples of the territories where we live and hike. Please consider donating to Indigenous-led organizations addressing community-identified priorities, such as Indigenous language revitalization, and learning about and supporting Land Back initiatives.

GIVE BACK

First Peoples' Cultural Foundation
fpcf.ca

Indigenous Women Outdoors Society
indigenouswomenoutdoors.ca

Kw'umut Lelum Foundation
klfoundation.ca

Lhaq'temish Foundation
lhaqtemishfoundation.org

PEPAKEṈ HÁUTW̱ Foundation
pepakenhautw.com

Sḵwx̱wú7mesh Líl̓wat7úl Cultural Centre
slcc.ca

Sníchim Foundation
snichimfoundation.ca

stal̓əw̓ Arts and Cultural Society
stalew.ca

Stqeeye' Learning Society
stqeeye.ca

W̱SÁNEĆ Lands Trust Society
wsanec.com

HIKES BY DISTANCE

Hike	Distance
33 Cirque Lake	4 km (2.5 mi)
86 shélkém (Mount Daniel)	4.5 km (2.8 mi)
91 Mount Erskine	5 km (3.1 mi)
93 Mount Work	6 km (3.7 mi)
67 Porcupine Rock	6 km (3.7 mi)
70 Wells Peak	6 km (3.7 mi)
36 Blackcomb Burn	6.2 km (3.9 mi)
57 79 Grind	6.5 km (4 mi)
92 Hwmet'utsum (Mount Maxwell)	6.5 km (4 mi)
22 Sea to Summit Trail	6.5 km (4 mi)
95 ȘELEꝀTEȽ (Mount Finlayson)	7 km (4.3 mi)
19 Deeks Bluff	7.5 km (4.7 mi)
101 Mount Erie	7.5 km (4.7 mi)
1 Devil's Peak	8 km (5 mi)
54 Evans Peak	8 km (5 mi)
103 Heliotrope Ridge Trail	8 km (5 mi)
2 Mount Seymour	8 km (5 mi)
69 St'ám'ya (Hope Mountain)	8.5 km (5.3 mi)
37 Decker Tarn	9 km (5.6 mi)
35 Flute Summit	9 km (5.6 mi)
15 Ken's Bluffs	9 km (5.6 mi)
65 Lhílheqey (Cheam Peak)	9 km (5.6 mi)
10 Mount Strachan	9 km (5.6 mi)
23 Neverland Falls	9 km (5.6 mi)
94 W̱QEN̦EL̦EȽ (Jocelyn Hill)	9 km (5.6 mi)
12 Black Mountain and Eagle Bluff	9.5 km (5.9 mi)
48 Pipi7íyekw (Joffre Lakes)	9.5 km (5.9 mi)
31 Brandywine Mountain	10 km (6.2 mi)
60 Campbell Lake	10 km (6.2 mi)
6 Mount Fromme	10 km (6.2 mi)
73 The Flatiron	10 km (6.2 mi)
13 West Knob	10 km (6.2 mi)
72 Zupjok Peak	10 km (6.2 mi)
63 Gloria Lookout	11 km (6.8 mi)
58 Hoover Bluff	11 km (6.8 mi)
17 Tunnel Bluff	11 km (6.8 mi)
105 Chain Lakes Trail	11.5 km (7.1 mi)
34 Crater Rim Trail	11.5 km (7.1 mi)
88 Emma Lake	11.5 km (7.1 mi)
55 Gold Creek	11.5 km (7.1 mi)
62 Qoqó:lem (Vedder Mountain)	11.5 km (7.1 mi)
32 Conflict Lake	12 km (7.5 mi)
14 Donut Rock	12 km (7.5 mi)
68 Flora Peak	12 km (7.5 mi)
66 Ford Mountain	12 km (7.5 mi)
9 Hollyburn Mountain	12 km (7.5 mi)
97 Mount Manuel Quimper	12 km (7.5 mi)
49 Mount Rohr	12 km (7.5 mi)
99 Pine and Cedar Lakes Trail	12 km (7.5 mi)
76 Skagit Bluffs	12 km (7.5 mi)
46 Valentine Lake	12 km (7.5 mi)
27 Tantalus View Lookout	12 km (7.5 mi)
52 Coquitlam Lake View Trail	12.5 km (7.8 mi
16 Mount Harvey	12.5 km (7.8 mi
71 Tikwalus Heritage Trail	12.5 km (7.8 mi

ike		Distance
41	Háwint (Tenquille Lake)	13 km (8.1 mi)
3	Mount Elsay	13 km (8.1 mi)
00	Oyster Dome	13 km (8.1 mi)
04	Yellow Aster Butte	13 km (8.1 mi)
37	Fairview Bay	13.5 km (8.4 mi)
20	Stl'álk̲em Stak̲w (Deeks Lake)	13.5 km (8.4 mi)
02	Sx'á7lex' (Mount Constitution)	13.5 km (8.4 mi)
42	Copper Mound	14 km (8.7 mi)
7	Goat Mountain	14 km (8.7 mi)
33	Mount Gardner	14 km (8.7 mi)
24	Siy̓ám̓ Smánit (Stawamus Chief Mountain)	14 km (8.7 mi)
81	Skyline Summit	14 km (8.7 mi)
18	Brunswick Mountain	14.5 km (9 mi)
50	Cinnabar Ridge	14.5 km (9 mi)
61	Kw'ekw'e'i:qw (Sumas Mountain)	14.5 km (9 mi)
4	Norvan Falls	14.5 km (9 mi)
45	Upper Fowl Lake	15 km (9.3 mi)
78	Windy Joe Mountain	15 km (9.3 mi)
43	Mount McLeod	15.5 km (9.6 mi)
8	Crown Mountain	16 km (9.9 mi)
59	Leq'á:mel (Nicomen Mountain)	16 km (9.9 mi)
96	Mount Braden	16 km (9.9 mi)
98	Mount Maguire and Babbington Hill	16 km (9.9 mi)
64	Mount Thurston	16 km (9.9 mi)
89	Crossroads Peak	16.5 km (10.3 mi)

Hike		Distance
85	Mount Steele	17 km (10.6 mi)
25	Watersprite Lake	17 km (10.6 mi)
21	Beth Lake	18 km (11.2 mi)
74	Illal Mountain	18 km (11.2 mi)
51	Little Horn Mountain	18 km (11.2 mi)
38	Rainbow Pass	18 km (11.2 mi)
40	Skywalk North	18 km (11.2 mi)
39	Skywalk South	18 km (11.2 mi)
11	Unnecessary Mountain	18 km (11.2 mi)
80	Skwa-kwa-eets (Lightning Lakes)	19.5 km (12.1 mi)
90	Confederation Lake	20 km (12.4 mi)
26	Elfin Lakes	20 km (12.4 mi)
84	McNair Lake	20 km (12.4 mi)
79	Frosty Mountain	21 km (13 mi)
28	Garibaldi Lake and Black Tusk Meadows	21 km (13 mi)
77	Three Brothers Mountain	21 km (13 mi)
53	Alouette Mountain	22 km (13.7 mi)
82	Lone Goat Mountain	22 km (13.7 mi)
75	Podunk Creek	23 km (14.3 mi)
56	x̣ɛ'ɛc'ɛnxʷ (Golden Ears)	24 km (14.9 mi)
5	Mount Burwell	25 km (15.5 mi)
44	One Duck Lake	25 km (15.5 mi)
47	Wetscín'atkwa (Lizzie Creek)	27 km (16.8 mi)
29	T'ak̲'t'ak̲'múy̓ín̓ tl'a In̓iny̓áx̱a7n (The Black Tusk)	27 km (16.8 mi)
30	Panorama Ridge	30 km (18.6 mi)

INDEX

Notes: Featured hikes indicated by page ranges in bold. Photographs indicated by page numbers in italics.

ABOUT THE AUTHOR AND PHOTOGRAPHER

Photo by Jeremy Moorhouse

STEPHEN HUI has been hiking, backpacking, and scrambling in the Coast Mountains of B.C. for more than 30 years.

Hui is the author of two number one B.C. bestsellers—*105 Hikes In and Around Southwestern British Columbia* and *Destination Hikes In and Around Southwestern British Columbia*—as well as *Best Hikes and Nature Walks With Kids In and Around Southwestern British Columbia.*

In 2022, Hui was named a fellow of the Royal Canadian Geographical Society. He serves as a Canadian commissioner on the transboundary Skagit Environmental Endowment Commission. Hui lives in Vancouver, B.C.—in the territories of the Musqueam (xʷməθkʷəy̓əm), Squamish (Sḵwx̱wú7mesh), and Tsleil-Waututh (səlilwətaɬ) First Nations.

Hui is currently on the trail to his fourth book.

105HIKES.COM

@105Hikes

@stephenhui

@StephenHui

@105Hikes

stephen@105hikes.com

#105Hikes